# A MOUNTAIN OF CRUMBS

Elena Gorokhova grew up in St Petersburg, Russia, although for most of her life it was known as Leningrad. At the age of twenty-four she married an American and came to the United States with one twenty-kilogram suitcase to start a new life. Now Elena is a writer and lives in New Jersey.

# A Mountain of Crumbs

Growing Up Behind the Iron Curtain

ELENA GOROKHOVA

✷ WINDMILL BOOKS

Published by Windmill Books 2010

2 4 6 8 10 9 7 5 3 1

Copyright © Elena Gorokhova 2010

First published in the United States in 2010 by Simon & Schuster

Windmill Books
The Random House Group Limited
20 Vauxhall Bridge Road, London, SW1V 2SA

Addresses for companies within The Random House Group Limited can be found at:
www.randomhouse.co.uk/offices.htm

The Random House Group Limited Reg. No. 954009

www.rbooks.co.uk

A CIP catalogue record for this book
is available from the British Library

ISBN 9780099537649

The Random House Group Limited supports The Forest Stewardship
Council (FSC), the leading international forest certification organisation. All our titles
that are printed on Greenpeace approved FSC certified paper carry the FSC logo.
Our paper procurement policy can be found at:
www.rbooks.co.uk/environment

**Mixed Sources**
Product group from well-managed
forests and other controlled sources
www.fsc.org  Cert no. TT-COC-2139
© 1996 Forest Stewardship Council
FSC

Printed and bound in Great Britain by
CPI Cox & Wyman, Reading, RG1 8EX

*For my mother,*
*Galina Konstantinovna Maltseva*

*A Mountain of Crumbs*

# CHAPTER I

# Ivanovo

I WISH MY MOTHER HAD come from Leningrad, from the world of Pushkin and the tsars, of granite embankments and lace ironwork, of pearly domes buttressing the low sky. Leningrad's sophistication would have infected her the moment she drew her first breath, and all the curved façades and stately bridges, marinated for more than two centuries in the city's wet, salty air, would have left a permanent mark of refinement on her soul.

But she didn't. She came from the provincial town of Ivanovo in central Russia, where chickens lived in the kitchen and a pig squatted under the stairs, where streets were unpaved and houses made from wood. She came from where they lick plates.

Born three years before Russia turned into the Soviet Union, my mother became a mirror image of my motherland: overbearing, protective, difficult to leave. Our house was the seat of the *politburo*, my mother its permanent chairman. She presided in our kitchen over a pot of borsch, a ladle in her hand, ordering us to eat in the same voice that made her anatomy students quiver. A survivor of the famine, Stalin's terror, and the Great Patriotic War, she controlled and protected, ferociously. What had happened to her was not going to happen to us. She sheltered us from dangers, experience, and life itself by a tight embrace that left us innocent and gasping for air.

She commandeered trips to our crumbling dacha—under the Baltic clouds, spitting rain—to plant, weed, pick, and preserve for the winter whatever grew under the rare sun that never rose above the neighbor's pigsty. During brief northern summers we sloshed through a swamp to the shallow waters of the Gulf of Finland, warm and yellow as weak tea; we scooped mushrooms out of the forest moss and hung them on thread over the stove to dry for the winter. My mother planned, directed, and took charge, lugging buckets of water to beds of cucumbers and dill, elbowing in lines for sugar to preserve the fruit we'd need to treat winter colds. When September came, we were back in the city, rooting in the cupboard for gooseberry jam to cure my cough or black currant syrup to lower my father's blood pressure. We were back to the presidium speeches and winter coats padded with wool and preparations for more April digging.

Maybe if I hadn't spent every spring Sunday ankle-deep in cold, soggy dirt, I wouldn't have been so easily seduced by the decadent sound of the English language that poured from the grooves of a record called *Audio-Lingual Drills*, my tutor's pride. I might have gone to medical school, like my mother, or engineering school, like everyone else. I might have even married a Russian.

Maybe if I could have attached the word "intelligentsia" to her weighty figure in a polyester dress made by the "Bolshevik Woman" factory, I wouldn't have had to escape to America on an Aeroflot flight, a startled face gazing from the passport in my hand, a ravaged suitcase on the KGB inspector's table packed with twenty kilograms of what used to be my life.

MY GRANDFATHER, KONSTANTIN IVANOVICH Kuzminov, was a peasant. The countess who owned his village on the steep bank of the Volga five hundred versts from Moscow, feeling guilty for the centuries of serfdom, provided him with a scholarship to attend engineering school. My grandmother was the daughter of a factory owner in the textile town of Ivanovo, who employed most of the men in the village. They married two years before World War I broke out and five years before the Bolsheviks stormed the Winter Palace and the country exploded into civil war.

By 1918, when the altruistic countess, among throngs of panicked nobility, sailed from the Crimea toward Turkey, my grandparents already had three children, my mother and her two younger brothers. The revolution, with its promise of liberation from the yoke of absolutism and paradise for all working people, seemed to offer the hope that Russia was on the mend, that centuries of inequality and slave labor were finally over and peace and prosperity almost within reach. But in 1920 food rations shrank yet again and the pall of famine settled over the country, a dawn to the six decades of terror already bleeding on the horizon.

That was when my grandmother invented the crumb game. At six and five years of age, my mother and her brother Sima were old enough to ignore their growling stomachs and make do with nothing but a piece of black bread and a cube of sugar, but three-year-old Yuva, my uncle who would die during the first minutes of the blitzkrieg in 1941, clenched his fists and bawled from hunger.

"Look at how much you've got," my grandmother would say as she broke a piece of bread and a square of sugar into crumbs with her fingers. "A whole mountain of crumbs." My mother and Sima, older and wiser, would exchange a secret look of pity for their baby brother, who allowed himself to be so easily fooled. "Two mountains," my grandmother would say. Yuva would stop wailing and rub the snot over his cheeks, pacified by this semblance of abundance, two whole mountains, more bread and sugar than the one sad little square on everyone else's plate, enough crumbs to pick at for a whole hour, to stick into his mouth one by one, plentiful and sweet.

By 1928 they lived in a two-story wooden house—my grandparents, their one daughter and now three sons, and Baba Manya, my grandmother's spinster sister, resourceful, doughy, and kind. She resewed old clothes for the children who grew too fast, kept three chicks in the kitchen until they were eaten by a cat, and later, during another famine, after World War II, bought the last rickety piglet off a horse-drawn cart that had stopped for a few minutes on their street. The pig lived under the stairs and saved them all from starvation the following year.

In 1929 my mother's younger sister, Muza, was born, the fifth and last child. "God gave us another girl," announced Baba Manya from the porch where she stood in the breath of Indian summer, wiping her hands on an apron. "Praise the Trinity in Heaven, in the name of the Father, the Son, and the Holy Spirit." She didn't know that a decree had come down from Moscow declaring religion dead—a sickly, fainthearted enemy kicked and stabbed and finally stuffed into the attic of the tsarist past.

"Not God," protested my fifteen-year-old mother, flanked by her three younger brothers, standing knee-deep in clumps of dandelions, watching as my grandmother swaddled a flailing Muza, who was rapidly disappearing under layers of old sheets. "Our mama gave us another girl."

"May your tongues fall off, all of you, godless fooligans!" yelled Baba Manya, hurriedly crossing herself. She meant to say "hooligans"—*hooligani*—but she either couldn't pronounce the *h* sound or didn't know the right word. That's what they all became, my mother and her three brothers—fooligans, ardent and naïve, resolute and reckless, inspired by a new god, a crossbreed of hooligans and fools.

IN 1931 MY SEVENTEEN-YEAR-OLD mother, who had inherited my grandfather's obstinacy and revolutionary fervor, pinned up her dark braids in hope of looking older and went to her first lecture at the Ivanovo medical school. Universities were now free, but candidates were accepted on the basis of their social class and not their merit: children of workers and peasants first, children of professionals last. Because my grandfather was no longer a peasant, my mother had to wait two months until a milkmaid's daughter dropped out, creating an opening. In November, when rain washed over the dust covering Ivanovo's roads and turned the town into lanes of mud, she became part of the first motley class of Soviet doctors, trained in the laboratory of the new state to be flung from their classrooms into the caldron of war.

In her first year of medical school she was taught by the novel "brigade" method: one student, the brigadier, took exams for the entire group of twenty. My mother pitied gangly Igor, who stood sweating in front of her class, craning his skinny neck over a textbook to read page after page in his monotonous voice, something about molecules and cells, a biology chapter he would be tested on at the end of the week. The test would either give credit to everyone in the group, now busy talking, daydreaming, and dozing off, or doom the whole lot to failure. Diligent and boring, Igor always passed.

By the second year, the brigade method was replaced with individual learning. A professor of anatomy arrived all the way from Moscow and promptly issued a failing grade to a former tractor driver. The days of dozing and daydreaming were over.

For the first time at the Medical Institute, my mother opened a textbook and by sheer force of will memorized the name of every bone, vein, muscle, tissue, tendon, and joint. She passed the anatomy final. She passed the surgery internship and the most serious exam of all, in scientific communism, a course hastily spun from quotes of Marx, Engels, and Lenin, a requirement for graduation in every university of the Soviet Union, across all its eleven time zones.

Three months after graduation, my mother was the chief and only physician of a fifteen-bed rural hospital thirty kilometers from

Ivanovo, near a factory that produced bricks of peat mined from the nearby underground swamps. Brimming with energy and the enthusiasm of the first socialist generation, she was eager to make things better. It was 1937, the twentieth year of Soviet power, the busiest year of the Gulag camps. It was the twenty-third year of my mother's life—when, for the first time, she left her parents' home, when her future rose on the horizon like the huge crimson sun over the swamp outside her new apartment window.

She set up a trauma point where she bandaged victims of accidents, mostly work-related: severed fingers, broken arms, bruised backs and shoulders. But she knew she could do more. Although most of the factory workers were women, there was no maternity ward in the hospital. To give birth, women had to take a horse-drawn carriage to a district hospital eight kilometers away, a long ride on a road often buried under snow or washed out by rain. There had already been two babies born en route, one of whom did not survive the trip. She made a call to the local health department and was told that maternity wards were not a top priority at a time when epidemics of typhus and tuberculosis were mowing down entire towns.

Indignant at such a lack of insight on the part of the local authorities, my mother sat down and wrote a letter to the real leader. General Secretary, Moscow, the Kremlin. "Dear Comrade Stalin," she began. "The patients at my hospital have no place to give birth to our new citizens. The Soviet women, who toil in peat swamps for our common bright future, deserve better." She stopped to consider how to word her request so that in one simple, effective sentence she would cut through the necessary layers of steel to what she knew was the leader's compassionate heart. "My apartment can easily be turned into a maternity ward with the help of a few necessary pieces of equipment (list attached). Please help."

She thought of the best way to sign the letter, vacillating from "comrade" to "citizen" to "physician." Comrade seemed too self-promoting: how could she be a comrade to the legend? Citizen was too impersonal. She finally chose her professional title, which still sounded strange, Dr. Galina Kuzminova.

The letter, she knew, was a gamble. Only months earlier, when she was living in the Ivanovo apartment with her parents, her siblings, and her uncle, there had been a knock on the door in the middle of the night. It was a loud, demanding knock, the kind that came only at two or three in the morning, the kind that everyone recognized even if they'd never heard it before. Two men in black coats marched straight to the room where her uncle Volya lived with his wife and fifteen-year-old daughter, turned the mattresses and all the drawers upside down, and announced that Uncle Volya was under arrest.

"For what?" asked Aunt Lilya in a ragged voice.

"You'll find out," muttered one of the men.

Uncle Volya stood in the middle of the room, in silly flannel pajamas, trying to quell an asthma attack. His round shoulders were slouched forward, and his mouth gasped for breath as he mopped his forehead with a handkerchief. "It's all a mistake, a misunderstanding," he whispered as soon as he could muster enough air, the handkerchief in his hand quivering. The men ordered him to put on a coat and escorted him to a van known as a *voronok*, or black raven, parked in front of their house. Weeks later Aunt Lilya learned that as part of his job in a propaganda agency, he'd taken a stranger from Moscow to a restaurant. There, sitting next to a good citizen dispatched by the NKVD —the People's Commissariat for Internal Affairs— to listen to conversations with strangers, Uncle Volya told a joke.

It wasn't even a political joke. *Two militiamen are invited to Comrade Kozlov's birthday party. What should we give him? asks one. The best gift is a book, says the other. No, says the first militiaman. Comrade Kozlov already has a book.*

They had all heard this joke before, but now it sounded unfunny and flat. Why did Uncle Volya even bother telling such a bad joke? My mother knew he should have been more careful around strangers. Pasted all over town were posters of a woman in a red head kerchief with a finger across her lips and a caption *ne boltai* in big red letters: do not babble. Babbling was only one step away from treason. Still, she believed that the NKVD had made a mistake. How could Comrade Stalin possibly have arrested an innocent man, her meek and soft-jowled Uncle Volya? Everyone knew that Comrade Stalin wanted everyone to have a good life, whether they were peasants or professors.

Yet there it was still fresh in her memory, the image of her uncle's trembling handkerchief and his arm missing the sleeve of his coat as the two men yanked all ten volumes of his collected works of Chekhov off the shelf, shaking them open, tossing them on the floor, angry that they could find nothing inside.

My mother also thought of my grandfather, who, in 1921, according to family lore, had telegraphed Lenin when a train full of wheat brought for the starving people of Ivanovo had been detained by a squadron of Red Army soldiers with shotguns. A few hours later, as the story went, the train was allowed to pass, thanks to her father's telegram.

In her mind, the scene of Uncle Volya being led away into the black *voronok* for telling a joke wrestled for a few minutes with the happy image of the Ivanovo citizens saved from starvation by a telegram. She stubbornly decided to believe that Stalin did not know of this obvious injustice, that it all happened as the result of an un-Soviet struggle for power among his crooked underlings.

But now she was writing directly to Stalin, the country's conscience and revolutionary glory. My mother signed the letter, folded it in quarters, and gave the envelope to Fyodor, who tended to the hospital horse Verochka and every other day drove the buggy eight kilometers to the nearest town.

A few weeks later, when routine traumas and illnesses had focused her attention away from the letter addressed to the Kremlin, she was called to the office of the head of the district health department. Comrade Palkin sat behind a desk, decked out in a military uniform like Stalin and thin-framed round glasses like the head of the NKVD, Beria. His head was small and bald, with wisps of down over the ears, and his thick forearms, which looked like they belonged to a bigger man, lay on the desk like logs. Leaning over the papers before him as if they were his prisoners, he failed to get up when my mother walked in, despite my grandmother's assertion that a man had no choice but to stand when a woman entered a room.

"Whom did you write to?" Palkin asked gravely, barely waiting for her to sit down.

"I wrote to Secretary Stalin," said my mother.

Palkin stared stonily from behind his glasses, and she thought of Uncle Volya. They still hadn't heard anything about him, despite the fact that Aunt Lilya took a week off to travel to Moscow, where she spent four days and nights standing in front of the Lubyanka NKVD prison, waiting to speak to someone, never allowed inside.

But my mother wasn't about to show that she was frightened, that her heart, contrary to all she knew about anatomy, was thumping somewhere in her throat. Showing what you felt was as dangerous as babbling. Lock up what you think, my grandmother had always said. What's inside you no one can touch.

"I've just received this order from Moscow," growled Palkin, baring bad teeth, stabbing a piece of paper with his finger while my mother imagined black *voronoks* and firing squads. "According to this order, Moscow is releasing fifteen thousand rubles to turn your apartment into a delivery room."

He might as well have said fifteen million rubles. My mother made three hundred rubles a month, a salary her former classmates envied, and since her largest purchase ever had been a woolen winter coat, she'd never seen a ruble note with more than one zero.

Back at the hospital, she went to the peat factory director's office and asked him to give her a room in the workers' dormitory. Only days after her meeting with Comrade Palkin, the needed equipment arrived and was installed in her former apartment with an efficiency she'd never seen before. By the spring a four-bed maternity ward was opened, where my mother delivered fifteen babies. During deliveries, she learned how to use forceps, turn a fetus, and manually separate the placenta. The women at the peat factory expressed their gratitude with string bags of cucumbers from their gardens and an occasional tin of lard.

My mother felt euphoric and important: what she'd done had upheld *poryadok*, order. The order that the country needed, that *she* needed. She described all this in her letter home, which, when she reread it, sounded as lofty and stiff as the front page of *Pravda*. Yet what she wanted to say was simple and short.

She'd survived.

# CHAPTER 2

# My Mother's Husbands

WHEN MY MOTHER MET my father in 1950, she had an eight-year-old daughter, my half-sister, Marina, and had already been married twice, two meteoric war marriages whose trajectories faded within months.

Her first husband was delivered to her by the short war of 1939 between the Soviet Union and Finland, laid out on her operating table with bits of shrapnel buried in his rear end.

"What a way to stop a bullet," said her former classmate Vera, who had been drafted into the same hospital.

My mother sliced open the buttocks of her future spouse and extracted pieces of metal, all except one, a shard lodged near the hip bone. She tried and tried, cutting and prodding, but finally had to leave it there, a lasting memory of their first meeting stowed deeply under his skin.

His name was Sasha Gladky, a graduate medical student himself all the way from Leningrad University, and he joked and laughed about his wound, basking in the attention of the female hospital staff. My mother, looking serious during the daily rounds, evaluated the healing process and checked the sutures. Being in full control of Sasha and his treatment—the expression of his broad-boned face with a slight cleft in the chin when she checked his temperature, the gratitude she could read in his gray, deep eyes—made her want to stay with him forever.

"I bet you he'll ask me to marry him," said my mother to Vera, nodding her head toward the door behind which Sasha lay surrounded by nurses. It was almost two weeks since she had operated, a few days before he was scheduled to return to Leningrad.

She liked Sasha's eyes following her around the room as she sterilized syringes in boiling water, trying to concoct a plan to keep him there longer. She was approaching twenty-five, rapidly getting too old for marriage. Her own mother had married when she was eighteen, her friend Vera when she turned twenty-two. The best childbearing age, as everyone knew, was twenty, and she'd missed that a long time ago.

Two days after the prescribed date, she signed his discharge order. Before leaving, Sasha waited for her in the back lot overgrown with thistle, where with a bashful smile, he announced that it was fate that had brought them together. He promised to send her a letter every week and a box of chocolates. "Chocolates!" marveled Vera. "For chocolates *I'd* marry him, too." A box arrived a few weeks later, embossed with Peter the Great atop a rearing horse, the famous Leningrad "Bronze Horseman" on the front. Since the beginning of the war, chocolates had completely vanished from the stores, and this huge box reminded my mother that it was her efforts and skill that had saved Sasha.

A few months later, when the Finnish War ended, Sasha came back to Ivanovo and they were married. Marriage was easy then, a fat purple stamp from the town hall on the third page of their internal passports and a name change for my mother from Kuzminova to Gladky. After four days Sasha returned to his studies in Leningrad. He sent letters to my mother once a week, then once a month. Then came a letter she did not expect: he accused her of having affairs while he was stooping over medical journals in the Leningrad library. Someone, an anonymous source, had informed him in a letter that his new wife—*stroinaya kak beryozka*, tall and slender as a birch tree—was, as he scribbled in a quick, slanted stroke, nothing but a tart.

My mother felt shock, then anger. She immediately grabbed a pen and wrote back to Sasha that if he could believe this, the two of them had nothing to discuss. If he could trust such toxic gossip, they were finished and their marriage dissolved.

She didn't really mean it. She simply wanted to register her indignation and discontent, expecting an apology and another box of chocolates. But no answer came. She waited two months and sent an angry inquiry to the anatomy department of Leningrad University, where he studied. The response came months later, in the fall of 1941, when German troops were already deep into Russia. Like all doctors, Sasha had been drafted to the front. On the map of the Soviet Union, where the black stain of German troops was rapidly expanding, there were already several fronts, and no one knew where they'd sent Sasha. No one would ever know.

NOW A DOCTOR AS well as an anatomy researcher at Ivanovo medical school, my mother was drafted, too, pulled away from her petri dishes and long-dead organs floating in jars of formaldehyde to sew up live, lacerated flesh at a frontline hospital. In her newly issued uniform, a khaki shirt cinched with a hammer-and-sickle belt over a narrow skirt, she looked too pretty to be part of the war, too willowy and long-legged, despite her black army boots that were two sizes too big.

All three of her brothers had been drafted during the war with Finland. They were stationed at the opposite ends of the country, Sima and Vova in the Far East, close to Japan, and Yuva on the border between the Soviet Union and Poland. On Sunday, June

22, 1941, when German tanks first rolled onto Soviet soil, my mother thought of Yuva stationed on the Polish border. Like every person in the country, benumbed and bewildered, she listened to Molotov's voice pouring from loudspeakers, announcing the invasion. She stood near the ambulance of the town emergency room, where she worked on weekends, its doors swung open, its engine choking. The humid smell of lilacs hung in the air, and the sun blithely beamed down through the lace of June leaves like an idiot laughing and dancing as flames gut his house. Why was it Molotov, the People's Commissar for Foreign Affairs, speaking to the country, and not Stalin himself? Where was Stalin when the German tanks were rolling over platoons of brothers and sons and even wayward husbands?

The hospital where she was drafted was no more than a railroad car pulled onto an auxiliary track a kilometer and a half from the town of Kalinin, occupied by the Germans. It was there that my mother first saw the indomitable infestations of lice. The wounded came in trucks from the front, a kilometer away, and although she scooped the lice out of the wounds with a teacup and rinsed the flaps of torn tissue as diligently as she could, lice festered in layers of dirty bandages, keeping the wounded awake and screaming through the night. They were younger than she was, those wounded boys—her brothers' age—and she peered into their dusty faces, clinging to a shred of hope that in some miraculous way her brother would be brought into her hospital for her to heal all the way from the Polish border seven hundred kilometers away.

Every week, in her squared-off handwriting, she wrote a letter home to her parents. *My dear Mamochka and Papochka, I hope everyone is well. I hope my sister Muza is a serious student and helping you with the house and garden in my absence. I hope our dear Yuva is fighting against the enemy as fiercely as our boys are fighting here.* There were always a lot of hopes in her letters.

What she really wanted to say was that she hoped her brother Yuva was not among the thousands of bodies she knew had been plowed into the warm summer earth of western Russia, but of course she couldn't write that to her parents. As she watched the front line ebb eastward on the map above the Hospital Commissar's bunk, she had to be careful that her letters did not sound as anxious and gloomy as she felt. *Military mail is very slow*, she wrote, making up an excuse for why they hadn't heard from Yuva in six months.

By the beginning of December, when the enemy was pushed out of Kalinin, an order came for the hospital to be transferred into a town school. The school stood at the end of the street, or what used to be a street. Its windows had all been blown away and were now hammered shut with plywood. In the courtyard, two soldiers were digging up the ground, unearthing German corpses buried there before the front line moved south. They piled the bodies by the entrance and then tossed them into a truck to be hauled away from the town center, privates in their underwear and barefoot, officers in uniform and full regalia. She had seen live Germans, too, but only from a distance, when the planes flew low to bomb and the pilots grinned from their glass bubbles and sometimes waved.

My mother's second husband swept in straight from the front lines. In his captain's uniform and a wave of blond hair, he was impossible to resist. From the minute she saw his sharp shoulder leaning against the stove in the Commissar's office, she wanted to touch him, to press herself into his tobacco-permeated military shirt and ask him to protect her. He was called Sasha, like her first husband, and she saw an irony in this coincidence, but also a consistency, a certain kind of order. One night, late, after she finished sewing up the last piece of torn flesh for the day, he accompanied her home to an empty, wind-swept apartment two blocks away and stayed over on the leather gymnasium mat she and a nurse had earlier carried in from the school to serve as a bed.

"Well, here we are," said my mother in the morning, although she didn't quite know what this "here" was or where it was exactly that they were. What she did know was that things had to be done in a proper way. A woman, once she went to bed with a man, had to marry him. Or rather, he had to marry her. Either way, they had to preserve *poryadok* because otherwise who knew what terrible anarchy would be unleashed by such unmarried permissiveness. Bitterly, she thought of her first Sasha, who had had the nerve to doubt her character.

Although the new Sasha resisted a little—rubbing his hairless chin, dragging out reasons why they didn't need to rush to the marriage bureau at the crack of dawn—my mother was unyielding. She needed order, she told herself, but she knew this was bigger than order. She was drawn to this blond captain like a fly to spilled honey.

This would be a real marriage, she thought, to a man who seemed gentle and kind. He was also a Communist Party member, an ideology leader of his division, undoubtedly a person of high morals and a definitive sense of purpose aimed at the future of the country as well as their own.

The marriage bureau was a desk in a small room where they registered deaths, births, and those missing-in-action. First, on a lined page ripped out of a school composition book, my mother wrote that she was declaring herself divorced from the first Sasha for the reason of "military cataclysm." She didn't know if he was dead or alive, and with the country occupied and ravaged, she couldn't—and didn't want to—find out. Then, on another page, she declared herself married to the Sasha standing next to her.

"Congratulations," said the puffy woman behind the desk, who was wearing a coat and an *ushanka* hat with the earflaps tied under her chin. After inspecting the purple stamps in their passports, Sasha and my mother went to her cold apartment, where the captain drank two tea glasses of vodka and passed out.

A few days later, my mother learned that in the northern town of Atkarsk, her new husband had a common-law wife and a ten-year-old daughter he hadn't seen since the beginning of the Finnish war. She also learned he had TB, in an open, most contagious form, which was the reason he had been sent from the front to the nearest hospital. Had she waited a little, she would have received a military transfer order with his chart.

It took her another month to figure out he was an alcoholic.

All too late, she thought of my grandmother's saying, *Pospeshish—lyudei nasmeshish*. If you do things in haste, you'll make people laugh.

SPRING BROUGHT WOUNDED CIVILIANS. When the ice on the Volga turned porous and frail, mines frozen into the river began to explode, touched off by the slightest shift, sending flocks of birds into the air and schools of fish to the water surface, belly up. Locals with buckets waded into the river to collect the unexpected harvest floating among chunks of ice, setting off more mines.

It was prohibited to treat civilians in a military hospital. But when a woman brought in an unconscious nine-year-old boy one April morning, my mother didn't hesitate. She unbuttoned his quilted jacket and muddy pants and carefully pulled them away from his perforated flesh, revealing blind belly wounds: entrances of shells with no exits. Together with the woman, whose son had been killed by the same mine, she carried the boy into the operating room, taking small, slow steps, the two synchronizing their walk. There she lifted a scalpel out of the boiling water, made an incision, and pulled apart flaps of skin, exposing multiple intestinal wounds, big and tiny holes in the coils of the boy's belly. She rinsed the boy's intestines with antiseptic and sewed up the holes, one by one.

As soon as she finished, the hospital Commissar stormed in, shouted that she was breaking a military order, and commanded her to report to the director's office immediately.

"Rules are rules," muttered Dr. Kremer, hunched over papers on his director's desk. "You had no right to operate."

"The patient is nine years old," my mother said. "He needs to stay here for three more days. After three days I can send him to the town hospital." She thought of how thickheaded and unperceptive he was, a typical man. In her mind, she returned to the child in the operating room, then tried to conjure up a ten-year-old girl somewhere on the other side of the Urals, the daughter of her new husband, coughing on their gymnasium mat. Or was it she who was thickheaded and unperceptive?

Dr. Kremer rubbed his forehead and looked around the room. My mother followed his gaze: a little metal stove empty of wood, boot prints across the plywood hammered against the window frame, a map of the pre-war Soviet Union on the wall left by the school principal, green and brown in the middle, blue in the north, with a big red star for Moscow, where Dr. Kremer grew up.

"Three days," he said. "That's all you have." He walked to the desk and leafed through several papers that looked like military orders, with ominous stamps and resolute illegible signatures. "And Dr. Gladky . . ." he turned to my mother.

"Maltseva," she said, surprised at how strange this new name sounded in her mouth as her own. "I just got married."

Staring at the director's grayish face across from hers, she thought that this might be the moment when he announced that she would be court-martialed for breaking military rules. My mother wasn't naïve about the swift hand of punishment. Uncle Volya, arrested five years earlier, had been shot attempting to escape from a camp in Vorkuta. That was what the NKVD letter said: "shot attempting to escape." As much as she tried, my mother couldn't imagine soft and asthmatic Uncle Volya climbing over walls or running. Was he guilty, after all? Was his punishment the price of maintaining order?

Ready to suffer the consequences of her insubordination, she watched Dr. Kremer get up and move the papers to the side. She watched the corners of his eyes crinkle slightly.

"Congratulations on your marriage," he said.

SEVEN MONTHS PREGNANT, IN September 1942, my mother was demobilized from the military hospital. She packed up the uniform that no longer fit and, with her sick husband, returned to her parents' Ivanovo apartment, now big enough for all since two of her brothers were gone. Vova was in the Far East, from where they recently received his letter. Yuva was still silent, and my mother's fear that he was dead had turned to conviction. The third brother, Sima, transferred to the Belorussian front, had been wounded and was now back home with complications from a piece of metal that had created an abscess and was beginning to cause an infection in his brain.

It made my mother furious to think that a doctor at a front hospital had failed to operate properly, leaving a shard of a grenade lodged in her brother's lung. She remembered herself at the beginning of her career, leaving a sliver of shrapnel in her first husband's butt, but a butt wasn't a vital organ, and although her first Sasha—she wanted to believe—may have felt an ache now and then, it wasn't her surgical failure that would eventually kill him.

But this, the fragment in Sima's lung, was killing him. Her parents, especially her *mamochka*, spoke of his recovery, but my mother knew he wouldn't survive. As Sima, now blind and delirious, lay in the room where all the three brothers grew up, she sat by his bed taking his temperature and peering into his throat, pretending that whatever small medical procedures she performed could make a difference.

Day after day, she sat by Sima's bed thinking about her brother and her husband, both dying. She couldn't cure them, so she concentrated on doing what she could do. She sold her ration of four hundred grams of bread and with that money bought fifty grams of butter, which, she hoped, might boost her brother's and her husband's chance for health. She watched Sima burn with fever and move his cracked lips as if wanting to say something; she heard Sasha's wet cough roll in his chest like the cannonade they heard at least once a day. Whom was she trying to fool? What she did was futile, she knew, but it required sacrifice, and that was the least she could do for her brother and her husband.

When Sasha began spitting up blood, he was admitted to the Ivanovo hospital, my mother's alma mater. She consulted the head of the TB clinic and her former professor, who concurred that after his release from the hospital, Sasha must leave home since he could not stay in the house with a newborn. But before he left, he took both the butter and the bread, added a few bars of soap from my grandmother's closet, and sold them to buy himself a jar of moonshine.

Sima died at home on November 1, 1942. My mother washed him and shaved him and dressed him for the funeral. Since she was eight months pregnant, her parents decided that it would be too traumatic for her to go to the cemetery, an invitation to premature labor. She stood on the porch, watching my grandfather crack a whip in a swift strike, watching the horse snort and jerk forward as the cart with my grandmother, slumped against Sima's coffin, slowly bumped onto the road, rutted by recent rain.

Sasha left on November 7, three weeks before my sister would be born, on the Day of the Great Socialist Revolution, which is in peaceful times an occasion for a citizens' parade, for people marching in rows, and banners flapping happily in the wind. In gray air pocked with drizzle, they walked through the ruins of her town and stood waiting for the train, my big-bellied mother and her second husband, who would die of TB in his hometown five years later, never having seen his daughter. When a plume of smoke billowed out of the stack and a spasm lurched through the cars, from the engine all the way to the mail wagon, she took a step toward the clattering wheels and raised her arm in a last good-bye. She waited until the train shrank to toy size, until the only smoke she could see was a streak of soot rising from an apartment building bombed the day before.

MY FATHER, FINALLY, PROMISED stability. He was fourteen years older than my mother, a widower with an eighteen-year-old daughter. During one of her Ivanovo hospital rounds in 1950, my mother's girlfriend Vera, who had tried to fix her up with men before, noticed a stomach-ulcer patient, undoubtedly a man of distinction because instead of an auditorium-size ward he'd been placed in a room with only three other beds.

"Ilya Antonovich seems like a very serious man," Vera whispered to my mother, respectfully using a patronymic after his first name. "He is a Communist Party member and has just been assigned to head a technical school in Leningrad. He needs a woman to take care of him," she added. "*Kozha da kosti*—skin and bones."

Perhaps it was the promise of Leningrad that did it. Her native Ivanovo had lost its luster—ravaged by the war, marred by the memory of one brother dead and the other missing, by the image of the train carrying away the husband she would never see again.

My father was reticent about his past. It was unremarkable and dull, he said. He'd participated in the collectivization from 1929 to 1933, when Stalin purged all of the wealthy peasants and turned the country's agriculture into collective farms, sad villages of desperate, perpetually inebriated country folk presided over by Red Army officers whose only experience with farming was riding the horses the army had supplied. Due to his political propaganda work, my father was exempt from fighting in the Great Patriotic War, but not from the scurvy he contracted in the mid-1940s. He was sent to Ivanovo to lift the people's spirit, damaged by the war.

He came from a tiny village in the most eastern part of European Russia, but he never spoke of his parents and no one in my family even knew if he had any siblings.

For a man of fifty-one he was good-looking—gaunt, sharp-featured, hazel-eyed. He walked with a light gait and spoke in unhurried sentences that made one forget the war was barely over. He sounded positive and solid. A two-room apartment on the top floor of a newly constructed building in Leningrad was already waiting for them, entirely their own, unlike other apartments where three families huddled in three rooms and regularly collided in a single communal kitchen and bath. With her recent PhD, my mother could easily find a job teaching anatomy in one of Leningrad's medical schools. Besides, my eight-year-old sister Marina, her second Sasha's daughter, needed a father.

My grandmother saw Ilya Antonovich's proposal as an upward move. He had a well-paid, respectable position, and a stomach ulcer was not TB. It was a manageable illness, a small cloud with a silver lining: it prohibited alcohol.

My mother agreed, despite a prickle of guilt somewhere in the area of her heart, a sensation reminding her she didn't feel the same fire as when she married her sick, alcoholic Sasha. But she was no longer daring or young: two defunct marriages and two wars and two brothers gone had dulled the edge of her enthusiasm and made her practical and prudent.

Leningrad was a true capital, Peter the Great's "window on Europe." It was the first big city she'd seen, with the baroque curves of the Kirov Opera and Ballet Theatre only two blocks from her new apartment. She liked walking from the streetcar stop to the medical school where she'd been hired to teach, past the eighteenth-century façades, past newspaper kiosks where Stalin's face still had two more years to glare from the front page of every paper. She liked the pearly-gray domes of Smolny Cathedral, so much like the Leningrad sky; she liked the broad avenues of the city's center and the mazes of its courtyards. She liked its grocery stores with their sawdust-covered floors and sweet smells of cheese, bologna, and sometimes even beef.

After the four hundred grams of war-rationed bread in Ivanovo, Leningrad seemed a gastronomic heaven. There were bread stores and milk stores and meat stores. Flour hung in the warm, fragrant air of bakeries; bricks of sour black bread shared counter space with loaves of white. On her dairy trip she brought a three-liter aluminum cistern to be filled with milk by an aproned woman behind the counter, and out of the three kinds of cheese, with the geopolitical names of Russian, Soviet, and Swiss, she would buy a kilo of Russian, the least expensive but the tastiest. There were stores brimming with sweets: cookies with patterns of spires resembling the new Moscow skyline, three kinds of sucking candy, glass counters full of *sushki*, dry tiny bagels so hard they could break one's tooth. There were even chocolate bars called "Soviet Builder" wrapped in silver foil that emerged invitingly from a paper sleeve with a picture of a muscular man brandishing a hammer.

My father provided what she'd craved, stability. But there was something else she wanted from this marriage, something that was as important as getting out of her hometown, something visceral and non-negotiable. Something my father dismissed as an impossibility. She was thirty-nine, too old to have another child, he said. And he was fourteen years older. If anyone saw him with an infant, they'd take him for a grandfather. *Dedushka*, they'd call to him, what a precious lovely grandchild you have.

My mother trotted out arguments, all in vain; then she simply stopped using contraceptives. She didn't tell my father until she was four months pregnant. He flew into a rage and told her to have an abortion.

"It's too late," she said. "At this point it's dangerous."

"Have an abortion anyway," he demanded in a high-pitched,

unfamiliar voice, as if he hadn't heard what she told him, as if she'd qualified someone else's condition, not her own, as potentially life-threatening.

"I will not endanger my life," she said sternly, enunciating every sound.

My father stopped speaking to her. She stopped speaking to him, too. She silently chopped beets for borsch, left a plate on the kitchen table and a pot under a warmer on the stove, and he silently ate and smoked his filterless cigarettes, immersing everything in the kitchen in sheets of smoke.

When she felt contractions and checked herself into a maternity ward, my father rang his driver, Volodya, and told him to drive to the hospital. Volodya, in his wrinkled brown suit, shiny in the back, had been waiting for this call, preceded by days of whispering among relatives and friends. Outside, the wet Baltic wind scoured the city, mopping cigarette stubs and used bus tickets into courtyards, rinsing linden branches in lukewarm air. On their way, they stopped by a metro station where a woman was selling flowers from a bucket—probably peonies, since it was the end of July—and with that bouquet, held like a whisk broom, my father marched into the hospital lobby, where a receptionist informed him that he was the father of a baby girl.

The announcement left him stunned, then livid. How could they, he thought. A girl! Turning on his heel, under the bewildered gaze of the whole reception area, he stormed out of the hospital with the peonies now clutched like a weapon in his fist. Not only did he have a baby—at his age—he had a baby girl! He got into the car and ordered Volodya to drive him out of the city, away from this double disgrace.

For six days he stayed at a friend's dacha with his chauffeur, who drove him to Leningrad in the morning and back out of the city at night. Finally, yielding to pressure from his own daughter Galya, my mother's surviving brother, and the friend whose dacha he used as a retreat, my father made an appearance at the hospital with a note for my mother. The receptionist folded the note and handed it to the nurse, who immediately delivered it to the third floor.

Don't be upset, my father wrote. Girls are all right, too.

# CHAPTER 3

# Vranyo, the Pretending

## Aunt Polya

E AT YOUR SOUP, GOROKHOVA, or you'll die!" shouts Aunt Polya over my head. She calls us all by our last names, and she is not really my aunt.

I am five, still a year and a half away from first grade, in a nursery school where thirty of us sit at three rectangular tables, pushed together at noon, and chew on buttered bread. It is 1961, and Yuri Gagarin, our Soviet hero, has just stepped out of his rocket that flew around Earth. Aunt Polya, in a stained apron stretched across her round stomach, holds a pitcher of milk and a thick-ribbed glass. The milk is warm, and the butter has absorbed all the rancid smells of the kitchen, but we eat and drink because we don't want to get into trouble with Aunt Polya. We don't want to hear her yell or see her aproned stomach loom over our faces.

Aunt Polya presides over the nursery school's kitchen, which is behind the big peeling door we are forbidden to approach. I fear she could be in charge of more than buttering bread, pouring milk, and dispensing soup, more than ordering us to chew and swallow and not waste a single crumb. She could be in charge of our lives, since what keeps us breathing and healthy, according to Aunt Polya, is food.

"If you don't finish your milk you'll get sick!" she screams, now towering over my friend Genka, and I almost believe her.

After we eat, we crowd into the hallway, where our coats hang on hooks hammered into the wall. When we are all properly bundled up, we go down to the courtyard, to the sandbox and tall wooden slide. Genka and I are the only ones who, in the winter, dare coast down its iced surface standing up. The slide is in the middle of the playground, and we are herded there in pairs, in scratchy wool leggings and galoshes over felt *valenki* boots, our throats cinched with scarves and our waists with belts over padded coats. With all that cinching, it is difficult to stretch my arms out as I glide down, whipped by freezing air, hoping I won't lose my balance and plop down onto what my mother calls my "soft spot" and what Genka calls my "ass."

But now it's late spring, a perfect time to explore the courtyard. We know there are vaulted hollows under the buildings— enticing, scary, and forbidden. While Raya, a girl with a red bow, wails over a collapsed sand castle that our teacher Zinaida Vasilievna is busy examining, Genka and I quietly creep out of the playground. We hide behind huge aluminum garbage bins and dive under an archway that leads through a damp tunnel to another courtyard separated from the street only by a metal fence. It is dizzying to think that we can simply walk through the gate and find ourselves on the sidewalk next to the street, so maligned by my mother for its dangerous streetcars and speeding trucks. But at the moment we are not interested in the risks the street can offer. We have just discovered a door under a dark archway, a rectangular sheet of wood upholstered in cracked black oilcloth that even Genka hesitates to touch.

I venture a guess that a paralyzed woman lives there. I see her in my mind, motionless and shriveled in her bed, yet still wicked, like an old, long-nosed witch from a tale of the brothers Grimm, or Baba Yaga from our own folktales, who lives in a hut that is perched on chicken legs.

Genka says that a paralyzed woman isn't a grotesque enough inhabitant for such a place, that a more horrible defect must lurk behind the door, like a deaf child or a gnarled hunchback.

Or the garbageman, I say, and we both fall silent. We stand there, unblinking and petrified. Without doubt, the garbageman is scary enough—the scariest of all because he is real—to reside inside this dark tunnel where beads of moisture slither down the slimy stone walls.

He works in the cellar across from the playground, shoveling raw garbage dropped from each apartment through chutes. The smell of rotting trash leaks from under the cellar door and rises to the sidewalk, six cement steps up. On rare occasions he climbs the stairs to crouch on the ledge, always with his back to the sun. Gnome-like, with black stubble sprouting through his cheeks and a nose like a wilted red potato, he smokes hand-rolled cigarettes, which he crumples in his crooked fingers before lighting. His clothes are so soiled and permeated with the stink of garbage that his smell hangs in the air long after he is gone. I've always thought he sleeps in the cellar, somewhere in a little nook he cleared of potato peels and fish skeletons in his underground sea of decomposing trash.

But now, frozen in front of this black door, we both realize that this is the place where the garbageman must live, in the middle of this damp tunnel, in the eye of darkness, where we are no longer protected by sunlight or Zinaida Vasilievna or even screaming Aunt Polya.

Just as my heart is stumbling at this hideous thought, the door creaks, and its oilcloth slowly begins to separate from the stone frame, making Genka produce a sound as if he were choking on a bone. His eyes are two black *o*'s, and we run as fast as we can, out of the tunnel, into the daylight of the playground and into the arms of our teacher, Zinaida Vasilievna.

She tells us to stand in front of her, straight up, arms down at attention, and explain why we are so special that we think we can just take off on our own. What makes you different from everyone else, she demands, from the rest of our collective, those who don't run around looking for trouble? What makes you different from those who are content with the sandbox activities?

Back inside, as everyone is herded into the bathroom to sit on tin potties, Genka and I stand in opposite corners of the room. We are told to face the corner, so all I see is a patch of paint peeling off the wall. I wish I could talk to Genka and ask him if he saw anything through the crack in the door, any hint of the garbageman—a gnarled finger or a glimpse of the quilted sleeve of his filthy jacket—but I hear Aunt Polya's lumbering steps and her voice behind me.

"Very good, Gorokhova," she thunders, a smell of sour butter wafting into my corner, "first you don't finish your soup, and now you run off where you please. Your mother, I'm sure, will be happy to hear this."

If my mother finds out, I'll face yet another corner, this one by the garbage chute in our kitchen, after a lecture on the need to march in step with the collective and on the perils of city streets. Serving my term of punishment by the garbage chute would be ironic, I think, especially knowing that the garbageman is six floors below, on the other end of the chute line, and that if I stand on my tiptoes and throw something down—anything, even an empty matchbox—it could land directly on his head and scare *him*, for a change.

The thought of scaring the garbageman makes me grin, but I bite my lip because I know Aunt Polya wants to see me upset and remorseful. I think of the worst thing that may happen, my cruelest possible punishment, the loss of a Sunday trip to the ice cream kiosk with my father: the ten-minute walk to Theatre Square, where from the frozen, steaming depths of a metal cart a morose woman lifts a waffle cup packed with ice cream called crème brulee, hard as stone.

"My mother has a sick heart," I say. "If she finds out, she may have a heart attack." This is only a half lie since I heard my mother complaining in the elevator to our neighbor that her heart isn't what it used to be when she was young.

"That's interesting," says Aunt Polya. Still facing the wall, I can only sense her presence from the kitchen smell and the movement of air giving way when she speaks. "You didn't happen to think about your mother's sick heart when you ran off into the street, did you?"

"We didn't go into the street," I say gloomily. I am telling the truth, but Aunt Polya isn't interested in the truth. She thinks I'm talking back to her.

"Listen well, Gorokhova," she shouts in her lunch voice, "you're a year away from real school, where they won't be so lenient. They'll kick you out with a *dvoika* in behavior, sick hearts or not." I am old enough to know that *dvoika* is the lowest grade you can get in real school. "You'll be lucky to end up sweeping the streets. I can just see you, an eighteen-year-old hooligan with a broom."

Standing in the corner, I contemplate my bleak future so succinctly fleshed out by Aunt Polya, afraid that in first grade my teacher, my principal, and everyone else will know not to trust me because I am the one infamous for placing the interests of the collective beneath my own. I will fail consistently: in handwriting, in gym, in keeping my hands folded on the desk, in scrubbing my collar white and then stitching it onto my uniform dress. I will not be allowed to become a member of the Young Pioneers and wear a red kerchief around my neck. My place will always be in the corner in the back, away from the teacher's attention, the place for those who cannot be relied on, for those with a *dvoika* in behavior. Aunt Polya will take care of that.

After an hour of standing, I am released from the corner. Later, when Aunt Polya is pouring milk as we sit around the table, she watches me more closely than usual to make sure I finish the bread. I know she's watching me, she knows that I know, and I know she knows that I know. We play this little game for a while: she gives me an unexpected glance, and I chew diligently, pretending I don't know she's looking.

The game is called *vranyo*. My parents play it at work, and my older sister Marina plays it at school. We all pretend to do something, and those who watch us pretend that they are seriously watching us and don't know we are only pretending.

The *vranyo* game of pretend chewing pays off. Neither Aunt Polya nor Zinaida Vasilievna ever tell my mother about my courtyard exploration, and on Sunday, my hand stuffed into my father's, we stroll to the ice cream kiosk and back, hard chunks of crème brûlée slowly melting on my tongue.

## Marina

"WHAT DO YOU WANT to be when you grow up, Lenochka?" asks Aunt Nina, who is my real aunt, although once removed—my mother's cousin. We are in Aunt Nina's apartment for her birthday, six of us, my sister Marina sitting next to me at the table covered with salads, appetizers, and Aunt Nina's special onion pie.

My sister Marina is seventeen: she is in her last year of high school and is concocting a plan to wrestle out of our parents their permission to apply to drama school.

"A ballerina," I say, jumping out of my chair and raising my leg behind my back.

"Sit down," says my mother, "and finish your potatoes."

I don't want any more potatoes. I'm saving room for the cake I glimpsed sitting in the kitchen, all studded with raisins and sprinkled with sugar.

I wish Aunt Nina would ask Marina what she wants to be, knowing that if she told the truth my parents already know, everyone would forget about my potatoes—and everyone else's potatoes, as well as the salted herring and beets with mayonnaise and thin slices of salami beginning to curl up at the edges. Everyone would sit with mouths gaping, wondering how such a stable family—the father the director of a technical school and the mother an anatomy professor—could have produced such an anomaly. At five, you are allowed to want to be a ballerina, or an actress, or a cosmonaut, but at Marina's age, you are supposed to be serious and think of a real profession, like nursery school teacher, or tram driver, or the local polyclinic doctor in the white hat over suspiciously blond hair who came to our apartment when I had the flu.

"What kind of a profession is acting?" my father wonders when we are home. "Standing onstage, making a fool out of yourself. *Gluposti*," he says, and waves his hand in dismissal—"nothing but silliness."

"But there were great actors everyone respected," argues Marina. "Stanislavsky, Nemirovich-Danchenko, Mikhail Chekhov. They even wrote books."

"Books are good," says my father out of a cloud of smoke. He is on his second pack of filterless Belomor cigarettes. "But learn how to read and write first. Go to a school where they teach you something useful—how to design an airplane, for example."

"And what will you do?" chimes in my mother. "Spend your life in some provincial theater so you can come out at the end of the second act to say, Dinner is served? I won't be able to help you find a job in Leningrad," she warns, practical as usual. "They'll send you to Kamchatka, and you'll be stuck there, with society's rejects, with sailors and ex-convicts, with those who can barely make it through a plumbing course, wishing you'd listened to what we told you."

My mother doesn't understand why anyone would voluntarily engage in such a disorderly and unsafe occupation as acting. First of all, it isn't serious work. What do you study in drama school, she wonders. Not chemistry, or biology, or even Latin. You don't contribute to the common good being an actress, she says; you aren't doing anything solid. It's all frivolous and chaotic, too unworthy a job for a serious citizen.

"Look at your sister Galya," adds my mother. Galya is my father's daughter who is ten years older than Marina and works as a pathologist at Leningrad Hospital No. 2. I don't know what a pathologist is, but it must be something solid since my mother often uses her as an example. "She has a proper, respectable job. Nine to five-thirty, six days a week."

On days when Marina is at meetings of her school drama club, my mother rattles the dishes in the sink, lamenting that it's all the fault of the radio. I prick up my ears, intrigued by the thought that the radio, with its piano banging, morning gymnastics, and solemn three o'clock news could have lured Marina into the trap of acting.

"It was that program," says my mother, *Theatre at the Microphone*. When they lived in Ivanovo, before I was born, Marina had spent hours standing in the corner under the radio, constantly punished for riding astride the bar in the back of a streetcar.

She would deliberately climb on when an adult was watching, says my mother, who thought she was punishing Marina. But that was my sister's plan all along—to end up in the corner, under the radio. All they used to broadcast in the evening were radio plays. She stood there for hours, like a totem pole. My mother could barely tear her away to eat dinner. And now here we are—she wants to be an actress.

I feel a new respect for Marina, for her enviable scheme of reckless streetcar riding in front of adults who would dispense the coveted punishment. I think of her standing under an old-fashioned radio with a wool-covered front, listening to the actors' voices, imagining them onstage, their eyes gleaming from under layers of greasepaint as they proclaimed eternal love, shed tragic tears, and died.

Then my mother changes her tone and tells my father that they have nothing to worry about. The competition to get into drama school is so fierce that there are a hundred applicants for one seat. "You must be a Sarah Bernhardt," she insists. "You must have extraordinary connections. You must be related to the minister of culture. No one gets in," she says and resolutely bangs a lid onto a pot of soup.

THERE IS A DOG in our house, a pedigreed Irish setter the color of copper. He is my sister's dog, although he couldn't have appeared in our apartment without my mother's consent. Both my mother and sister constantly brush the dog's long curls and let him sit in our armchair so he can look at the grainy images on our TV that flutter behind a thick, water-filled lens. When the dog is in the chair, I climb up next to him and we both watch figure skaters glide across the screen.

The dog's name is Major, and when it is time to breed him, a man rings our doorbell and introduces himself as Ivan Sergeevich Parfenov, the head of the Leningrad chapter of an organization devoted to Irish setters. Ivan Sergeevich is soft-jowled, just like Major, and somewhere around my mother's age. As he steps into our hallway, he bows slightly, takes off his felt hat, and hangs it on a hook across from the refrigerator.

"Who is the dog's owner?" he inquires as my mother shows him into the kitchen, where she is already boiling water for tea.

"Marina!" she yells, and my sister appears from her room,

where she was pretending to be busy with calculus problems. She is in her senior year of high school, tenth grade, and her future is set. She is guaranteed acceptance at both my mother's medical school and my father's technical institute. She doesn't need to kill her summer cramming for college entrance exams or tremble at the end of August in front of lists of the accepted, pinned to the dank walls of college hallways. In my mother's words, the future has been served to her on a silver platter.

To Marina's surprise, Ivan Sergeevich stands up from his chair and shakes her hand. She is even more startled when he addresses her with the formal pronoun *vy* reserved for adults and not the casual *ty*, which is used with children and family members.

He makes small talk about the final exams that are looming in June and asks Marina where she is planning to apply after she graduates from high school.

It is no secret that my sister does not care for either medicine or technology. We all know that what makes her heart melt is standing on the stage of her school's auditorium, her voice projected and her soul transformed by tragedy from the pages of Chekhov, or Gorky, or some other important playwright whose name I haven't yet learned.

For a second she hesitates, not knowing if she should reveal the truth in front of this stranger, but Ivan Sergeevich calls her *vy* one more time and smiles so openly that she glances at my mother and bites her lip. "I want to be an actress," she says looking at her feet. "I want to apply to drama school."

My mother, busy pouring boiling water from a kettle into a small porcelain pot filled with tea essence, stops and drills her eyes into Marina, who is still staring at her feet with such concentration that I creep out of the hallway to see if anything extraordinary has attached itself to her slippers.

Ivan Sergeevich becomes agitated, as though this is the best piece of news he has heard in a long time. "I can help you, dear girl," he exclaims enthusiastically, pressing his hands together in front of his chest as if begging Marina to take advantage of his offer. "I have a wonderful old friend, an actress, who could listen to you read. She can tell you if your talent is suitable for theater. She can advise you on what pieces would work especially well." He names the actress and Marina stops examining her shoes and looks up. It is a name she has heard many times, first on the radio in the old Ivanovo house, and later in Leningrad, a name attached to a voice that delivers a story every day at three, for which Marina sometimes skips the last period of school.

He gives Marina the name and the telephone number, oblivious of my mother's ominous teacup clinking and tensed back as she roots in the cupboard for a jar with strawberry jam. My mother has brought the good dishes from the other room, the set with rosebuds and a golden stripe that makes its appearance on the table only when we have guests, and we drink tea with slices of bread loaded with butter and jam while Ivan Sergeevich explains the steps in the breeding process. When we finish, he carefully sweeps breadcrumbs off the oilcloth into his palm and offers it to Major, who all this time has been waiting for a handout under the table. Then we all crowd into the hallway, and as Ivan Sergeevich reaches for his hat, my mother pulls him back into the kitchen and shuts the door.

My sister and I stand under the coat hooks, hiding in the folds of wool and crinkly raincoats, unable to hear anything but the hum of voices. I try to breathe very quietly in order not to test Marina's patience. She wouldn't normally let me share such a moment with her, but now, intent on unbraiding the strands of two voices behind the kitchen door, she tolerates my presence.

When the door finally opens, we skitter into Marina's room and peek through a crack between the hinges. Ivan Sergeevich, looking uneasy, aims a little smile toward my mother, who unbolts the front door with aggressive efficiency.

The next day Marina calls the number, and the actress gives her a date for a reading. My sister's face burns with the same feverish energy I see in my friend Genka's face when he comes up with another plan to outsmart Aunt Polya.

"This is nothing but childish blabber," says my father at supper, smoking the last of today's pack of Belomors, annoyed at the noise my mother makes rattling the silverware in the sink. His head hurts, he says, because Uncle Volodya, his chauffeur, couldn't fix his twelve-year-old *Pobeda* today, and he had to take a bus and hang out of its doors with other commuters like a bunch of grapes. He stubs out the cigarette and gets up. "This actress, whoever she is, will yawn through a couple of poems and send her home."

I'm glad Marina cannot hear this since she is with her school drama club tonight.

"Maybe it's all for the best," sighs my mother, as she picks up a rag and starts drying the dishes. "Maybe she needs to be told by an actress that a theatrical career is out of the question. Like my *mamochka* always says, everything that happens, happens for the best." A diminutive *mamochka*, which she uses instead of *mama*, sounds strange to me since I can't imagine my wide, ancient grandma as anything miniature or slight. My grandma's philosophy sounds strange, too: if everything happened for the best, why are there so many things around that aren't so good?

All week I hear Marina practicing in her room, reciting and singing. Loudly and with inspiration she reads Lermontov's "Sailboat" and Paustovsky's "Basket with Pinecones." Leaning on her door, I try to memorize the lines so I can repeat them later for my friend Genka in the same tragic and melancholy voice, a voice destined for somber theater audiences wrapped in velvet and furs.

After the audition, my mother receives a phone call. She tells my father about it while Marina is sent out to the bakery, but this time the kitchen door is open a crack, and hiding in the tangle of coats,

I hear every word. The actress called her at work, at the faculty room of the anatomy department since we don't have a phone at home. For about five minutes, under the gaze of a bored pathology professor, my mother heard about Marina's outstanding talent. You must understand, the actress said, that she has a gift for acting. You must allow her to go to drama school.

My mother reports that she felt angry to hear the judgment that instantly shattered the family's plans and legitimized, to an extent, such an unworthy profession as acting. But at the same time she can't deny she felt something that resembled pride. For a minute, while the actress went on praising Marina's innate gift, the anger and the pride bumped against each other, with pride unexpectedly taking the upper hand. My mother said "Thank you" and hung up.

When Marina returns home with a loaf of bread, she goes directly to the kitchen and starts setting the table. She doesn't usually set the table unless she is told, but she knows the actress is going to call mother any day now, so she is being preemptively helpful and sweet.

My mother watches her move across the scuffed linoleum, swing open the cupboard doors, and take out four plates.

"Elena Vladimirovna telephoned me today," she says, calling the actress by her name and patronymic, the only way an adult can be addressed in the presence of a child. "You're going to Moscow," she says. Marina's hand stops in midair and drops a fork on the floor. My sister has a stupid expression on her face, a look you should never show, a look I would never let Aunt Polya see—half confusion, half fear. Maybe she thinks she's being punished for having publicly revealed her ambition to be an actress. Maybe she thinks she did so badly at the audition that the actress has recommended that she be banished from Leningrad altogether.

"To Moscow?" she stammers out.

"Yes, to Moscow," my mother says impatiently, not wanting to repeat the words she wasn't happy to say in the first place. "Elena Vladimirovna said you should go to the best school there is, and Leningrad drama school is not that good."

# CHAPTER 4

# *Dacha*

M Y GRANDPARENTS COME TO visit every summer. From June to September they stay in our dacha thirty kilometers from Leningrad, a little house squatting on a half-acre of land behind a wood fence. It was my mother who initiated buying the dacha soon after I was born, despite my father's uncertainty about added responsibilities. I'm already eight, and I can conjure up how it happened. The baby needs fresh air, she would have declared in her teaching voice, the same voice that tells me I must finish every crumb on my plate.

My father probably hesitated, since no one wants to do right away what the teaching voice tells you. But his deepest passion was fishing, and the dacha stood a mere four kilometers from the Gulf of Finland, where you could catch pike and perch and sometimes even eel. In a rowboat, he felt at peace, enjoying the solitude infinitely more than he enjoyed the catch.

Now the boards of the dacha have been bleached to gray by years of snow and rain, with only several leftover patches of the original green paint scattered over the wood. A porch, sinking to the left, leads to an enclosed veranda with a table and two long benches in the center. The rest of the house is always dark, since the two small windows sifting light into our tiny bedroom and kitchen are shaded by branches of a sprawling lilac bush. When I enter, my eyes need a few seconds to adjust to the twilight, to make out the contours of a fat, wood-burning stove propping the low ceiling.

Another stove, this one flat-topped to accommodate pots and pans, dominates the kitchen. Its cast-iron body seems to grow out of the floorboards, rooted somewhere in the depths of the earth below the foundation. A metal sink—connected to nothing since there is no plumbing—hangs underneath a washing device, a pot with a hole in the middle plugged with a metal stem. When I jiggle the stem up and down, water trickles onto my hands and, through a hole in the washbasin, falls into a pail underneath. The sink makes you think the washing device is really a faucet that drips water into a pipe instead of a stinky pail—another example of *vranyo*, which Aunt Polya taught me in nursery school.

Dedushka, my grandfather, loves gardening. Tall and white-haired, his body thick as an oak tree, he turned a half-acre of waist-tall grass into a showcase of neat beds of strawberries, cucumbers, and dill. He planted apple trees, whose branches now bend under the weight of apples, and bushes of gooseberries, their sour fruit covered with soft white fur. In the back, he built a tomato hothouse, a sheet of plastic perched on a wooden frame and held down by bricks.

Dedushka loves to be in charge. The commander, my grandmother calls him. She looks at him out of the kitchen window, washing plates in a kettle of warm water, the skin around her eyes folding into deeper pleats with a smile from behind her glasses.

"Time to water!" he commands precisely at seven, when the sun begins to roll down the sky toward our fence. Obediently, as if she has suddenly become a different person, docile and quiet, my mother carries two watering cans from the barn. Dedushka cranks the rusty handle of our well until a chained bucket falls into the water. Leaning onto the well frame, I look down, but it is so deep I can never see the water; I only hear the bucket twitching on its chain and then a splash. With both hands, Dedushka draws the bucket up, into daylight. Two bucketfuls, one after the other, to fill two watering cans that my mother drags to the beds of radishes, carrots, and beets and then to the hothouse for the tomatoes. She walks slowly, her shoulders pulled down by her load, and I wish it had rained so Dedushka wouldn't make her do all this lifting and lugging.

Dedushka would like to commandeer my father, too, when he arrives on Saturday night with Uncle Volodya, but he knows better than to try. There's no road, so they drive up the field dotted with the blue stars of cornflowers and buttery cups of yellow flowers called chicken blindness. If eaten, I am told, these flowers can cause instant blindness, especially in chickens. My father and Uncle Volodya bump on ruts, announcing their arrival with rattling we hear all the way from the veranda, and leave the car by the back gate, next to the compost pile. I run out to meet them, to inhale my father's smell of tobacco and the car's odor of gasoline that laps around it in thick, sticky waves. Aside from compulsory watering and weeding, so little happens in the dacha that any distraction—a trip to the grocery store or a truck hurtling by—makes the day memorable. But my father's arrival is special. A whole Sunday is in front of us, with possibilities that seem infinite, with Uncle Volodya stroking his thinning hair and telling a story about a militia traffic post, with my father at the head of the table, all mine, slurping spoonfuls of cabbage soup.

When my father is in the city working, the head of the table becomes Dedushka's place. Right now Dedushka is outside. He doesn't like to give up his commanding post at the table, so the minute Uncle Volodya's car rattle reaches the house he remembers that it is time to prune or weed or fertilize. I glance out the window and see him by the currant bush, inspecting its branches and sifting white powder from a small bag onto the leaves, pretending he didn't see the car drive up the field.

"Want to go fishing tomorrow?" My father puts the spoon down and looks at Uncle Volodya.

"I want to go fishing!" I shout and jump off the bench.

"Sit down," says my mother. "You haven't finished your compote."

I don't want any more compote. I want to go fishing.

"What kind of fisherman are you?" asks my father. "*Ot gorshka dva vershka.*" Two inches taller than a potty.

"I'll be the best fisherman," I promise and press my palms to the sides of my sundress, standing at attention for a moment. "I'll catch a fish this big." I open my arms as wide as I can and push my shoulder blades together to increase the span.

"The house needs painting," my mother says. "Last Sunday it rained."

Uncle Volodya, who already heard this argument a week earlier, feels in his pockets for cigarettes and goes out onto the porch.

"No," says my father. "You'll catch a fish this big." He holds his thumb and forefinger an inch apart.

Dedushka walks up the porch past Uncle Volodya, waving away the cigarette smoke.

"Do we have enough paint?" my mother asks, directing her question to Dedushka, who is now conveniently within earshot.

"Let's go, I need some help with the stove," says grandma, and she pulls Dedushka by the sleeve toward the kitchen, away from the painting debate my father doesn't like.

He pulls his elbow out of her grip. "We have five liters in the barn," he says and straightens his shoulders. "That should be enough."

"I want to go fishing," I wail after my father as he gets up, leaves the veranda, and joins Uncle Volodya on the porch.

"Please, please, please." I know he left because he doesn't like to take orders from Dedushka, who thinks he can be the commander of all of us.

My mother and Dedushka are on the veranda alone now. No one else wants to think about painting the house, not with Sunday almost here, not with my father clattering inside the barn in search of fishing rods.

AT NIGHT, I DREAM about fishing. In my hand I am holding an oar, heavy and damp, which silently cuts into the dark water beneath the boat. I cannot see my father's face under the visor of his cap: he has lowered his head to his cupped hands, trying to light a cigarette. Writhing on the bottom of the boat, in an inch of murky water, are two purple worms that have escaped from a tin filled with dirt. We dug them up at five that morning, from the boat keeper's compost pile.

The clouds over the Gulf of Finland glimmer with a lemon tinge along the line where they roll into the water—a hint of the sun still hidden away, like a row of dimmed stage lights.

"Look beyond that light," says my father. "Look hard and you'll see people filing into the theater. You'll see ushers run up and down the aisles; people talk, programs rustle—you'll hear a murmur. When the lights start to dim, the murmur rises, and then, just a moment before the curtain goes up, the noise stops—everyone in the house holds their breath, everyone knows what is going to happen. This is the moment I've always loved most: the anticipation of magic, the expectation of illusion."

I don't know why my father is speaking about theater as if he were an actor, or even a devoted fan, but I don't question it. I cannot see his face because he is looking away, at the horizon, into the audience. "Don't let the magic slip away," he says, "or you'll sink into the quicksand of the ordinary."

"How will I recognize the magic?" I ask, but I have no voice, and I just keep opening my mouth, like the perch I caught last summer, twitching on the bottom of our boat.

Somehow, in a way that happens only in dreams, he hears the question. "You will know," he says and looks at me from under the visor of his cap. "You will know because the noise will stop."

I WAKE UP WHEN light has already bled into the air and made the sky blush. I am petrified that I may have overslept and missed the fishing trip, all as a result of wallowing in weird dreams about theater and fishing.

It is almost seven. A kettle begins to whistle on a hot plate and my mother, her hand wrapped in a rag, takes it off and pours boiling water into a teapot. I run to the veranda in search of my father.

He sits in his place at the head of the table, with his glasses on, reading the *Pravda* he brought with him from the city as though this is an ordinary day with nothing planned.

"When are we going fishing?" I demand.

He lowers the paper and his glasses, peering at me from above the rims, which gives his face a slightly facetious look.

My mother enters the veranda with the teapot in one hand and the kettle in the other. "Who is it that is going fishing?" she asks. Her tone is too familiar, the voice of a professor admonishing a student.

I look at my father. "You said yesterday we could go." I try not to glance at my mother pouring boiling water into his cup. "You said we would go fishing." I see her straightening up, preparing to speak. "You promised," I say, bending what was said yesterday in the veranda a few millimeters to my advantage.

"You're not going anywhere," says my mother, looking directly at me. "You're staying right here, helping us with the painting." She scoops two teaspoonfuls of sugar out of the sugar bowl, pours them into my father's cup, and gives the tea a couple of swirls.

This is so unfair that I burst out crying. I wail and sob. My nose begins to run, and I rub the tears and snot around my face.

My father doesn't know what to do. Crying makes him uncomfortable, sending him out of the veranda, his shoulders curled forward, glasses off his nose, crushed in his fist. I see his figure, smudged at the contour, move toward the barn where Uncle Volodya is sleeping in the hayloft.

Hearing my wailing, Grandma sails in from the garden, where she has been cutting off strawberry shoots. Whiskers, she calls them, as if strawberry plants were aristocratic gentlemen out of Tolstoy. "*Nu, nu,*" she murmurs, circling her arms around me, holding me pressed to a stomach so soft that my mother's diminutive term *mamochka* suddenly fits her. She mutters her line of wisdom, "Whatever happens, happens for the best."

This is the perfect example of the absurdity of her philosophy because painting the house on Sunday is obviously not better than going fishing with my father. But I don't say anything since her arms feel warm and soft as a blanket.

My mother is back in the kitchen, clomping between the bucket with drinking water on one end and the table on the other. I hate her, I hate these peeling walls, I hate this ruined Sunday. I hate Dedushka, whom I see in the garden yanking yellow suns of dandelions out of a scallion bed. When he is done with the last one, he straightens up and stares at his palms, which I know are black and sticky with dandelion milk. Then he takes a ladder out of the barn, carries it to the house, and leans it against the outside wall.

I wipe my face with the back of my hand, wriggle out of Grandma's embrace, and march out of the gate into the field where the flowers known as chicken blindness are in full bloom. The grass around me is protective and soft, like grandma's arms. I'll eat the yellow flowers and go blind, which will prevent me from helping my mother and Dedushka paint the outside of the house. Feeling the air in front of me with my feeble hands, I'll be walking around our garden, stumbling into the apple trees, tripping over the hothouse bricks, wavering precariously on the lip of the well. "Look at her," kind neighbors will whisper behind my back, out of my mother's earshot, telling their children not to stare. "Once her mother didn't allow her to go on a fishing trip . . ."

BY THE END OF August the dacha chores change. There is no more watering and weeding; all our forces, under Dedushka's command, are charged with gathering and preserving. When the strawberry season ends in July, it is time for raspberries and currants. Currants become translucent, with white veins running through their flesh, ready to soak in the ripe sunshine of August. Raspberries soften and blush in the sun, little flashlights among jungles of nettle plants. Raspberries and nettles always together.

No matter how hard I try to avoid the burning nettle leaves, my arms swell in welts every time I venture into a raspberry patch with a bowl. And if, miraculously, I manage to avoid being stung by the nettles, I get scratched by the thorns of the raspberries themselves. Yet it is impossible to pass the raspberry patch without dipping my arm into the midst of it, into the heart of the bushes, where berries grow the biggest and sweetest. If my mother sees me, she'll bunch her eyebrows together and say I am an *egoistka*, one who fails to think about other people.

I know I am not supposed to eat the berries, one of the dacha's unwritten rules. All of them—strawberries, raspberries, red and black currants, hairy gooseberries, and purple plums—are collected in pots and baskets, cleaned, sorted into piles on the kitchen table, and turned into jam for the winter.

The giant kitchen stove is ablaze, snake-tongues of fire hissing through the metal rings of burners. Next to it is a stack of firewood—you have to feed the stove constantly, you can't let it feel even a twinge of hunger. Every fifteen minutes Dedushka opens the blazing throat with an iron stick and shoves another log into the flames.

Otherwise the jams that are boiling on its top in big copper bowls will not take: the alchemy of sugar and fruit comes together only at a constant temperature.

My mother is wearing an old apron across her belly. Underneath the apron is nothing but a cotton brassiere and pink underpants that come down to her knees. Her face glistens with sweat, beads growing above her upper lip and rolling down her chin. She stirs the boiling jams with a ladle, keeping them from getting stuck to the bottoms of the bowls. The raspberries are boiling more and more slowly, until they start to bubble with a sighing sound, a lazy noise of exhaustion—my mother's readiness test. She fills a spoon with hot jam and slowly spills its contents back into the bowl: if it spills easily, in a stream, the jam needs more boiling, but if it drops hesitantly, one heavy drop at a time, it is ready.

This is the moment that makes everything—cranking the old well, the nettle burns, the kitchen heat—worth enduring, the moment when I can lick the bowls after the jam has been transferred into three-liter jars to store for the winter. The thick film coating the bowls, a gooey mixture of cooked sugar and fruit, is the ultimate reward.

A soup spoon in hand, I savor every scrape, especially the abundance of sticky treasure that nestles along the seam where the walls of the bowl meet the bottom. When the spoonwork is done and I know from experience that scraping will not yield another drop, it is time to start licking. The sidewalls are easy. It is reaching to the bottom that is a challenge, and I stick my tongue out as far as I can until it reaches the sugary ridges left by the spoon on the bottom. My whole head is inside the bowl now, my hair sticking to the walls, the copper sides leaving gummy marks on my neck and ears.

SOMETHING HAPPENS AT THE end of August: summer curls like a scorched leaf, folding into itself, shrinking. The breeze from the Gulf of Finland turns into an icy wind, and the sun becomes cool and distant as if it has lost interest in our dacha and our garden.

It's my father's last chance to go fishing, and he plans a real fishing trip—no children, no one allowed but him. He leaves at night, sleeps in the boat keeper's barn, and sets off at three in the morning, in pitch blackness, before the sun is even contemplating getting up. We see him off at the gate, my grandma, my mother, and I, waving vigorously and then watching him walk across the field, three fishing rods bobbing on his shoulder in synch with his steps.

He doesn't return the following morning. At noon my mother stops pinching gooseberries off the bush, sets the basket down on the veranda floor, and checks her watch against the alarm clock on the table. With Grandma, they go over the times again: how long it should have taken him to take the boat out into the Gulf, how many hours to bring it back, pull it into the boat keeper's barn, and then walk four kilometers back home.

"He might be talking to the boat keeper," offers Grandma. "Maybe he's fallen asleep. Or decided to clean the fish there, right away. With men you never know."

Her voice is sweet and thick as honey, but my mother is hard to fool. She gets up, spreads a newspaper on the table in the veranda, and pours the gooseberries out to clean. Instead of cleaning, though, she sits in front of the berry mound and pulls off bits of skin around her fingernails.

They don't say anything for a while, and we watch Dedushka outside pruning the old pear tree, clipping off branches and rubbing the fresh cuts with something white from a can.

Then it's two in the afternoon, and three, and four.

"I shouldn't have let him go. I felt something would happen, felt it right here," says my mother and drives her fist into her chest.

"Men are men," Grandma says. "They'll do what they want."

She shuffles around the veranda, back and forth, pausing by the window to look at Dedushka, who is now pulling out the last handfuls of dill. They are wilted and sinewy, good only for pickling, with yellow umbrellas of blossoms on the top.

"I should have said no," says my mother. "Just no, you cannot go. And now—here we are." She opens her hands as if presenting us with the news we already know. Lamenting her own softness, she seems to take this anxious waiting, this possibility of the unspeakable, as punishment for her lenience. Had she been a little stronger, a bit more willful and persistent, the three of us wouldn't be in the veranda now, avoiding looking at the clock.

"There could've been a storm. It's the Gulf of Finland. It's the Baltic Sea, after all," says my mother, adding another log to the blaze of her worry.

Although I participate in this restless waiting, I know my father is safe. Nothing could have happened to him. Nothing could ever happen to him. He is a fisherman, he has three rods and knows how to hook a perfect worm. He knows how to work the oars so that the boat glides noiselessly and turns at a slightest nudge from his hand. In case of a storm, he will simply row hard and fast, stronger than the waves. He is invincible, my father. I know he is waiting somewhere, tired of being told what to do, sick of Dedushka's commandeering, testing them all with his absence.

At eight, when dusk begins to dissolve the trees' contours, he staggers across the field, lumbers up the porch steps, and collapses on the couch. I wiggle next to him, but he waves me away. My mother brings him tea, but he waves that away, too.

I glare triumphantly at both my mother and Grandma, letting them know with my eyes that my father stretched on the couch is an indelible proof that I've been right all along, that the only thing their worrying did was make him seem weak and vulnerable, as if he could ever succumb to a storm. As if he could succumb to anything.

"So what happened?" asks my mother, her voice tinged with the remains of anguish but also with a demand to know what it was that kept her and Grandma looking at the clock, forced to come up with reasons why a man would be hours late to return home.

There was a storm, he says, a storm he survived by being able to maneuver the boat into a marshy creek—a piece of damn luck—where he tied the boat to a tree and huddled until it was safe to leave.

My mother gasps, but I am the only one to see it because she quickly turns away, and the hands that she held up to her chest are now wiping her dress at her thighs.

I watch my father close his eyes and fall asleep. I watch my mother bring a blanket into the veranda and spread it over him and tuck the sides under his shoulders and his knees. He turns on his side and puts his elbows over his ears as though he doesn't want to hear any more ruckus over his absence.

I knew my father was stronger than the storm, stronger than anyone here thought he was. I knew he would be all right.

# CHAPTER 5

# Lenin and Squirrels

M Y THIRD-GRADE TEACHER, VERA Pavlovna, is bony and tall, a brown cardigan trailing from her shoulders, stiff as a clothes hanger. She teaches arithmetic, Soviet history, and Russian. In her class we copy exercises from the textbook into lined, skinny notebooks as she walks around the room, peering down over our heads, praising the uniform strokes of our handwriting.

Most frequently, her praise falls on Zoya Churkina, who sits in the row to my left, two desks closer to the front. Zoya is blond and perfect, her long hair arranged in two tidy braids with bows at the ends, her black apron buttoned over her smart brown dress with a white collar, always starched. "Our diamond," Vera Pavlovna calls her as Zoya blushes, trying to suppress a smile.

She never calls me a diamond, although I finish the exercises as fast as Zoya does. The best nickname I ever receive is "our gold nugget," which she bestows on me when I decline all the participles without a single spelling error. I resent Zoya, with her exemplary braids and her permanent diamond status. Although none of us has any idea of what a diamond or a gold nugget looks like, we are all aware of the diamond's supremacy and thus of my second-place standing.

When the bell rings, Zoya erases the board and makes sure everyone goes into the hallway. She is the class monitor, the only one allowed to stay in at break time, the one to ensure that Dimka, the class hooligan, doesn't instigate any fights.

Dimka is a *dvoechnik*, the one who gets a *dvoika*, or failing grade, in everything. The opposite of *dvoika* is *pyatorka*, a five, the grade Zoya and I get. "Most likely this Dimka is a plumber's son," says my mother, who just recently had an encounter with plumbers. After a week of daily visits to our apartment building office to complain about a water leak, my mother finally prevailed, and two plumbers were sent to fix the problem. But by the time they arrived they were so drunk that when my mother opened the door, they could only sink to the floor of the stair landing, their heads propped against the elevator shaft.

IT IS ONE DAY before November 7, the anniversary of the Great October Socialist Revolution, a topic Vera Pavlovna is passionate about in our history class. Stretching her long arm forward, like Lenin in the statues scattered around the city, she tells us how the retired World War I cruiser *Aurora*, which is now permanently anchored on the other side of the Neva, fired a blank shot signaling the storming of the Winter Palace.

"Workers and peasants," she says, "ruthlessly exploited by the Tsar, climbed over the palace gate, ran up the October Staircase, and arrested the Provisional Government." The part about the Provisional Government remains murky since she never explains how this government came to replace the Tsar, and why it, too, needed to be overthrown if it was the already de-throned Tsar who had plunged the country into the pitiful abyss requiring revolutionary intervention.

As her voice trembles describing the arrest, I try to picture a crowd of workers and peasants inside the Winter Palace, the home of the Hermitage, stomping their boots up the October Staircase with its inlaid marble floors and Italian paintings, hurtling past the throne of Peter the Great with their hammers and scythes. I cannot help thinking that, despite Vera Pavlovna's ardor, they wouldn't allow anything of that kind today, when simply to enter the Hermitage you must put on cloth slippers, cinch them around your ankles, and glide slowly under the gaze of a million babushkas in the corner of every room, making sure that you don't come too close to the royal china or priceless oils.

"Tomorrow, November seventh," she says, "all across the Soviet Union, from our glorious capital to the permafrost of the Siberian taiga, we will celebrate the anniversary of the Great October Socialist Revolution."

"Why is it the October Revolution if we celebrate it in November?" asks Dimka the hooligan from the last row.

Vera Pavlovna stops in the middle of her story and looks at him with disbelief. The Julian-Gregorian calendar change is first-grade information, but even back then Dimka obviously wasn't listening.

"Shame on you," she says, pointing at him Lenin-style. "Shame on you and your ignorance."

She pauses to let Dimka's shame and hopelessness sink to an appropriate depth in each of us. After a minute of silence, as the train of her narration is irrevocably off track, she turns to more recent happenings.

"In two days, when we return to school after the holiday, we're going to have a celebration of our own. A great honor will be bestowed upon you—you will all become Young Pioneers."

Every year in the school gym, three sections of third-graders, lined up in perfect rows, take the Young Pioneer Oath and have red kerchiefs tied around their necks by the seventh-graders, who in their turn, at fourteen, rotate out of the Pioneers to join the Young

Communist League. It's as much a school ritual as the annual visit to the dental clinic, a day in the middle of March that everyone hates.

"All of you will take the oath in two days, the first step on the great road to becoming a communist," continues Vera Pavlovna as she looks at Dimka. With a shake of her head she lets us know that, despite school policy, he is obviously undeserving of this honor.

The Code of Young Pioneers, which is posted on our classroom wall, requires good behavior and good grades of all its prospective participants, so technically Dimka is not eligible; but in reality every person in every class gets a red kerchief, and Vera Pavlovna can do nothing to stop Dimka from joining in. We all know, of course, that she would never try. She understands the necessity of diverging in practice from what's been written on paper, of rules being something you recite and aspire to, not something you follow. It is clear to everyone that it wouldn't look proper if some people during the ceremony remained unkerchiefed, raising all kinds of questions about their intent and allegiance.

"Look at our Pioneer hero of the past," says Vera Pavlovna and points to the portrait of Pavlik Morozov hanging on the wall next to Pushkin. His story is in our textbooks, but Vera Pavlovna recites it again. "A son of wealthy peasants, Pavlik found out that his father was hiding sacks of wheat in his cellar—while people were starving. At night, this brave boy ran across the fields to the local Soviet and told them about the grain. The next morning the soldiers came to his house and confiscated the wheat. The local Commissariat gave Pavlik Morozov a medal." Vera Pavlovna nods her head to punctuate the last word.

I glance at Pavlik's solemn head looking down on us in a red Pioneer kerchief and a halo of righteous superiority, as perfect as Zoya Churkina's.

"What happened to the father?" asks Dimka from the last row. Vera Pavlovna pauses and looks at him with a hopeless smile. Even if you don't know what happened to Pavlik's father, everyone knows what *should* have happened to him for hiding wheat from starving people.

"For this serious crime, and for breaking Stalin's decree to give up all the harvest to the people, Citizen Morozov the elder was arrested and served ten years in the camps," announces Vera Pavlovna.

I am not sure that ratting on your father and having him shipped to Siberia is a heroic thing to do, even if it saved someone from starvation. But I don't say anything, and no one else does either, to contradict Vera Pavlovna in praising Pavlik Morozov's vigilance and valor. We all know that some things are so obvious you just don't debate them. You don't debate what's written in history textbooks. You pretend you think that Pavlik Morozov was a true hero deserving a medal, just as in nursery school we pretended to chew the bread with rancid butter.

But Dimka, because of his ignorance or stupidity, does not know the unwritten rules. Unlike the rest of us, he doesn't weigh what to say before he says it. He doesn't rehearse in his mind to make sure that what rolls out of his mouth will fit the Code of Young Pioneers. So, once in a while, he can ask an interesting question.

AT HOME, THE NIGHT before the Young Pioneer initiation, I wash my white uniform collar and my mother irons it and sews it back on. In the morning she braids my hair with two white nylon bows and stands me in front of a triple dressing mirror in our room. "What a pretty Young Pioneer," she smiles. My father is fumbling through the armoire looking for his jacket. He left it hanging on the back of a chair, a fine place for a suit jacket, but my mother put it away and now he'll be late for work. He tugs on a hanger, spills a tangle of cardigan sweaters, and pulls his jacket out of their midst. "Let me see the salute," he says, the result of my mother's orderliness crumpled by his feet.

I straighten my right hand and bring my thumb to my forehead, as our school's Pioneer counselor has taught us.

"*Molodets*," says my father. "Good for you." He is standing in front of my mother, who is knotting his tie.

"We're all joining in," I say, "even Dimka the *dvoechnik*."

"I don't know about that," says my mother and shakes her head. "What kind of a reward is this for a *dvoechnik*?" she says, and I know she is still fuming over the two drunk plumbers who have yet to fix our water leak. She threads the tie under the collar of my father's shirt. "What do you think, Ilya?" she asks.

"What difference does it make?" he says. "It isn't what it used to be." He pats himself on the pockets to make sure he has his two packs of Belomor cigarettes for the day. "We used to believe in something. You went through the war, you know," he motions toward my mother. "For motherland, for Stalin. Remember?"

My mother loops his tie back and forth and nods.

"There's nothing to believe in anymore. You open *Pravda* and everything is so much better there than it was yesterday. And yesterday was better than the day before. At this rate, everyone will be out of communal apartments by next week, driving their own cars to load up on *kolbasa*. You know the joke about *Pravda* and *Izvestiya*?" he asks to no one in particular. "There's no news in *Pravda* and no truth in *Izvestiya*."

I think it's funny—no news in the Truth and no truth in the News—and I laugh, but my mother looks at my father with reproach because, I know, she doesn't want to disillusion me before I even join.

"Be a good Pioneer," says my father, taking his briefcase and opening the front door. "And don't forget that salute."

"Listen well to what Vera Pavlovna says," instructs my mother as we go down in the elevator, letting me know that, although what my father said may be true, it does not apply in school.

OUR MORNING CLASSES ARE canceled. Lined up in our special uniforms, white aprons instead of black ones for girls, white shirts under gray suits for boys, we stand at attention in the gym and solemnly promise to live, study, and struggle as the great Lenin bequeathed that we must do.

We stand in rows, the three sections of our third grade, a hundred and twenty of us, with Vera Pavlovna straight as a pole, her eyes on the principal at the podium. In front of us, along the other wall of the gym, are the three sections of seventh-graders, red kerchiefs stretched on their palms. When the principal is finished with her speech—the Pioneer duties and responsibilities we all know by heart—our music teacher signals a fifth-grader with a horn to play a few notes, and the boy tries so hard to hit them right that his face turns as red as his Pioneer tie. This is the signal for the seventh-graders to move forward and bind the kerchiefs they are holding around our necks. With inadvertent pushing and bumping as each fourteen-year-old moves toward each of us, our identical rows instantly collapse into a crowd. When a seventh-grade boy approaches, freckled and red-eared, he fumbles with my kerchief, tying it so that it hangs too long on the left, but that's not important because the kerchief is all mine now and I can set it right or untie it altogether and make a brand-new knot.

I turn my eyes sideways to look at Zoya's white bows obediently lying on her shoulder blades, at Dimka staring into space as he, along with all of us, bends his elbow in salute. Then the school's Pioneer counselor, who is about twenty but who looks twelve and is in charge of orchestrating the whole event, takes in a lungful of air and yells out, "Be ready!" It is a signal to recite the Young Pioneer motto that we rehearsed so many times after classes and during the big break, pretending we had red kerchiefs tied around our necks. But this is the real thing. Little flames of polyester bloom around our collars, announcing to everyone in our school that we are no longer eight years old. We all breathe in, count to three, and shout as we were taught, "Always ready!"

After the ceremony, there is another opportunity for Vera Pavlovna to tell us about heroism and valor. She stands in front of our four rows of desks, talking about the Great Patriotic War. Stalin, she says, got his name from the word *stal*, which means "steel," because he was as strong as steel. "Got his name," she says, as though names were given out at some name-dispensation fair according to people's character.

I wonder how Lenin got his name. According to our history book *Eternally Alive*, he chose it in honor of the great Siberian river Lena. But Lena is also my name, and this coincidence makes me uncomfortable. Am I somehow, in an odd way, related to Lenin? Does it oblige me to be as fervent as Vera Pavlovna in believing what our third-grade history lessons teach? Does it oblige me to admire Pavlik Morozov, who chose the starving people over his father and now sneers down at me from the wall?

My shoulders sag under the weight of this historic liability.

IN MARCH OUR THIRD-GRADE class is scheduled to go to a dental clinic. Vera Pavlovna writes the date on the board, in cursive letters uniformly bent to the right, and tells us to copy it into our school journals—Wednesday, March 10.

I hate the dental visit. I wish I could expunge the date we all wrote into our journals, eradicate it from the page and from existence. I wish I could cancel all future trips, one per grade, that will loom in the third quarter of each year, dampening the anticipation of International Women's Day, when all the boys in my class timidly produce little mandatory presents for all the girls and the last period on March 7 is dedicated entirely to the distribution of pencil sharpeners, erasers, and pocket combs.

Last March, the dentist poked and prodded inside my mouth, looking angry when she didn't find any cavities to fill. This time, I suspect, she won't be so disappointed. You cannot be lucky two times in a row, says my sister, who is studying acting in Moscow, and she may be right. I think of the kilograms of Squirrels—chocolate candy wrapped in blue paper with a picture of a brown squirrel holding a huge nut—that I've cajoled out of my mother over the past year. My mother pretends she doesn't want to buy the candy, but I know she likes to unwrap a Squirrel with tea, so every time we walk into a grocery store we play the same game I learned in nursery school.

"Please, can I have some Squirrels, please," I whine as she stands in line to pay for bread at the cash register. The counter with sweets is right next to the bakery counter. Behind an indifferent saleswoman, ignorant of the fact that she has unlimited access to such treasure, sit chocolate candies called Red Poppy, Polar Bear, and Kara-Kum Desert, with camels trotting across the yellow wrapping papers. Under the wrappers is a thin layer of silver foil that crinkles under my fingers when I open a piece and a dark brown side emerges in all its nut-and-chocolate glory. "Please," I beg, "only two hundred grams."

"Candy is bad for you," says my mother as the cashier gives her a receipt, which she must now take to the bread saleswoman. "I let your sister eat all the candy she wanted and now look—she's studying acting. Maybe she'd be an engineer or a pathologist like Galya if I wasn't so soft on her."

The idea that Squirrels lead to acting makes little sense, but this is not the time to argue with my mother. "Just a little bit," I wheedle. "A little tiny bit for the evening tea."

At the bakery counter she exchanges the receipt for a brick of black bread and a loaf of white *bulka*.

"For the tea," I whimper. "*Chut-chut*—just the tiniest bit."

She glances at the line to the cashier, which now consists only of an old babushka and a woman with a baby in her arms. With just two people, you can't even call it a line.

"All right," she concedes and takes out her purse, just as I knew she would. "But only *chut-chut*."

*

ON MARCH 10, THE thirty-eight of us pile into a streetcar that takes us to Dental Clinic #34. In pairs, we file into a fluorescent-glaring waiting room with a sharp odor of something that smells like the ether they use to kill rabbits in my mother's anatomy lab.

We are told to sit down and wait. My partner, Sveta Yurasova, and I, still holding hands, take the two end seats, away from the door with the sinister sign "Treatment Room," away from Dimka the hooligan, who glides across the linoleum pretending he is skating.

Vera Pavlovna lifts her arm, asking for our attention, but it isn't her gesture that makes us all quiet down. The door into the Treatment Room opens and reveals rows of drills, ominous and still silent. In the doorway stands a square woman in a white gown and a cotton hat neatly ironed into creases that make it rise on her head like a meringue pie. We are all quiet now, frozen in our last gesture before the door to the Treatment Room opened, as if we were all actors performing the final scene of Gogol's *Inspector General*, the most famous silent theater scene of all time.

"Antonova," reads the woman from a file in her hand, and our eyes all turn to Anya Antonova, a girl with a red braid down her back who gets up and obediently follows the woman into a vast room behind the door.

"Alphabetical order," says Sveta, and she smiles an embarrassed smile because she will be the last one to be called. I know she is thinking about all the things that could happen between A and Y, hoping for a sudden power outage, or a swift lethal disease that exclusively affects dentists, or even an emergency history test that Vera Pavlovna remembers she has to administer by the end of the day.

I don't have Sveta's luxury of hoping and waiting. My name is at the front of the alphabet, G being the fourth letter, after A, B, and V. Yet I know that even if I had the guts to run out of here, the first militiaman on the street would drag me back, to Vera Pavlovna's scolding. I am nine and I've already learned that there is no escape from this waiting room, from this annual dental punishment, from this order of life.

But the worst drawback of being at the front of the alphabetical list is that no one has yet returned to tell the story. They are all still inside, the A's, B's, and V's, pressed into cotton-padded chairs, cringing away from the drills.

The door opens again and the first dentist, the woman in the meringue pie hat, is staring into another folder. "Gorokhova," she barks, my last name only, in a voice that suddenly sounds like Aunt Polya's. I creep across the waiting room and Vera Pavlovna, who is now standing by the door, pats me on the back.

The room is the size of our school cafeteria, with twelve dental chairs arranged in two rows, although the drills make it look less like a cafeteria and more like a factory floor. A factory for neglected teeth compromised by too many Squirrels. I see my three classmates, small inside the tall chairs, their open mouths gaping in faces twisted with fear. As I follow the meringue hat around the towering drills, I see Anya Antonova, the first one called, her hand over her cheek, climbing out of the chair now designated for me.

"Sit down," says the dentist, and she begins to study my chart. I hope she studies it well enough to see that I had no cavities last year despite all those chocolates my mother pretends she doesn't like. I hope she decides I am an exceptional case and lets me out of this chair with padded arms and the drill looming on my right.

She stops reading, puts down the folder, and sinks onto a stool next to the chair. She is so close I can see little black hairs over her upper lip and creases radiating from her eyes into her hair. From the table that is out of my sight she picks up something long and metal. "Open wide," she says and starts poking inside my mouth, tugging at my teeth with a metal hook, wheezing into my face with a breath of cabbage and black bread.

Then she stops, puts down the poking instrument, and starts writing in the file. She writes and writes, and the more she writes the lower my hopes sink until they cannot sink any lower, hitting the bottom of the dental abyss. I hear someone scream through the whizzing of drills, and it begins to smell like burning wire, or maybe smoldering bone.

"Open wide," says my meringue-hatted dentist as she packs my mouth full of chalk-tasting rolls of cotton. "And stay open."

I shut my eyes and stay open. I hear the drill roaring to life; I taste its metal heat as it bores into one tooth, then the second one, then the third, and then I lose count. The drill seems to gouge into the center of every tooth, burning and coming too close to something soft and unprotected that I know would hurt much more than I can tolerate. I clench my fists and think of my father. I think of how strong he had to be to survive the Gulf of Finland storm. I imagine him being pummeled by the waves, struck by the oars flying in the wind. I imagine him clenching his fists around the wood and rowing as hard as he could, hard pellets of rain whipping him in the face. He withstood it all. Not even for a moment did he think of crying or moaning or showing that it hurt.

When the buzzing of the drill finally stops and I feel the soaked rolls of cotton being pulled out, I open my eyes and see Vera Pavlovna standing in front of me, smiling.

"*Molodets*," she says. "Five cavities and you didn't even cry."

I know she is being generous because I feel the hot path of two tears that rolled down my cheeks. But I know they were silent tears nobody heard, and that makes them unimportant because my dentist with the meaty hands didn't notice them or pretended she didn't as she drilled the teeth decayed by too many Squirrels.

The rest is easy. After the dentist mixes the ingredients on her table, she dips something cold and ether-smelling into each drilled hole. Then she scoops the mixture and packs it into each tooth, pressing hard with her metal hook. It doesn't matter that the ether stings and makes my tongue go numb; it doesn't matter that the scraping makes me wince. If I can withstand the drill, I can be like my father. I can withstand anything.

Back in the waiting room, I see Sveta Yurasova crouched in the corner. She is impressed by my valor, but her eyes are all pupils. I know she has realized that nothing extraordinary is going to happen between G and Y that will save her.

As I sit there waiting for everyone to be drilled and patched, I find out that five cavities wasn't actually that bad. Dimka the hooligan, as it turns out, had twelve and is still sweating in the dentist's chair. Zoya the diamond wailed so loudly and jerked her head so much every time she heard the drill start that the dentist screamed at her, kicked her out of the chair, and told her to come back with her mother. And Anya Antonova, the first girl to go in, has had a dose of arsenic crammed into the root of her tooth and is required to come back in three days when the nerve is dead so that the meringue-hatted dentist can perform a root canal.

My partner Sveta, the last one to go in, turns out to be the luckiest of all. She takes on my role of last year, the girl with perfect teeth, and even the meanest dentist, the one who yelled at Zoya for crying, fails to find a single cavity in her frightened mouth.

AT HOME, WHEN WE have our evening tea, I tell my father about the dental visit. He sits in his usual place at the head of the kitchen table, across from my mother, his knee drawn up to his chin, a pack of filterless Belomors next to his teacup. My father doesn't like sweets, so he has a slice of black bread in his hand, a big piece my mother cut off the center of the loaf and slathered with a thick layer of butter. My father takes a pinch of salt with his fingers and sprinkles it all over the buttered bread.

"I hate *zubniks*," I say, using a word I've made up, a tooth person instead of a dentist.

"Don't call doctors names," says my mother. "They are dentists, not *ʒubniks*."

I like the word I've made up because it's precise. Dentists are tooth people, that's all they are, prodding around your mouth every March in desperate search of reasons to pull on the cord of a rusty drill and step on a pedal to grind it to life.

I wonder what my father thinks about *ʒubniks*. His teeth look perfect and white, undoubtedly because all his life he's probably eaten black bread instead of Squirrels with evening tea. Maybe he can teach me something I don't know. Maybe he can tell me a dental secret that only people with perfect teeth know, the secret that goes beyond staying away from chocolate candy.

"I want your teeth," I say to my father. "Perfect, with no cavities."

My mother gives him a look across the table, the look that makes my father reach for matches and shake a cigarette out of the pack.

I feel I need to take a closer look at his teeth, at the teeth that should be mine because he is my father, so I get off my stool and wiggle into his lap and tug on his lips. I pull them apart so I can see his flawless teeth, uniform and straight as in a poster for dental hygiene. In comparison, my mother's teeth, which are full of metal fillings, should be a reminder of black bread's superiority and a deterrent against buying more Squirrels.

But are perfect teeth worth giving up candy in favor of black bread? Is it worth suffering for years and denying myself the pleasure of Squirrels so I could end up with my father's teeth, or is it better to succumb to guilt and a yearly dentist's drill?

I'm proud of myself for asking these philosophical questions about guilt and pleasure, but I know that there is one big unasked question hiding behind this oratory. The question is this: are these perfect teeth real? Once or twice, when my father stayed in bed because he didn't feel well, I saw a glass on the bathroom sink— something that was there only when he didn't go to work—filled with cloudy water and chunks of pink, curved plastic sprouting something that looked suspiciously like teeth. Are his own teeth so full of cavities and metal that he has to cover them up with this pretend façade that needs to be kept in a glass? Is this just another instance of *vranyo*, like our dacha's fake sink or my mother's insincere disdain for Squirrels?

My father pulls away from my hands and lights a cigarette. He doesn't want any more bread, he says, when my mother picks up a knife to cut off another slice. "You want my teeth?" he asks, lifts me from his lap, and puts me down on the floor.

My mother looks up, a frown on her face, as if she were uncertain about what she should do next.

"What did that *ʒubnik* say when she patched up your five cavities?" he asks, using my made-up word, ignoring what my mother said about not calling doctors names.

"Nothing," I say. "She was silent and mean. She put arsenic in Anya Antonova's root canal."

"Did she say anything about this?" He picks up a Squirrel from the little metal vase on the table and dangles it between his fingers as if it were poison.

The Squirrel looks so enticing in its blue wrapper that I decide it isn't worth suffering. Next March is a century away, and I have a whole *ʒubnik*-free year stretching ahead of me, a year that can be sweetened with kilograms of Polar Bears and Red Poppies and Squirrels blooming on the shelves of our grocery store.

My father can sense that I've decided not to care about ruining my teeth, that I'd rather live with my mother's metallic smile than give up chocolates.

"Do you want to see what happens when you ignore your teeth?" he asks and stretches his arm to put the piece of candy he is holding back into the vase.

I don't know if I do. I stand in the middle of our kitchen, between the cupboard with jars of our dacha jam and the stove with a pot of borsch under a warmer, not knowing if I want to face the truth. And then, as my father leans forward and drops the candy back, as the sleeve of his flannel pajamas brushes against my empty cup, I do know. I'm certain now that I don't want to see his real, damaged teeth behind the fake perfect ones. I'd rather fool myself into thinking that his teeth are healthy and white; I'd rather pretend that my father is invincible and faultless.

"Your father had scurvy during the war," my mother says, preempting whatever she thinks might come next, seeing from my face that I don't want to see anything that would blemish him. "That's why he lost his teeth, because of hunger and a lack of vitamins. It happened to a lot of people during the war."

War and hunger are the two words we hear everywhere: in our classrooms, in our news, in the conversations of babushkas on the benches of our courtyard. They are nonspecific and worn out, something that happened not to individuals but to the entire country. Yet, it occurs to me, my father's lost teeth happened specifically to him, to this bony man sitting in his chair under the shelf on which the radio is cheerfully dispensing Tchaikovsky's "Dance of the Little Swans." In a quick move, I dash toward him and dive into his lap again, wrapping my arms around his neck, burying my face in the flannel folds on his chest. He smells of the brown soap my mother uses to scrub the laundry in the bathtub against a wooden washboard with metal ribs, and of his Belomor cigarettes, and of warm skin flushed with tea.

These are comfortable smells that make me press even deeper into the flannel of his pajamas, but I know it's dangerous to lull yourself into a sense of false safety. I'm no longer in second grade and I just had five teeth drilled. I think of war and hunger, not the hunger that happened to the country, but the one that took away my father's teeth. The specific hunger as opposed to the abstract hunger my teacher Vera Pavlovna lectures about in our history class. I think of the hunger that made Pavlik Morozov a hero, but I also think of what happened later, the part I learned from Marina, the part Vera Pavlovna never talks about at school. Despite Pavlik's heroic status, his own uncle—in cold disregard of all the people Pavlik had saved from starvation by denouncing his father—picked up an ax and delivered his own, personal justice to his nephew's head. And that unsanctioned, private act left a far greater impression in my mind than all the stories about saved people and triumphant collectives crammed into our history textbook.

But aside from partitioning the individual loss that affected my father from the collective loss that affects nothing but our grades in history class, I have a more weighty question knocking in my head. Despite his perfect fishing cast and expert rowing and powerful arms, there was something even stronger that was able to harm him. Something that even my father didn't have the power to prevent. So as I sit in his lap breathing in tobacco and soap, the question is a distraction from these cozy smells of home. If he could succumb to war and hunger, what else is lurking out there, what else is so deeply hidden and unmentionable that it makes my mother press her lips together and sigh?

# CHAPTER 6

# *Theater*

M Y MOTHER AND I are going to Moscow to see my sister's graduation performance. She has been away for four years, studying theater and acting at the drama school named after the famous dead actor Schukin. It's June, my mother has given the last exams, and I've just said good-bye to Vera Pavlovna and my third-grade class. I am a year older, content in the knowledge that Dimka the hooligan was held back, hoping that I will no longer be the gold setting for Zoya Churkina's diamond.

We travel on an overnight train and stay in Marina's dormitory room, which is itself an adventure. I've never traveled anywhere but to the dacha, where everything is dull and familiar. The dorm is the dacha's opposite, with its large corridors and white walls, with its foreign smells of impermanence and other people's clothes.

"To the end of this corridor and then two flights up," says Marina, sprinting in front of us, her ponytail swaying as vigorously as the two string bags in her hands. The string bags are filled with *pirozhki* my mother had baked the day before and chunks of salami and cheese, all wrapped in last week's *Pravda*.

Marina's hair is long now, and she has bangs that fall down to her artfully curved eyebrows. Last summer, when she was home for two weeks before she took off for her first film role, I saw her pluck her eyebrows with tweezers in front of a hallway mirror, ruthlessly yanking the little hairs out of her face, biting her lip with each vehement tug. It looked barbaric to pull out your own hair, but Marina said that it was what the stage required, and I was as impressed with her courage as with the art's severe demands. Other than her hairstyle she is the same Marina—loud voice, big eyes my mother calls photogenic, and a pudgy nose that my sister says typecasts her into character roles.

I don't look anything like my sister. That's because she is my half-sister and we have different fathers, which also gives us different patronymics. She is Marina Alexandrovna, the daughter of Alexander, and I am Elena Ilyinichna, the daughter of Ilya.

I don't know when I learned that my sister had a different father. I didn't know it when I was five, but I already knew it in Vera Pavlovna's history class. I knew it when she told us about Pavlik Morozov, who had a living real father, which made me think of Marina, who didn't.

Marina's father died in 1947. Last year, when we were getting ready to join the Young Pioneers, I tried to imagine her father's heroic death, worthy of Vera Pavlovna's history lesson on valor. I saw him stopping a tank with a grenade or throwing himself over an artillery trench until I heard my mother say that he'd died of TB, not at all a heroic way to die, according to our history books.

Marina doesn't seem to care that my father is not related to her by blood and calls him *papa*, just as I do. He is the only father she has ever known, my mother says, since her real father, that unknown Alexander, sick with TB, died shortly after the war. There is a murky period of five years between Marina's birth and her father's death, the time my mother doesn't talk about, a time long enough, in my estimation, for Marina to have known and remembered her father.

"*Papa* couldn't come," says my mother, panting, as she climbs the stairs, heaving our black square suitcase from step to step. "Lately he hasn't been feeling well." She says this with a sigh, probably from lugging the heavy bag up the steps.

When we get to Marina's room, my mother drags the suitcase into the corner and opens it immediately because she needs to hand to my sister what she's brought for her—an iron, a set of thick rubber curlers the color of rust, and a cylindrical package of cotton for which my mother says she stood in line for a whole hour.

The room has three metal beds and an armoire. Luckily, one of Marina's roommates just got married and went to live with her new Moscow in-laws, so we move the third bed next to my sister's for the three of us. At night, I dream of living in the dorm and of long corridors that lead nowhere, that all end in brick walls keeping me away from what I know is behind them, the stage.

MY SISTER'S GRADUATING PERFORMANCE is tomorrow night. This performance is like a final exam, my mother says; you'd better be ready to show everything you've learned, or you'll get a *dvoika* in acting and they'll ship you straight to Pinsk to organize a theater club for street cleaners in their local House of Culture. My mother is still unsure that she made the right decision in allowing Marina to go to drama school. Now and then she shakes her head, saying that Marina should've listened to what she was told and chosen a real profession. She could have become a pathologist like Galya, my mother laments. She could be building airplanes.

My sister's performance is a vaudeville, which, as Marina explained to me, is a short romantic comedy with music. Her play is called *Little Orphan Susanna*. She plays Madame Pichard, a widowed matchmaker unsuccessfully trying to find a husband for the orphan of the title.

In the morning Marina wakes with a scratchy throat and hoarse voice, and all day my mother has been heating milk in the dorm kitchen, adding chunks of butter into the pot. The best remedy for voice restoration, she says, carrying cups of buttery swirls up to our room.

"I can't sound like a crow," Marina cackles, swaddled under a blanket in bed. "This better work."

I press my fingers into tight fists and wish for my mother's remedy to work. We all understand the importance of tonight's performance for, as my mother summed it up, Marina has to demonstrate everything she has learned in four years. I'm not sure it's fair to judge eight semesters of schoolwork by an hour-and-a-half vaudeville, but these are the rules of the drama school and, I begin to suspect, of all schools.

A few hours later, I see Marina draw black lines along her eyelids with a tiny brush, paint little red spots in the inner corners of her eyes. I see her spread a layer of beige all over her face and neck and then rub little puddles of rouge she'd prepared on her dressing table into her cheeks and her chin. I see her put the rubber curlers my mother brought from Leningrad into her hair; I see her lift another brush and outline her mouth in crimson. I watch closely and Marina doesn't mind, peering intensely into the mirror, stroking her eyelids with a little brush in elegant, exaggerated movements of her hand, utterly enjoying the attention.

I would give anything to do what she's doing and watch my face change from a familiar Young Pioneer with braids to someone completely different, someone you couldn't find in Vera Pavlovna's textbooks. This is Theater, the real make-believe, exciting and meaningful, not at all like the everyday make-believe we all have to live by. This is the game that only the select few, those blessed with talent, one out of a hundred, are chosen to play.

My mother helps Marina lift the heavy burgundy dress, as rough to the touch as my winter coat, its skirt held wide by three metal rings, and pin a headdress of black plumage to her curled hair. Fascinated, I watch this transformation of my sister, two hours earlier wrapped in a dorm blanket, into a stranger called Madame Pichard.

Then we are sitting in the second row, my mother biting her lip as Marina performs an opening scene. She speaks her lines confidently and loudly, holding a fan in one hand and lifting her long skirt just a little bit to expose the tip of her pointy shoe.

Her voice is holding up in the first and the second scenes, but my mother and I both know that it is her song, the main number of this performance, which is going to be the test. Music starts out of the orchestra pit, which is two meters below the stage, and Marina steps onto the rim, a foot-wide strip running around the orchestra toward the audience.

I press my fingernails into the palms of my hands and in my mind call Marina all the curse words I know because this is what you are supposed to do if you want someone to have good luck. Unfortunately, I don't know any curse words, so I can't think of anything better to call Marina than an idiot, a fool, and a hooligan, although the latter is not even a curse since my teacher Vera Pavlovna uses it all the time.

My sister starts singing, reining her voice in a little, but only my mother and I know that she is afraid to strain it. Her voice rings out, filling the theater. She walks along the whole length of the stage rim, holding up her dress in one hand and a fan in the other, making small dancing steps with her pointy feet, driving her voice up and down the scale to coax the orchestra music out of its two-meter depths. "Little orphan Susanna, little orphan Susanna," she sings in the wise, experienced voice of Madame Pichard, "let me find a man for you." Her dress falls in glamorous cascades of fabric, brushing the stage behind her, as if it were made of fine silk and not of the scratchy polyester I held two hours earlier. She takes a breath and soars to the final roulade, my mother clasping her hands around the chair arms, my fingernails driven into the skin of my palms so deep they hurt. The audience is silent for a few seconds, as if they've collectively forgotten to exhale, but then we all realize that she is done and break into a frenzy of applause.

I clap so hard my palms begin to burn. This is the moment when I feel proud to be related to Marina, when I love her stage voice because it is powerful and sublime and isn't directed at me. My mother claps and smiles, too, and there is pride beaming from her eyes, the same pride she must have felt when the famous actress told her about Marina's gift.

I imagine myself on that stage, curtseying and bowing and graciously smiling, but as much as I want to be up there, in full makeup and a crinoline dress, I know in my gut that I could never do it. I could never perform in front of one pair of eyes, let alone five hundred. Maybe it's genetics, our different fathers. Marina's father gave her the acting gift and the operatic mezzo-soprano; mine gave me wooden limbs and two big front teeth.

Or maybe it isn't genetics at all. Maybe it's me, my own lack of that special talent that makes theater and its world of make-believe so thrilling and real. Without that natural gift I'll always be doomed to being a part of the other, common, make-believe, the dull and phony pretense of Vera Pavlovna with her heroic valor and Aunt Polya with her rancid butter and mandatory chewing, the pretense of our history textbook that canonized Pavlik Morozov for the brave deed of turning in his father and of our school that bent the Code of Young Pioneers to allow Dimka, the *dvoechnik* and hooligan, to join in.

With this pitiful truth staring me in the face, all I can do now is clap my hands and shout "Bravo," just as my mother and the other mothers are doing all over the auditorium. All I can do is admire and applaud this real make-believe, Theater, and within it my sister, who stands on the rim of the proscenium—batting her photogenic eyes and curling her crimson mouth in a smile, her arms outstretched toward the audience—fully aware that she isn't going to be sent to Pinsk to work in the local House of Culture because her final exam performance deserves nothing less than *pyatorka*, a perfect five.

The next day, as we pack up to leave, I find out that a perfect five is not all her performance deserves. My sister says she has received an invitation from the chief artistic director of the Leningrad Comedy Theatre to join the company starting in the fall. "Imagine this," says Marina as she folds her housedress and her nightshirt. "The director turned out to be married to that famous actress Elena Vladimirovna, for whom I auditioned in tenth grade." My sister stuffs her folded clothes, the curlers, and the iron into a suitcase because she is leaving with us on the night train to begin her acting career in Leningrad.

My mother looks satisfied but not surprised, which makes it clear that my sister has already told her, that my mother knows about this favorable turn in Marina's future.

It makes it clear that the only person who doesn't know anything is me.

# CHAPTER 7

## Simple Past

MASHA MIRONOVA IS THE only girl I know who wears nylon tights. The rest of us put on vest-like *lifchiks,* under-bodices that sprout elastic suspenders with rubber clips, and pull on ribbed cotton stockings that twist around our legs like snakes. Masha's cut hair, held back by a hair band, is a challenge to another institution: braids. Braids and bows keep our hair long and innocent of barbers. When Masha walks, her shining hair bounces above her neck, and every time I see her cross the courtyard on legs covered with perfectly aligned nylon, my own ankles thickened by cotton instantly turn into lead weights.

Masha is unique in other ways, too. Of all my friends, her mother is the only one who wears high heels. Every morning she clicks across the yard on her way to work: a tailored skirt, teased hair, red lipstick. She teaches college English: the word "English" sounds majestic and alien. In my family no one speaks a foreign language, especially one as foreign as English. My mother knows the names of all the body parts in Latin, but Latin isn't exotic, it's ancient and dead. My father speaks nothing but Russian. My sister studied French at her Moscow drama school, but French is so ingrained in Russian history that even my provincial Aunt Muza sometimes says, "*Merci beaucoup*."

Besides her bold appearance and her high-heeled mother, Masha has another quality that makes me admire her: she can speak this rarely heard language of mystery. Every morning, when the rest of us walk to our district elementary school, Masha takes Bus 22 to an English school, one of the few in the city, clearly a place for the chosen. In addition to Russian, math, and biology, she studies literature, history, and geography—all taught in English. Every morning my heart skips a beat when I glance out my window at the bus stop, when I see her nylon-clad legs climb into the crowded bus.

MASHA'S LAST NAME IS her mother's, Mironova, and not her father's, Finkelstein. Uneasy to ask Masha herself about this discrepancy, I ask my mother.

"Mironova is a Russian name," my mother says, not going into any explanation, as if what she said were self-evident. I know that names ending with *-ova* or *-ov* are Russian and that names ending with *-stein* are Jewish. Realizing that I am waiting for more, she adds, "Parents can choose which name to give their child, father's or mother's. It's usually the father's, but Masha's parents wanted her to have an easier life."

I am relieved. My own name is Russian, so maybe I'll have an easier life, too.

WE ARE SITTING IN Masha's apartment leafing through glossy magazines her mother has brought from work. There is Bulgarian *Burda*, with toothy women perched on skinny heels; there is Polish *Moda*, thick as *Crime and Punishment*. I look at the beaming models, who undoubtedly all wear tights and have never heard of *lifchiks* and snaking stockings. Masha and I are trying to figure out why in Bulgaria and Poland, countries much smaller than ours, people can be so interested in fashion that they publish whole magazines dedicated exclusively to appearance.

"My mother's friend from work went to Sofia as part of cultural exchange," says Masha. "She lived in another teacher's apartment. She says there were flowers blooming in the lobby of the apartment building."

It is difficult to imagine flowers blooming in such an unfitting space. The entrances to our apartment building are cement, with broken light bulbs and a smell of pee.

"What's a lobby, anyway?" says Masha.

I don't know about lobbies; I only know about stairwells, so I shrug.

"I also know someone who took a trip to Prague," says Masha nonchalantly, which in my eyes raises her to an even higher level of worldliness. In the overseas ranking order, Czechoslovakia is above Bulgaria, although both are way below England.

"Wouldn't you like to go to England?" I ask wistfully. "With all the English you're learning?" We both know it is a purely rhetorical question because England is the West and going there is completely out of the question.

"I'd like to see the Beefeaters," says Masha, who just finished a lesson on the Tower of London. "And a Laura Ashley store."

We saw a picture of a Laura Ashley façade in *England*, the only Western magazine we find in her mother's heap. It is published in both Russian and English by the Moscow house Progress as a joint British-Soviet venture and is available only to reliable readers like Masha's mother.

The Laura Ashley dresses are so bold in color that they hurt our eyes. They resemble gardens in full bloom, colors merging, rolling into one another, making fantastic arrangements, like bouquets of resplendent flowers. They would fit well, we think, in a lobby of an apartment building in Sofia.

I love sitting in Masha's apartment. It is similar to hearing English—mesmerizing. Soft yellow armchairs caress my elbows the same way palatalized *l*'s and rolled *r*'s caress my ears. A floor lamp with an appropriately foreign name, *torchier*, soars over the armchairs like a rising tone at the end of English sentences and then suddenly curves down in one bold jazzy stroke, pouring light on *Moda* and *Burda* and *England* scattered on the coffee table. And the coffee table—a round, dainty thing, the epitome of decadence and luxury, serving no purpose whatsoever—is as alien as the English language itself.

What amazes me most about Masha's apartment is that it contains a room not serving a basic function, a room not used for cooking or sleeping, a room where we can simply sit and talk and gawk at exotic magazines. The word "living room"—*gostinaya*—sounds as strange as "coffee table," evoking frilled ladies in chestnut curls and whiskered gentlemen puffing on cigars. Its four syllables, slick and cool, linger on my tongue, as foreign as ice cubes.

In my apartment there are only two rooms, neither defined by name. One room has two beds covered with a silk bedspread, pink doves embroidered on a purple background, my mother's pride and joy. My father was forced to make a call to a department store, where she'd seen it delivered and then hidden by a saleswoman under the counter. A bright red couch, my bed, flames against the wall. A television sits on a chest where linens are kept, and next to it stands a dressing table with tall triple mirrors that no one ever uses for dressing.

In the other room, my sister's, gleam two pieces of furniture required for every respectable home: a cupboard filled with cut crystal and a piano. Everyone I know takes piano lessons, whether they have an ear for music or don't, and every apartment boasts a black upright called Red October. Ours is covered with a lace runner and porcelain ballerinas bending in the poses of dying swans.

I hate dusting the dressing table and the piano. I hate practicing the piano, too, and that double aversion keeps me away from my sister's room, which suits us both. When I come home from Masha's apartment, my parents' purple beds, and my red couch, and the undusted triple mirror where nothing interesting is ever reflected, seem sorry-looking and old, mismatched pieces of furniture forced into cheerless coexistence.

I AM IN A streetcar, on a seat made of wooden slats varnished yellow, too hard and straight for a fifty-minute ride. It's a morning in July, and we are clattering along Leningrad streets that are nearly empty. All the citizens who could get out of the city are in their dachas, tending to strawberry shoots and tomato seedlings, shivering on the windy beaches of the Gulf of Finland between watering and weeding.

It's the first summer in my ten-year-old life that we are staying in the city. My father, who has been home for the last two weeks, doesn't feel well, my mother says, because he's been working too much. He sits in bed in his long underwear, light blue like the pale sky behind the window, staring into the television screen.

"You want Channel One or Channel Two?" asks my mother, ready to turn the knob. Channel One is from Moscow: news, figure skating, a travel show. A combine rolls across a field, over acres of wheat, with a truck crawling behind it, filled with tons of grain. A couple glides over a skating rink, a woman pirouetting on one foot, her back almost touching the ice in a movement called "the death loop." A herd of zebras is galloping across African savannah. When my father shakes his head—a slight, exhausted movement—my mother switches to Channel Two, the Leningrad station, where we see the same combine roll across the same field of wheat.

Looking out the streetcar window, I think about my father back home, sick of the black-and-white television images, reading

*Pravda* from beginning to end, all four pages. He scoffs at figure skating and says that if they broadcast soccer as often as they show ice dancing, the country would come to a halt.

"A bunch of silly men chasing a ball," my mother says. "Give each one his own ball if they're so desperate to have one."

My father doesn't dignify her remark with an answer. He focuses on the screen, where a sports commentator talks about the republic championship. His favorite team, Zenith, has just lost to a pathetic Dynamo, and he mutters in a barely audible voice, "*Sudiu na mylo!*" which is what they shout at soccer matches, a demand to make soap out of the referee. I don't know if any referees have ever been turned into soap, but it occurs to me that if I could substitute my teacher Vera Pavlovna or Aunt Polya for a referee, it would be a pretty neat call.

I am in the city in the middle of July because of my English lessons. Every weekday I take a streetcar to a tutor's apartment, where I memorize words, decipher grammatical rules, and contort my mouth around strange sounds until it hurts. During my two-month summer vacation I have to learn what my friend Masha has been learning in her English school for three years. In August, I'll take an exam to enter the fourth grade of Masha's school.

The backs of my thighs are glued to the wooden slats of the streetcar seat. My hands are sweaty, too, and I notice that I have left damp marks on the envelope I am clutching. Every ten lessons I hand my tutor, Irina Petrovna, a rainbow of bank notes—green threes, blue fives, red tens, and an occasional purple twenty-five, the largest note I've ever seen.

Irina Petrovna is my sister Marina's age, and I think it's funny that she could also be my sister. She has short hair and thick eyebrows and isn't as erratic as Marina, who can benevolently let me use her desk to listen to my English records one day and yell at me for leaving my dictionary on it the next. Irina Petrovna is predictable but strict. She teaches me the tenses, the most difficult part of English grammar, which do not seem that bad compared to the conjugations, declensions, and six case-endings a foreigner would have to sweat over to master Russian. "You're lucky you were born here," she says. "Look at those poor Vietnamese and Cubans who come to our universities and have to learn Russian in one summer."

The thought of the Vietnamese, who don't have an alphabet anyone understands, makes learning English easier. If some Vietnamese can learn Russian in one summer, I can certainly learn English. For an hour and a half I listen to Irina Petrovna, to her melodious English voice that sounds so much more thrilling than the familiar Russian cadence. In the evening, I write out the exercises she gives me for the next day, after reading five pages from Kipling. It is the same routine, six days a week, until the end of August.

In addition to the envelope with my tutor's money, I hold a three-kopeck coin, my streetcar fare back home. The coin is copper, darkened by many fingers, and I roll it around my palm until it inadvertently slips out of my grip and disappears between the wooden planks of the floor. Squatting between the two seats, I peek into the dark, but the coin has vanished, lost in the guts of the streetcar.

At the end of the lesson, I know I should ask Irina Petrovna for three kopecks—a minuscule amount, the price of a glass of water with syrup squirting out of vending machines at every railway station. As I linger in her apartment doorway, she asks if I need something, giving me a perfect opportunity to word my request, but my tongue refuses to move. I cannot bring myself to ask for money, even for three kopeks, so I shake my head and say good-bye.

Outside, for about five seconds I contemplate stealing a ride. Since there are no conductors to collect the fare, it's an easy thing to do—simply ignore the box where you are supposed to drop the money and quietly sit down, pretending you're so distracted by the unfolding landscape that you absentmindedly failed to buy a ticket. But then there are inspectors who could expose your guilt and question your honesty, putting your character in doubt in front of the whole car as they demand a five-ruble fine. It is ultimately fear that guides me past the streetcar stop and along the tracks, the only way I know to find my way home.

I walk for hours through the afternoon haze, then the evening twilight. Streetcars are flying past, screeching at the turns, sparks bursting on the electric wires above. Finally, after one more bridge and one more turn, a familiar street extends before me, with my apartment building looming at the corner. The courtyard seems to be waiting. It does not reproach me for my stubbornness, for my silly fears. As I walk to my door, a gust of wind puffs in from the street, as if the yard is breathing a sigh of relief: I am three hours late, but I am home.

MY MOTHER TEACHES A late class at her medical school and isn't back yet. I don't have to make up an improbable story she won't believe or admit that I couldn't bring myself to ask my tutor for a three-kopeck coin. My sister isn't home, either: after graduation from drama school she has been working at the Leningrad Comedy Theatre. It makes me feel important to have an actress sister, but it also makes me feel jealous and resentful.

The only person at home is my father. He is out of bed, sitting in a kitchen chair in his long blue underwear with one knee drawn up to his chin. His knee is so sharp that I can see the outline of his bones under blue cotton, the skinniest knee I've ever seen, even for his reedy frame.

He is smoking his Belomor, although it's a half a pack a day now, instead of the usual two. In the cloud of smoke around his face, his nose seems sharper, too—another angle protruding out of his body, in addition to his elbows and wrists and long, bony fingers. "I can teach anatomy on you," my mother said ruefully the other day, looking at him sitting up in bed. This is what she usually says when Marina or I refuse to eat another slice of bread with dinner, although we both know we aren't so skinny that you can see the outline of our bones. But this time, with my father, she actually could teach an anatomy lesson: his body is nothing but skin shrink-wrapped around bones.

There is a plateful of salad in front of him on the table, cucumbers and radishes sliced by my mother's expert hand, mixed in with wisps of dill and scallion chopped into bits so small they look like dark green paste. In the summer, when fresh vegetables appear in the markets and in all the gardens, my mother insists on a plate of salad every single day, the same way she insists on a bowl of soup. The salad is necessary for our nutrition, she says, and the soup for our digestion.

"Cow chow," says my father each time, pushing the salad away, which never stops my mother from chopping up another plateful.

"That's the reason you lost all your teeth," she says, banging a knife on the cutting board, reminding him that had he understood the nutritional value of vegetables he wouldn't have had scurvy during the war.

Next to his untouched salad is a saucer with caviar, which my mother has recently started buying at a deli three blocks away. It sits on the deli counter in two-hundred-gram packages wrapped in wax paper, above a pile of *kotlety*, palm-sized patties of ground meat, and a pot of borsch, next to a handwritten price tag of two and a half rubles. Two and a half rubles is a lot of money, the price of one hour with Irina Petrovna, but my mother doesn't think twice. Nutritionally, caviar trumps the soup and even the fresh vegetables, so she divides the package into three equal parts and every morning sets down a portion in front of my father, next to the plate of salad he never eats.

"Here, Brother Rabbit, come here," he calls. *Brother Rabbit* is the first book I read on my own, at five, perched on his lap. "Have a bite. Mother says it's really good for you."

He lifts me onto his thigh and spoons some caviar from the saucer. It's salty and rich, melting on my tongue, and I eat it all because he keeps feeding me spoonfuls, smiling and pleased. Inside my mouth it now tastes like fish, and I think of our fishing trip on the Gulf of Finland, the only one we took last summer. I had my own rod, with a round bobbin painted half red and half white, and my father hooked a worm for me because it had been wriggling in an inch of water on the bottom of the boat and I didn't want to impale it. We sat on two boards, and he cast my line without getting up, without tipping the boat. The line whistled in the air in a perfect arc and plunked down ten meters away. He hooked worms on his two rods, his fingers black from digging them up in the compost pile, and cast them on the other side of the boat. We sat and waited, silently, because fish, as he'd explained, could hear the slightest sound you make, even your coughing, even a dripping oar. We sat for a long time, the gray water swirling in small ripples, until the red half of my bobbin plunged beneath the surface and my father whispered, "Pull." I pulled, astonished by how heavy the rod had become, leaning back so far that the boat tipped and the oars grated against their metal casings. He guided my arms until I could see the fish sparkle just a few centimeters below the surface. In a precise, meteoric movement he whipped the line, and the fish vaulted through the air and thumped to the bottom of the boat. It was small, too small for the force of the tug and the resistance it had worked up in the water. I watched it thrashing against the boards, with a comb of spikes on its spine. My father grabbed the fish by the head, avoiding the prickly fins, and I saw the hook in its open mouth as it gasped, gleaming far down its perforated jaw. He yanked the hook down and out, and the fish stopped gasping and lay still. "A perch," my father said. "Your first catch." I picked up the perch and held it between my palms, its scales hard and glistening silver, its eyes like glass. I held it the same way I'd held a dead duck my father had once brought from a hunting trip, stroking the shiny scales the same way I stroked the green feathers of the duck's neck that lay in my fingers, soft and docile as a piece of rope.

My father never cleaned the fish he caught and never ate them. It was my mother who opened the bellies, scraped the guts into a garbage pail, and plopped the fish onto a frying pan. I never knew, though, what she'd done with that duck.

The strong taste of caviar in my mouth stays after I swallow the last bite, when my father circles his arms around me and lowers his cheek into my hair. He smells of tobacco, and I feel his stubble pressed against my head. I like his stubble and his smell and the fishy taste in my mouth, all happening at the same time, but he lets this feast of senses last for only thirty seconds, and then releases his hold and puts me down on the floor.

"Let's hear you play," he says. "Some Tchaikovsky or something."

I don't like playing the piano. I don't have an ear for music, as my piano teacher reminds me every week as he tries to teach me bits of *solfeggio*. But now it is my father asking me to play, and I follow him into my sister's room, where our Red October piano gleams against the wall.

He shuffles across the hallway and slumps onto the couch as if he'd walked up six flights of stairs, watching me fold the lace runner and open the piano lid. The book of sheet music, *Works for Secondary School*, is open to Tchaikovsky, just as my father asked, to the piece my teacher has been assigning to me for weeks, "A Doll's Funeral." I don't like it very much because it's too slow, all in the low range of the left hand, but it's the only piece I can play well, so I begin, making it more upbeat, banging the keys to turn the funereal notes into a march.

"Good, good," my father whispers with his eyes closed. "Nice tune."

Through my chords I hear a key in the door, my mother getting home. Without taking off her raincoat, she walks into my piano banging, her face tense with worry, demanding that my father immediately get back into bed. In one sweeping glance she surveys the kitchen, her eyes pausing on the untouched salad and the saucer empty of caviar. "Keep practicing," she tells me, wiggling her shoulder under my father's arm to help him lift himself off the couch and walk to the other room.

I close the piano and pull the chair to the desk to do my English homework for tomorrow. My father is in bed now, with tea on his night table and grainy figure skaters floating across the TV screen. I carefully pull a record out of its cardboard sleeve and set it on the turntable. After a few moments of hissing, the needle falls into the groove and a voice, British and familiar, announces the lesson: the simple present tense. When we started classes, Irina Petrovna allowed me to borrow the British-made set, her pride, telling me to listen to two pages of each lesson a day and write down ten sentences of my own using the lesson's grammar.

"I go to school by school bus," the voice says, giving an example of a habitual action characteristic of the simple present. I don't know what a school bus is, but I can easily substitute Bus 22 that my friend Masha takes to her English school. I hope it will also be my English school this September, after I take the entrance exam, and with audacity, I write in my notebook for Irina Petrovna, "I go to school by Bus 22."

My mother walks in, critically regards the room, and unfolds the lace runner from the couch to place it back on the piano lid. She draws the curtains closed, straightens pots with aloe and scallions on the windowsill, and looks into my notebook as if she could read the English sentence I just wrote. Her eyebrows are mashed together in an exasperated look, as though she cannot understand why I am doing something so different as learning English; why, despite her hopes for me to enter the medical field just like her, I would spend a whole summer glued to a seat—in a streetcar, at Irina Petrovna's, at the desk in my sister's room. I'm glad she wasn't home earlier to ask why I was late, to lament my obstinacy, to have another chance to say I am stubborn like my father.

I AM IN IRINA Petrovna's apartment for our last class. Two days from now I'm scheduled to take the entrance exam for Masha's English school.

"Here is a chart of all the tenses," says my tutor, unfolding a poster-size paper with auxiliary verbs and past participle forms. Four groups of tenses—present, past, and future—twelve in all. "Don't kill yourself over the perfect continuous; it's seventh-grade material anyway." She quizzes me on the form for each tense, satisfied with the answers. "Concentrate on the simple tenses," she advises. "Especially the irregular verbs of simple past."

She checks my last homework, an exercise from the British book and record set I've brought back to her.

"What is privacy?" I ask as she scans over the page.

She looks at me and I point to the sentence I copied from the text, "Helen and her new husband lost their privacy when her mother moved across the street." After consulting my English-Russian dictionary I figured out it had to do with the word "private," as in the "private property" that plagues all capitalist countries, according to our third-grade history book. Perhaps they lost some money, I thought, some essential part of their private property, but it was still unclear how it was caused by the mother's move. I tried a couple of other possibilities, but no matter how I turned and twisted it, the loss Helen and her new husband suffered refused to reveal itself.

Irina Petrovna squints at the sentence and I notice that her cheeks are turning pink. She has always answered my questions with confidence, everything that had to do with tenses, infinitive constructions, uncountable nouns, and even articles, the most mysterious grammatical element of all. She has distinguished participles from gerunds in a fraction of a second and recited all three forms of every irregular verb we've ever encountered. But now, gazing at the sentence I copied from the last lesson in her British textbook, she doesn't know the answer to my question.

She opens her English-Russian dictionary, the same edition I have at home, which I know doesn't contain the word "privacy." Then she climbs onto a chair and pulls a tome off her shelf, *The Oxford Dictionary*. It is as fat as an encyclopedia, all in English. She bends over it, carefully rustles the pages to *P*, and we both stare at the foreign word. "1. The condition of being secluded or isolated from the view of, or from contact with, others," we read. "2. Concealment; secrecy."

The phrase still makes no sense. Did Helen and her husband want to be secluded or isolated? And if they did, how could the mother, all the way on the other side of the street, affect their isolation? If they all lived in one apartment, like my aunt Muza with my three cousins and my grandparents, I would understand. But across the street? We think, bent over the page side by side, clueless. And if it's the word's second meaning we need to consider, were the two of them secret agents or spies whose cover the mother had exposed?

Irina Petrovna, back to her normal color, finally shrugs her shoulders and says that we don't have the word "privacy" in Russian. "It simply doesn't exist," she proclaims. "We do have seclusion, though, as well as isolation."

She makes me think of the time when a neighbor in the communal apartment on our landing had diphtheria and all three families were put under isolation by a local polyclinic. There was a handwritten sign, "Diphtheria," posted on their front door so that no one, not even a telegram delivery woman, would think of ringing their bell and having that door opened.

Standing on her toes, Irina Petrovna squeezes *The Oxford Dictionary* back into its spot on the shelf. "Seclusion and isolation, yes," she confirms. "But no privacy."

How strange, I think, that an English word has no translation. Does that mean that the English people know something we don't? Is this mysterious "privacy" an invention of the capitalist West, something that we, the only people destined to inherit a bright future, lack?

WHEN I WALK INTO our apartment after my last lesson with Irina Petrovna, I immediately sense that something is not right. My sister is in the kitchen pouring hot water from a teakettle over a folded towel in the sink. My father is in bed, stretched under the blanket with eyes closed, his arms on top of the duvet cover, nut-color on white.

"Where is Mama?" I ask, struck by her absence in this moment of trouble.

My father opens his eyes and tries to smile.

"She's at the neighbors', calling the hospital," says Marina, walking in with the towel and stretching it over Father's head. "They finally agreed to admit him. Forty years in the party, and we had to beg and plead with every idiot in the District Committee."

"Come over here," says my father and taps the blanket with his fingers. He doesn't try to sit up, and that's unusual because he hates lying in bed. "Come here, Brother Rabbit."

I sit where his hand patted the cover, and he peers into my face, his eyes dark in the electric light, deep as the water under our fishing boat.

"How is your English?" he asks, words barely audible, a small whistling coming out with every breath. "When is that exam?"

"Monday," I say. In two days one test will decide if I take a city bus to a new school or stay in my district elementary with Vera Pavlovna, who likes to talk about Stalin and the heroic valor of the Great Patriotic War.

"You're a smart Brother Rabbit," says my father and covers my hands with his palm. His fingers are cool and leathery, and they smell of tobacco when I lean down and touch them with my cheek.

MY MOTHER AND SISTER walk him to the elevator and then down to the waiting taxi. With his arms around their shoulders, he hangs between them, an open raincoat thrown over his long underwear, as if it no longer matters what he wears, as if his relevance to the world dressed in street clothes has ceased to exist. My mother lowers him into the car without any seeming effort, as if he were a feather. I see him through the glass recline across the backseat, stalky in his blue underwear, wispy and pale as the sky.

As soon as my mother gets into the front seat, the car begins to move, and Marina and I both start waving, but neither Mama nor Papa turn to look back.

ON MONDAY, MY MOTHER goes with me to the new school, but she is only an escort. This is my test. This is between me and the English language.

The school's hallways are empty, its wide stairway both inviting and intimidating. The testing classroom is small, very different from the huge rooms of my school that must accommodate forty students. "*Zdravstvuite*," I say as politely as I can to a solemn-looking woman at the desk. "How do you do," she replies.

She gives me a story in English from a book about animals, which I must read and retell. No dictionary is allowed, but I can take notes. At first the words blur like tiny black figures in a crazy dance. I close my eyes and think of my father, and that slows the words down, structuring them into a pattern. I sit there for as long as the woman allows, rereading the story about a tiger and a monkey, rehearsing its retelling, which requires desperate searches in the book for the words that are hard to remember.

Finally, she calls me to her desk in the corner, a very modest, very British desk. In her solemn English she begins to ask questions. I describe from memory the tiger who lived in the jungle: his appearance, his character, his habits. The teacher's questions echo in the small space of the room, her pronunciation majestically foreign, swollen with rolling and lilting sounds so uncharacteristic of our docile Russian. Her elastic mouth moves in a mysterious way, lips parting and stretching sideways, to produce something that looks like a pretentious smile, although I know well enough that she is not smiling.

"*Hu-els* lived in the jungle?" she asks, and I realize with horror that I don't understand the question. I don't remember any *huels* in the story, although if she is asking this question, there must have been at least one. I keep silent, desperately trying to recall every character, and even furtive peeks at the book do not help. She repeats the question; I keep silent; she repeats the question again. I faintly hope that at the last moment, as in a fairy tale when the princess is about to perish, there will appear a handsome *huel* on a white stallion, a savior who will deliver me into the shining kingdom of English. I stare down at the desk in hot, shameful horror, hearing my own blood rushing through my head, realizing that this may be the end of everything that has not yet begun: I will never have a living room or a coffee table, my hair will always be long and braided and my stockings cotton.

"How was the test?" asks my mother, who used the time while I was inside to go to a farm market and buy the nutritional delicacies to take to Papa's hospital. Her arms are weighed down by string bags with pears all the way from Azerbaijan, huge scarlet tomatoes from Georgia, and bouquets of cilantro and other greens my father will never touch.

"All right," I say, and start walking in the direction of the exit.

"What did you have to do?" She hurries after me.

"A story." I keep walking. "To read and retell."

"Were there any words you didn't know?"

"A couple." I push open the front door and take a breath of air. "Can we go home now?"

At home we don't talk about father's illness. We talk about the nourishing value of the chicken bouillon my mother boils on the stove and pours into pot-bellied jars, in which it cools on the windowsill, forming a yellow crust of fat under the lids. She'll take the jars to the hospital because the food there is all stolen by the nurses and orderlies. We talk about the absence of direct streetcar routes to the hospital, which makes her, and sometimes my sister, too, lug the string bags with the jars of bouillon and the harvest of her market trips from the last stop to his ward almost a kilometer away.

She never takes me: children are not allowed in the hospital. The closest I can get to my father is to trail her downstairs to the phone booth in front of our apartment building and wait, leaning on the squeaky door, during the daily call to a woman in Hospital Information.

ON OUR WAY DOWN to the phone booth, the elevator lurches between floors, threatening to get stuck. Outside, clouds seep through the gaps between buildings, promising more rain tomorrow.

I stand outside the phone booth, leaning on the door. I don't want to hear the words my mother is saying; I don't want to guess the answers. All I want is to stay outside—out of what's happening, on the fringes of the actual events, of what I am not told.

This time my mother stays on the phone longer than usual, her lips slowly falling into a new, unprotected curve. She seems to be asking questions; she covers her eyes with her hand while listening to the answers.

"What, Mama, what? What did they say?" I ask. I want to know and at the same time I don't.

"Nothing new, really." She is trying to pull her mouth back into a controlled position. "They're going to change Papa's medicine. The old one isn't working so well. That's all."

She grabs my arm and pulls me across the broken asphalt of the courtyard so fast, her pace so resolute, that I have to skip after her to keep up.

Back home I hide under the coat hooks, between the crinkly raincoats, alone, because my mother and sister are both in the kitchen pretending to be busy with dinner. I'd rather not hear what they're talking about, and yet I stand there straining my ears. Nothing much escapes from behind the closed door, only the drone of their voices and splashes of separate words.

"Oxygen," I hear, a word not normally used while cooking dinner. "Didn't let me stay," my mother says more loudly, moving from the stove to the sink near the door. "They knew I'm an anatomy professor, so they told me the truth," I make out, my hope buoyed by this complete sentence, yet immediately suspended by the banging that begins in a cupboard near the door. I hold my breath, but nothing audible escapes from under the kitchen door, until my mother clinks plates onto the table and says something ending with "too young to understand anything."

At night, pretending to sleep, I hear her sniffle in her bed, which is next to my father's, unopened and empty.

"WE'RE GOING TO CALL the hospital early today," my mother says in the morning.

The three of us chug down in the elevator, staring at the floor, mother clicking two-kopeck coins for the phone in her palm. It starts to pour again as we walk across the courtyard, around the puddles, and into the street, where the green phone booth gleams under the rain. We stop in front of it, and Marina tightens her fist around a piece of paper with the hospital phone number.

"Here is the number," she mutters, glancing sideways, avoiding my eyes, stuffing a piece of paper into my hand. "You call today."

With fingers as wooden as my legs, I dial the six digits scribbled on the paper, my heart pounding, my stomach queasy. I don't recognize my voice when I say my father's name; it whistles out of my throat, barely audible, like his voice before the taxi took him away to the hospital. On the other end, I can hear the Information clerk rustle through paper, slipping a funny remark to someone, chuckling in response.

"Died last night," the voice resounds from the other end of the city, a normal female voice accustomed to delivering abnormal messages. It sounds a little like Irina Petrovna's, only much harsher because the woman is speaking in Russian. I hear a click and then a long tone, flat, droning, and endless.

We are silent on the way back up. In the apartment, Mama trudges into the bathroom and thoroughly towels her face and hair. Slowly, she fills a watering can and makes her way down the hallway to water the plants on the windowsills. She moves carefully and methodically, her rhythm and silence dictated by a long-practiced habit of survival.

"The latest news from the fields," barks a voice from the radio. "Collective farm number fifty-four of Oktyabrsky region is happy to report the largest ever harvest of . . ." Marina reaches up and turns the knob, but the voice continues humming from the neighbor's apartment behind the wall.

Death, I know, makes people cry, but no matter how I fumble inside myself, I cannot locate grief. Uncharted on the map of my ten-year-old life, it belongs to the theater and movies, to the world of my third-grade teacher Vera Pavlovna and the textbook valor of the Great Patriotic War she declaims.

Strangely, life outside my body continues as before, reeling out scenes with the same predictability and order: my mother shuffling around the apartment; my sister trailing after her, as if waiting for orders; the brakes screeching when a car on the corner fails to make the light; the smell of fried onions oozing from a neighbor's kitchen through the cracks around the door. I mechanically register everything, as if I were Irina Petrovna's British record, but I don't know how to feel.

My mother goes back to the bathroom and refills the watering can. She keeps watering the plants, walking from one windowsill to the next, not noticing that the water is rising in the pans around the flowerpots, spilling out onto the sills, dripping on the desk in Marina's room. It's dripping onto my English notebook, the only evidence left of my summer of vocabulary lists, irregular verbs, and the twelve tricky tenses.

I lift my notebook to save it from the trickling water, and it opens to the lesson on simple past. The simple past that now contains my father. Yesterday he was still in the present, yesterday and every day for the past ten years, when I watched him dip the oars into the gray water of the Gulf and stroll across the field of our dacha, three fishing rods bobbing on his shoulder. The past has won over the present, the warped irregular past, the most incomprehensible of all the twelve tenses, as inexplicable as the English word "privacy."

I feel that something has cinched my throat and I know I'm crying. I cry because I was the one who held the phone and dialed the number. I was the one struck by the word "died." Not my mother, the anatomy professor who was privy to everything about his illness. Not my sister, the actress, who knows how to bring out tears and how to hide them.

I cry because my notebook glares with the past tense, the tense that now contains not only my father but everything my father and I have done. There is a part of me trapped in that past along with him, and I don't know what that means. Maybe I will die, too— whether I eat salad or don't, whether or not my dinner includes soup and bread every single day without fail.

What I do know is that I won't smell tobacco on his hands or feel his stubble or be "Brother Rabbit" ever again, and that knowledge makes me cry even harder, so hard that my mother breaks out of her watering trance and presses me to her soft breasts and whispers to Marina, "*Vsyo ponimaet*," which means I've instantly grown up and now understand everything.

# CHAPTER 8

# *Mushrooms*

"NOBODY BUT ME CAN find the *belye*," says my sister as she and my mother examine different-size baskets piled by the entrance to our dacha. "I bet you all the best ones will be mine."

It is our first dacha autumn without my father. The three fishing rods are still in the barn, leaning against the splintery boards, but they are now behind the row of spades and hoes, pressed to the wall by the more essential tools. Because of my father's illness, we planted nothing at the dacha in June, and to my infinite joy, we have almost nothing to harvest. That's why we can devote a whole Sunday in September—my second week in the fourth grade—to mushroom hunting.

*Belye* are at the top of the mushroom Olympus, their dark-brown caps clamped down on solid stems. Rare and difficult to find, they are treasures my mother sautés with sour cream, shreds to infuse pungent fragrance into soup, and hangs on thread over the stove to dry for the winter.

The next most prized are red caps, their stems flecked with black, trailed closely by birch-tree gray caps on long, skinny legs. Under the caps of all the best mushrooms is a hard sponge, and it is that underside that separates the noble mushrooms from the peasants with hollow stems and silly umbrella heads lined with spokes of pale flesh.

These second-rate mushrooms are good only for salting. Drops of acrid milk bead on their stems when my mother cuts them, so they need to be boiled to flush out the bitter taste. Then she layers them, limp but still full of color—gray, pink, and the rarely found orange—in an aluminum bucket between yellow umbrellas of dill flowers, garlic, and black currant leaves. When the bucket is full, she pours a pot of hot water up to the top. The mushrooms will be ready to eat by early fall, an essential appetizer in every gathering, a complement to boiled potatoes and black bread. The bucket, impossible to fit in any refrigerator, will sit on our balcony in the city, frozen from November to the end of March, when we will need a hammer or Marina's strong fist to break the crust of ice over the top.

A mushroom hunt, as everyone knows, must start early, when tentative brightness bleeds from under the horizon, setting alight the stubble of forest across the field. Like fishing, it is a ritual that must be performed at sunrise.

My sister knows the spots. To find mushrooms, especially noble ones, you must know the spots, not necessarily geographically but intuitively. My mother and I meander around the forest looking under every tree, turning up every brown leaf, while Marina walks straight past us to some dinky-looking ditch, where she digs up a perfect family of *belye*.

The three of us start when the sun appears above the treetops. We walk past the unpainted house where the Gypsies live, past the Gypsies' bull, whose tail has been chewed off by rats, past the piles of boards dumped here a long time ago for a project that never happened. As we walk through the damp field, toward the forest still hazy with night fog, birds rustle out of bushes, and grasshoppers, as if on cue from an invisible conductor, begin to trill in the clumps of grass.

As we approach the far end of the field, just before the forest begins, we come to an island of birch trees surrounded by blueberry thickets, a good spot for birch-tree mushrooms. I dip my hand into the middle of a bush, part the hard little leaves, and a slippery cap emerges from under my fingers—and another one, smaller, right next to it—resilient and perfect. I sink my fingers into the moss and dig the mushrooms out at the root, their stems sturdy and white.

"I got two!" I yell to Marina's back zigzagging between the trees far ahead of me. I run until I catch up with her at the line where the real forest begins and where fir trees and oaks tower overhead, screening out the sunlight. I hold out my hand and Marina lifts and examines the mushrooms. They are flawless, with flecked stems and stout caps, and there is nothing to find fault with except for one thing—they are not *belye*.

"Wait," says Marina as she hands them back to me, "wait until I get to my spots." She slips into the forest and vanishes behind an oak trunk.

What secret sense led me to that blueberry patch under a birch tree? My small victory tickles my nose, hones my senses, makes it possible to smell my own way to the hidden treasures of *belye*.

I step into the forest. Musty leaves marinate in thick loam; dead branches and old pine needles slowly become part of the forest floor. I follow the crackling of Marina's steps, swift and resolute. My mother's rustling on my left is slower and less determined. Although most of my senses are alerted to the ground, my ears are still tuned to the territorial shifts of my mother and sister. Their sound is my only compass under the tree roof.

Beyond a clump of old firs the ground slopes to a ravine with steep sides overgrown by grass. I squat on the rim and jump onto the bottom, crunching pinecones under my feet. My eyes are level with the rim, and I see that the sides of the ravine are reinforced by logs, half-rotten and splintery. A World War II trench. There are many of them in the woods, trenches and bomb craters, their sides smoothed by time. There used to be hundreds of old shells, mines, and grenades buried under layers of forest compost, but those are hard to find nowadays.

I want to show the trench to my mother. Every Victory Day, on May 9, she takes her three medals out of the drawer, carefully lifting them from brown boxes. The medals look like the chocolates in gold foil we all get for New Year's, but they are bronze, attached to trapezoid badges of striped cloth.

I wonder what it was like to live in a trench like this because I suspect that those who fought in these woods during the nine-hundred-day siege of Leningrad were not always attacking under red banners or dying heroically from German bullets, as my third-grade teacher Vera Pavlovna wanted us to believe. Nine hundred days is an awfully long time to live in a trench, especially if it's winter and there are no mushrooms or berries or even old leaves because everything is under a meter of snow.

I think of my mother's brothers Sima and Yuva, whom I cannot regard as uncles because they'd died long before I was born. No one actually saw Yuva die, so he is still listed as missing in action. Several times my mother has written to the archives of a town, now in Poland, where he'd been stationed when the war started, but there is no trace of anyone from that division guarding the border at the onset of the blitzkrieg. "They might as well have never existed," my mother says bitterly. "They didn't even have guns."

I don't understand why the soldiers on the border, right before the Great Patriotic War, didn't have guns. They have guns now, at a time of developed socialism, as our textbooks call it, which seems far less dangerous than June 1941.

"Not a pistol, not a rifle, not even a shotgun," confirms my mother. "So what could he do against a division of tanks? Mowed down in the first few minutes. He didn't even have time to get scared."

My mother's brother Sima is not among those missing. He died in plain view of the whole family, a few months after he had been wounded on his first day at the front, a piece of shrapnel lodged in his lung. "That sliver of metal resulted in a metastatic abscess in the brain," my mother says, deliberately using medical terminology to hide her anger at the doctors who had failed to take the piece out, wishing perhaps that Sima had been brought into the front hospital where she worked and where she would certainly have been more fastidious in removing every shard.

Before going to war and dying, Sima had studied painting at the Leningrad Academy of Art. His canvases hang on the walls of our apartment: a portrait of my young mother, a soldier throwing a grenade at a tank. He must have been thinking of fighting the war even before he was drafted into the army, painting a soldier in front of a rearing hunk of steel, a soldier just like his brother Yuva, only armed with real weapons. Looking at the portrait of my young mother, at her crinkled eyes and her mouth open in a half-smile, I make a discovery: there was a period, even during the war, when my mother was cheerful and ironic, before she turned into a law-abiding citizen so much in need of order.

When did this transformation take place, I wonder, from the woman in Sima's portrait into my unsmiling mother? Was it during the war when Marina was born, or when Marina's father died of TB? Did Marina know a different mother, someone who would let me go fishing with my father instead of making me paint the house, someone who wouldn't frown at a drama school or learning English? It doesn't seem fair, the fact that I didn't have a chance to know this other mother—another advantage my sister has, in addition to her acting gift and her ability to find the best mushroom spots.

Now the remnants of war are buried in the ground. Ten years ago, when my grandfather was turning up dirt for the first strawberry bed in our dacha plot, his shovel struck metal—a foot-long artillery shell, unexploded, hibernating since 1944. A sapper brigade loaded the rusted jacket onto an armored truck and hauled it away. I hear the story each time a new guest is given a tour of the dacha grounds, my mother's voice ringing with pride that it was our plot that was blessed with such a close danger.

For years, stories have been floating around the countryside about boys who found shells in the woods, threw them into camp-fires, and had fingers blown off their reckless hands. Supposedly there was a boy in a nearby village whose face was burned by bullets he'd tossed into a fire, and another whose foot was severed by a land mine.

I've never seen boys with missing fingers or feet, or anyone with a burned face. But on my mushroom-gathering trips I see enough craters and trenches, like the one I'm standing in now, to know that the war was really fought here, that it cut wounds in the flesh of the earth deep enough to require a quarter-century to heal.

On the rim of the trench I see a tall mushroom, a bright red umbrella with white dots, a splash of color among pale blades of grass and sparse strawberry bushes. It is called *muhomor*, death to flies. My mother chops it up in a saucer with a little water and sugar—and the next day there are piles of dead flies around the saucer on the windowsill and on the floor. It's always perfect, untouched by animals; it can afford to be conspicuous and bright. And right next to it, under the shade of the polka-dot umbrella, is a small brown-top only two centimeters out of the ground, and a bigger one next to that, and another—like a row of nested *matryoshka* dolls lined up on the downward curve of the slope. Eight altogether—a perfect family of *belye*.

Dizzy with success, I jump up and down on the bottom of the trench, pinecones crunching under my feet. To find eight *belye* on one mushroom-hunting trip is almost impossible. For the first time, I have managed to beat Marina.

Carefully, one by one, I wiggle them out of the ground. The biggest one is about ten centimeters tall, with a velvety head the color of chocolate. I stoop to line my basket with fern leaves from the bottom of the trench, as I've seen Marina do so many times; a prize like this must be padded against the bristling twigs.

I climb out of the trench, head spinning, knees scratched from the splintery wood of the slope. For a minute I stand on the rim, trying to get my bearings. The most important thing is to think back, to remember. I approached the trench from a clump of balding fir trees, but as I look around I see that there are firs all around it. And the sun has moved; it is oozing through the treetops from the left now. I stand still and listen hard, listen for rustling of leaves and crackling of dead branches, for signs of my mother and sister.

I listen so hard that my own breathing gets in the way. Leaves rustle high above my head, but everything below seems to exist in silence: blueberries, mushrooms, moss spreading over crumbling stumps. No sounds, no human movements intrude into the calm of the forest.

"A-ooo!" I yell at the top of my lungs, turning in different directions—a cry of being lost in the woods. The only response is a murmur of leaves high above my head. It is still morning, I say to myself, it's sunny outside the forest, and my mother and sister are probably already looking for me. Besides, in my basket I have a perfect row of *belye*.

Suddenly it strikes me: the last field we crossed to come into the forest, where I found my first two mushrooms, must not be far. It didn't take me long to walk from there to the trench. If I turn back, I will find the field and retrace my way home.

I start walking away from the trench, toward a patch of light glinting through a tall opening between trees. The light is deceptively close, but every time I come near, it floats away, further and further, until I realize that what seems like an open space must be a play of light and shade, an optical illusion resulting from sunlight sifting into shadow.

I walk for a long time, for what seems like an hour, before I understand that I am not approaching the edge of the forest. The biggest opening of light before me turns out to be a small grass meadow dotted with blue flowers and surrounded by trees.

I plop into the grass, a purple flower before my eyes, like a tiny bell. The last of the wild strawberries are glowing along an ant path that leads to a hill of sand and pine needles. I know a trick: if I spit onto an anthill, the ants will stand on their hind legs and squirt their liquid onto my palm, a sharp yet irresistible smell. Then I sniff my palm, again and again, until no odor remains, until I've completely drained it out of my skin.

It's cozy in the grass, so I close my eyes and the image of the purple flower bell floats on my eyelids. And then I am at home, in our tiny dacha kitchen, where a smell of sizzling mushrooms tingles my nose. My mother has piled the most noble of them from our baskets, cleaned and cut up, into the biggest frying pan we have. Now the cubes of white stems and spongy yellow caps absorb the melting butter, and it begins to smell like dinner and home. In a few minutes my mother, a kitchen rag wrapped around her hand, will lift the pan off the burner, lower it onto a wooden cutting board, and scoop the fragrant stew onto my waiting plate. All the gray and red caps we found today, and the biggest of my *belye* mushrooms, all melt into a steaming mouthful balanced on my fork.

But then something happens. The mushrooms piled in the basket on the kitchen floor begin to move, their heads rising, turning from brown and red to gray, growing tails, all turning into mice. As they dart in different directions, I see that they are bigger than mice, or are they growing bigger as I look? They are now as big as those rats that chewed off the tail of the Gypsies' bull last winter. The tailless bull watches me out of the corner of his bloodshot eye as I carefully walk past the unpainted Gypsy house. Anita, a Gypsy girl whose father owns the bull—a girl with yellow curds of pus in the corners of her eyes—tells me that rats are so hungry in winter that they will eat anything, even if it is alive. Those must be Gypsy rats; it's too scary to think that they could be the same rats that scurry at night under our own floorboards.

Then Anita gets angry with me. Her father, she says, will steal me and stuff me in a sack. I laugh in her face, but she knows I'm terrified. Anita's father grins and unfurls a Gypsy sack, its inside black as the winter night. His hands are hairy, with gnarled fingers and black nails, and I know that, like all Gypsies, he has a knife in the back pocket of his pants. I try to run, but my feet won't move. I see Anita smirking as her father extends his arm to grab me around the back of my neck, just as he grabs blind kittens before he drowns them in a ditch.

I scream—the loudest scream that has ever escaped from my throat—and my eyes pop open. Something is tickling my neck: a couple of ants have climbed over me on the way to their hill.

"Le-na!" A faraway call is getting louder and now it is unmistakably the voice of my mother. "Aa-ooo!" comes Marina's voice, slightly to the left of me. I yell back, turning in the direction of the voices. Then I hear the crackling of dead branches and the rustling of leaves. I grab my basket and run toward the sounds, scratched by the bushes, whipped by the firs, stumbling on pitted soil. I run straight into my mother's stomach and bury my face into the pillows of her breasts. We stand like that for a few minutes, without moving, without saying a word, enfolded in the smell of mushrooms and damp leaves.

Out of the forest twilight my sister comes into view. Her forehead is puckered and her eyes glare. "We've been searching for you for an hour!" she shouts, but as she approaches I glance inside her basket. She knows where I'm looking and stops shouting. There are only a couple of birch-tree mushrooms, scattered on the bottom, and a few commoners, too big and old even for salting.

She tries to ignore what I have in my basket, her eyes barely skirting its contents, but I make her look. I parade my family of perfect *belye*—the eight trench warriors—in front of her face, and she squeezes out a smile because there is no one in the entire world, not even my older sister, who could ignore their splendor.

We walk back, meandering on a narrow footpath through fields, my mother clasping my hand in her hot palm. We walk close together, as if connected by an invisible thread, unto trailing each other home.

# CHAPTER 9

# *About Love*

OUR FIFTH-GRADE LITERATURE TEACHER, Ludmila Ivanovna, is short and round, wheeling from one corner of the classroom to the other on tiny feet. We call her Couch Legs. She is the opposite of our English teacher, who is bony and tall and rarely moves.

With Couch Legs, we are studying the father of Russian literature, the Shakespeare of the Russian language. There isn't much in Pushkin that can be shrouded in ideology: he is simply a classical poet whose sharp profile and ringlets of hair are familiar to every student within the borders of the Soviet Union. But Ludmila Ivanovna, her plump face framed in tight chemical curls, is doing something unauthorized and daring: she is entertaining us with an extracurricular analysis of the reading preferences of Tatiana, the virtuous heroine of *Eugene Onegin*.

"Tatiana adored romantic novels," pines Ludmila the Couch Legs, basking in the rare spotlight of our attention. "She read in French, as all Russians did back then, and immersed herself in the love adventures of young dukes and ladies-in-waiting."

We perk up at the sound of the word "love," which is never mentioned in school, at least not in its romantic meaning. We hear a lot about love for the motherland and love for the Communist Party, but never about love for one another. It is almost scandalous that Tatiana, the example of chastity in Russian literature, was fond of such improper novels.

"Do you think she knew how to kiss?" I whisper to Larissa, my neighbor. We are seated two to a desk, thirty of us, encased in a stuffy classroom where dust whirls in the shafts of April light slanting through the windows. "I mean, before she married that general?"

Larissa giggles, then arches her eyebrows in bewilderment. Who knows what you can trust if Pushkin's Tatiana could exhibit such astonishing frivolity.

Couch Legs, bathing in the intensified light of our attention, waves her short arms and rolls her eyes, a requirement for delivering the tragic story of a French countess. Her eyes sparkling, curls shaking, Ludmila is indignant and triumphant in the delivery of a story about this love of the unmentionable kind.

I do, of course, know about that love, although my mother, just like my school, pretends it doesn't exist. After all, I will be twelve and in the sixth grade next September. In my courtyard, where things are more real, I see that love lurking over the rusty radiators between flights of stairs, where sixteen-year-olds pluck at guitar strings and sing of heartbreak, lighting the dark with their cigarettes.

In the middle of this Pushkin rapture, when our attention is piqued by Ludmila soaring to the climax of her story, the door opens and, as solemnly as always, in walks our principal. She is tall and stern, with a perfect crow's nest hairdo on top of her serious head. No one I know has ever seen her smile. She sits at an empty desk in the back for one of her surprise class observations.

Couch Legs abruptly stops rolling around her makeshift stage, and the spotlight of our attention shifts, leaving her to flounder in the dark. I kick Larissa under the desk, and she skews her eyes in my direction, eyebrows bunching in a frown. No one dares to say anything, even in a low whisper, with the principal looming in the back.

We can smell Couch Legs' distress. It exudes out of the pores of her flushed face and moistens her fine hair, tightening the ringlets over her temples. After a minute of leaden silence, Ludmila desperately hobbles from the breezy affairs of the French court to the curriculum-prescribed role of women in society, her voice a dull monotone.

I doodle on the desk with my fountain pen, a shameful thing to do since purple ink is impossible to erase. I scribble the word "love," pressing the pen into the wood so that the letters stand out among other students' desk comments on teachers and life. Thick and juicy, they pulsate like the hearts of the young lovers in Ludmila's interrupted story.

The lecture on the role of women in nineteenth-century Russia floats quietly past my ears and out an open window, where the sun breaks into rainbow shards inside dripping icicles. As soon as class is over, I will run downstairs at breakneck speed and then, catching my breath, casually walk along the hallway past Room 11, where seventh-graders have a zoology class every Thursday. If I am lucky, I may see Nikolai Gromov, the boy who smiled at me in the coatroom two weeks ago.

Nikolai has just exchanged his Pioneer scarf for a Komsomol badge. This means he has turned fourteen, the age that assures every student a passage from the Young Pioneer Organization to the Komsomol, the Young Communist League. I can't believe that a fourteen-year-old boy smiled at a mere fifth-grader in the coatroom.

The bell saves Ludmila from further attempts to breathe life into the mortuary of the social order in pre-revolutionary Russia. No one stirs. We are not allowed to move until the teacher gives permission, and the principal's presence serves as an unspoken reminder of this unwritten rule. In one stately movement the principal stands up, collects the papers she has been covering with notes, and silently walks out. I don't think I have ever heard her speak other than through a stage microphone during formal school functions.

"The lesson is over," sighs Ludmila, who then sits down at her desk and begins to leaf through the roll book, her plump hand over her eyes. As I pass by her on the way out, I notice that her stubby fingers are trembling.

TODAY, ALTHOUGH OUR CLASSES are over at two-forty, we cannot go home. We have a quarterly Young Pioneer meeting, and to assure mandatory attendance the doors to the school building have been padlocked since two. The assistant principal stands guard, letting out only Komsomol members, whose necks are not adorned by red scarves. Two boys from my class try to slip past him by mingling with a group of Komsomolets, but he immediately plucks them out, shuts the door, and gives them a quick scolding.

From where I sit on the hallway window ledge, I wistfully watch Nikolai Gromov putting on his jacket and boots in the coatroom. Inside, all students are required to wear school shoes that we keep in cloth bags on assigned hangers. His shoe bag hangs on the far end in the "senior" corner, with "Gromov" cross-stitched in red across the coarse linen.

Nikolai walks toward the door without so much as a glance in my direction, and for a moment his tall figure is etched in a diamond of sunlight when the door is briefly opened; then it is just as hastily shut. Through a grimy square of the window, I see him lift stork-like legs over puddles as he crosses the gray pavement of the courtyard.

The yard is dotted with spongy piles of dirty snow, the only reminder of the long winter that for six months kept us wrapped in wool and fur. On the chilliest mornings, my nose shielded by a scarf my mother wrapped across my face, I climbed onto the bus that bumped along streets encrusted in ice, past frozen canals, petrified trees, and snow-capped monuments. That is how wintry Leningrad is carved on the template of memory: shimmering like a cameo, seen through a five-kopek-size circle cleared by my breath on a frosted bus window.

Now, the spring snow is porous and frail, and Nikolai Gromov, the first boy I ever liked, leaves without acknowledging my existence.

"The Pioneer meeting is starting in five minutes," erupts the loudspeaker in the enthusiastic voice of Natasha, the school's Pioneer activities organizer. Natasha is twenty, but she wears a Pioneer scarf and generally behaves like a zealous fifth-grader trying to score *pyatorka*, a five. A five is the highest grade bestowed on work that is indeed perfect, not marred by the slightest error. I earn straight fives in both English and Russian. Ludmila the Couch Legs adores my compositions in which, in guerrilla-like fashion, I snake around the prescribed interpretations of stories armed with quotations from Russian classics. I pride myself that in the two years I've been at this school I have never received a satisfactory three, let alone a two, or *dvoika*, a failure.

I sense that Nikolai Gromov, too, is far from ever receiving a *dvoika*. He has a spark in his eyes, a glow radiating from within. Our two-year age difference raises him even higher above the rest, an older boy whose long neck and measured gait make me feel limp and think about my father.

There is no way I can escape through the padlocked door guarded by the assistant principal, so there is nothing left to do but trudge into the auditorium already brimming with brown dresses and gray suits, our uniforms. The noise of grades three to six, three sections to each grade, bounces off the walls, clamor and laughter rising from rows of stacking chairs. Attendance is perfect; the padlock worked.

"We are gathered here today to report on our successes during this quarter." Natasha's voice, amplified by a microphone, rings with enthusiasm worthy of a more prominent audience than a flock of young Pioneers from the English school of Oktyabrsky district. She seems to be as competent in addressing a crowd as she is in coordinating our after-school craft projects, and she looks comfortable onstage, eloquent and entirely in charge. "Our first speaker is the head of the Soviet of the Young Pioneer Commune of our school."

Tamara Kuznetsova, a heavy girl with hair braided in two rattails down her back, lumbers to the microphone with a stack of notes in her hands. Slowly but predictably, the surf of our voices calms, though never fully retreats. For me, Tamara's significance lies solely in her being a classmate of Nikolai Gromov. She also turned fourteen recently, but will fulfill her head-of-the-Soviet duty until the end of the year.

In a dreary monotone, Tamara speaks about the 23rd Party Congress, reciting its accomplishments, which are familiar to all of us because they are painted on red banners looming over the most impressive buildings of the city. When she is finished quoting from the General Secretary's speech, she switches to a recitation of our own school's triumphs worded in much less sophisticated prose, a report she probably wrote herself between homework assignments the night before. I feel sorry for Tamara, who is sweating onstage in front of us, instead of following Nikolai Gromov out of our padlocked school.

As the thrill of falling in love floods me, I feel like telling the whole world about Nikolai. I need to share this brimming lightness, this buoyancy that spills out of me with every move, with every new thought about him. I even consider telling him.

I quietly pull a small notebook out of my book bag, a secret notebook in which I write what cannot be said. In which I wonder, for example, when it was that my mother metamorphosed from a young, daring surgeon into a union member who wouldn't now be looking for a way to escape from this dreary meeting. In which I wonder why I wonder about this at all. Am I afraid that this transformation may just as easily happen to me? That one day I may become like her, voluntarily going to meetings instead of following older boys into the sunshine of the courtyard?

As Tamara's voice fades out, I begin to write what I think about Nikolai, soon realizing that I am writing to Nikolai. Words stream out onto the page, weaving disparate strands of feeling into the trim braid of a letter.

Thin applause, initiated by Natasha, stirs up another wave of din from the audience as Tamara collects her notes and plods down the stage steps. Natasha, who has been lurking in the wings all the time, flies up to the microphone and taps on it with a pen. In a short navy skirt, with the red flame of a Pioneer scarf around her neck, she looks exactly like one of us, only more enthusiastic.

"The next issue on our agenda is of a personal nature," says Natasha, and waves of hushed giggles rapidly subside. Matters of a personal nature seem out of place at this gathering of three hundred students packed in here as a result of a padlocked front door.

Someone keeps giggling in the front row, and Natasha patiently waits, looking down with mild reproach at two third-grade chatterers.

"Although trivial at first glance, this matter seems quite serious after deeper examination." All the giggles have died down now, and our whole Pioneer commune is unusually quiet. "I am going to ask Lubov Petrovna, the homeroom teacher of grade 5B, to come to the podium and join me."

Lubov Petrovna, a stout old woman in a blue suit she wears every day, ascends to the stage and installs herself next to Natasha, severe, thick-rimmed glasses adding importance to her size. She exudes a sense of power, and it streams, like smoke, down from the stage, silencing all of us. She does not need a microphone.

"One of us," says Natasha in a somber voice reserved for personal matters, "wrote a note incongruent with the Code of Young Pioneers." We perk up our ears the same way we did in literature class only a few hours earlier when Ludmila the Couch Legs began to spin her love stories.

"Fortunately, the note was intercepted by Lubov Petrovna so that the person who wrote it now has an opportunity to apologize in public." It is so quiet that we can hear the voices of first-graders playing tag in the schoolyard. "The person who wrote the note, come onstage now."

A current of whispers and shuffles drifts through the auditorium, grows stronger with every second of waiting, merges into the cloud of authority enveloping the stage. The sun breaks through the windows and dilutes the glare of incandescent lighting into a shade of watered-down tea.

"Come, come," repeats Natasha, resolutely and persistently, a voice of a righteous older sister. A girl rises in the third row, her hair blonde and shining, her face almost as red as her scarf, and walks up the three steps to the stage, into the realm of power, slowly approaching Natasha and Lubov Petrovna, both straight and solemn. She seems very small, almost rickety, in front of Lubov Petrovna. She looks as if she could burst into flames at any moment, cinder instantaneously into a small mound of ashes.

"I am sorry," mouths the girl, looking at her feet.

"Louder," says Lubov Petrovna.

"I am sorry," repeats the girl at a higher pitch, her mouth conforming to the words but not pleading.

"And I will never do it again," says Natasha, orchestrating the scene.

"And I will never do it again," repeats the girl in a voice so high and tense it could pop any second like a taut violin string.

Lubov Petrovna bends down and pats the girl on the shoulder. The girl turns on her heels and runs down the stage steps, past our greedy glances, past the rising clamor, out of the auditorium.

"The meeting is over," says Natasha, smiling, voice ringing with satisfaction.

IN THE POST-MEETING TURBULENCE no one seems to want to leave, and I find my desk neighbor Larissa surrounded by a tight ring of classmates. By her elbows clenched to her sides and her squinted eyes I realize that she is telling the girl's story. Larissa somehow manages to know all the school's scandals, and that is why, despite my smoldering desire to know all about Nikolai, I have hesitated to ask her about him.

"And then she passed the note to the boy, Valerii I think is his name, and the teacher saw it and grabbed it!" sputters Larissa, and small bubbles of saliva fizzle in the corners of her mouth.

I think of my first English tutor, Irina Petrovna, and the mysterious word "privacy." I even remember the sentence from her British textbook, "Helen and her new husband lost their privacy when her mother moved across the street," the sentence even my tutor didn't know how to decode. Only now it seems to make perfect sense: Helen and her husband parted with the same privacy the girl with blonde hair has just lost. Helen's mother across the street was like Lubov Petrovna, who intercepted a note to a boy and made the girl who wrote it apologize in front of the whole school. I wish I could get on the tram and tell Irina Petrovna; I wish I could enlighten her with this newly acquired knowledge that even her fat Oxford dictionary didn't contain.

"What was in the note?" asks Dina from grade 5C, elbowing her way closer to Larissa.

Larissa purses her lips and pauses in order to heighten the anticipation. For a second, all movement in our circle stops as Larissa glowers at us, the owner of a piece of exclusive information.

"I love you. K.," she finally announces to an eruption of giggles. "And her name is Kira," she continues so fast she almost chokes on her own words, "so they quickly found who it was. Can you imagine? I love you! Right in the middle of the class! And this boy Valerii, to whom the note was addressed, immediately told them it was her."

"What an idiot," says Viktor, who sits next to me in math, and everyone understands that he means Kira to be an idiot because he uses the feminine form, *idiotka*.

"And she denied it when she was caught," blurts out Larissa, "but this Valerii told them it couldn't be anyone else!"

Now I am glad I haven't told Larissa anything about Nikolai. Like Natasha and my mother, she doesn't seem to understand much about love.

Would my father understand? What would he think about my own unsanctioned letter?

"And what if it was you?" demands Dina, now standing straight in front of Larissa. "Would you like to be put onstage in front of Lubov Petrovna?"

"I would never have written the note," declares Larissa, unclenching her fists and putting her hands on her hips. She looks around to see whether anyone would dare question her integrity. "And if I did, I wouldn't send it to him in the middle of the class."

My letter to Nikolai, also contrary to the Code of Young Pioneers, blooms in my notebook, and neither Natasha nor Lubov Petrovna can make me apologize for writing it. If I add some rhyme, it will be as beautiful as the one Pushkin's Tatiana wrote to Onegin.

He will read it, meticulously copied on lined paper, signed with my full name. Sublime and dignified, this letter will haunt Nikolai for the rest of his life. When he reads it in middle age, in his late twenties, he will realize that he looked past something remarkable, something he could have touched by just stretching out his arm, by just casting a glance. He would realize how big and simple it was, this love that sprang up next to him in our school hallways.

But it will be too late. Like Pushkin's Tatiana, I will then be married and faithful. It will be too late.

# CHAPTER 10

# *Human Anatomy*

Every year, during school recess in November, my mother takes me to her medical institute, where she teaches in the department of human anatomy, and I spend ten days in the museum. She is trying to indoctrinate me early into the serious world of medicine because she doesn't want me to become an actress like my sister. The museum is silent and empty and, like the rest of the human anatomy department, stinks of formaldehyde.

I breathe in, and the thick chemical air fills my lungs. A diagram of the lungs, with blue and red vessels tangled up inside a faceless man's chest, hangs on the left wall. Below, in a large jar of cloudy liquid, floats a pair of real lungs, like gray, deflated chunks of rubber, a Latin caption underneath. I walk around the room gazing at the exhibits. Half a head stands in a jar with the nasal passages revealed, the gray hemispheres of the brain cracked like parched earth. What thoughts, I wonder, lived in the grooves of its caverns? In another jar floats a heart, colorless and limp, with stumps of arteries suspended in the liquid—a misshapen pear.

Flaps of skin, naked muscles, wrinkled genitals—nothing is frightening. They are all transformed, bloodless, dissociated from the life they are supposed to represent. Grainy and monochromatic, parts of human bodies float in jars like images behind the thick glass of TV screens.

During these anatomy visits, my mother places me in the care of a lab assistant, Aunt Klava, a shriveled babushka with clumps of gray hair bursting from under a white hat. Everyone here wears a white doctor's coat and a cloth hat, even lab assistants, even first-year students who silently creep into the museum and carefully pull their chairs away from desks with exhibits, hesitating to sit close to the jars with formaldehyde.

Aunt Klava smells of tobacco, and when I hang out in the hallway, I see her puffing on a cigarette on a stair landing, near the toilet. She shuffles, and wheezes, and clangs keys. She fishes into her pocket and pulls out three pieces of sucking candy—for me, for stringy-haired Zina, who busily peers into a microscope every time someone opens the door into her small lab in the basement, and for Volodya, who works in the morgue and who clumps along the hallway in a rubber apron and big rubber boots. Zina and Volodya are eighteen, straight out of school, but the six years that separate us are light-years. They acknowledge my presence, but they look right past me. They are adults, they work for a living, and they know things I don't know.

My mother's students are starting their practicum: they will be learning dissection. Volodya and another morgue assistant, Dima, in rubber aprons and gloves, carry a cadaver up from the morgue in the basement and lay it on a high marble table in the dissection room. The body is brown from formaldehyde, as far beyond life as the museum organs. As my mother begins her class, I slink closer and see that it is a man. I gaze at the limbs stretched along the torso, at the angular face with skin tight around the cheekbones, at the stomach sunken under the rib cage. At the lump of shriveled flesh in the crotch.

My mother looks up and tells me to go to the museum. Although I want to watch the dissection, I know I cannot argue with her in the middle of the class. Instead of the museum, I go down to the basement and walk along the narrow corridor, past the closed door to Zina's lab, past the opened door to the morgue. The inside of the morgue is shrouded in twilight, two bulbs throwing dim light on huge tubs with wooden lids where bodies are kept. These are the bodies of people who have no relatives, whom nobody wants, my mother told me. The lids are connected to hand cranks by thick wire cords, frayed and discolored. The smell of formaldehyde is so intense here that it burns my nose and makes me cough.

In the corner, I see Zina, the lab assistant, sitting on a tub lid and Volodya pouring tea out of a kettle into her cup. They don't see me, or pretend not to, engrossed in their tea break among the cadavers. I would like to sit with them, quietly, preferably next to Volodya, eavesdropping on their freshly acquired adult wisdom, but they continue to be oblivious to my presence. I pretend I am Zina, sitting on the wooden tub lid next to Volodya, talking matter-of-factly about mysterious grown-up things, glancing in the direction of the door, where a clumsy twelve-year-old with big feet is pathetically vying for his attention.

I go back to the dissection room and lurk in the doorway. My mother's students are cautiously poking at the Man's forearm with their scalpels, prodding his flesh in pursuit of the inner tubes of vessels, threads of nerves, clumps of muscle tissue. Even from where I stand I can see that the students are tentative, awed by their own audacity, by my mother's confidence. Under her steady fingers, the Man's body is slowly shrinking, cut up into museum exhibits spread around in petri dishes. I realize that the Man is disappearing at the rate of my mother's lesson plans from an anatomy textbook, a chapter a day.

*

I SIT IN THE museum, drawing a big diagram of blood vessels my mother asked me to copy from a textbook. My desk is under the jars marked "Female Reproductive System." Red arteries and blue veins crisscross their way from the heart to the perimeter of the skin. Red—fresh blood, full of oxygen; blue—old and used, on its way back to the filter of the heart. I must be careful and precise: one centimeter off, and the exact clock of the internal mechanism will creak to a stop and collapse. I am in charge of the organism's complex wiring, of its smooth operation.

I think of a man I'd seen hanging around our dacha, a tall, dark man who approached me this summer at the bus stop while I was waiting for my mother to come back from work. I had seen him cutting grass in the field by the fringe of the forest, his movements broad and fierce as his scythe fell and whistled with a hypnotic rhythm. He was sitting in the grass, by the paved patch of the field where the bus ended its route, smoking and watching me with his hard, black eyes. I felt flattered that he was looking at me, a twelve-year-old in a homemade sundress, as if I were worthy of this attention, as if I were one of those older girls who painted their eyelids and teased their hair and went to dances on Saturday nights.

A dot at the end of the road grew into a bus, coughing and rattling, but even before it stopped, I knew my mother wasn't on it. The three people on the bus climbed down the steps and started walking away, one toward the electric train station, the other two in the direction where the Gypsies lived. The air was grainy with gathering dusk, although it wasn't even six. The bus waited a few minutes, screeched around in a plume of exhaust, and drove away. The man got up. He was wearing black pants and a checkered shirt, sleeves rolled up to his elbows. I needed to occupy myself with something, so I squatted near where the asphalt ended and grass began, pretending to study a patch of *podorozhnik*, a medicinal plant commonly known to stop bleeding. It had thick, dark-green leaves that were heart-shaped and veined.

From the corner of my eye I saw the man stretch, walk a few paces the width of the road, and stop, gazing in the direction of the forest as if estimating how long it would take him to get there. I kept sitting on my haunches, hesitant to move now that he was so directly in my field of vision, although the pose was uncomfortable and I could feel tiny needles of numbing pain beginning to tingle in my leg. Then I saw him look directly at me, and I quickly turned away and stared hard at the thick, dusty leaves.

"What is it you're looking at?" he asked from about six feet away, his hands in his pockets. He used an informal *ty* for "you," a form used with children or people you are on close terms with, and I wasn't sure which one he meant.

I got up, my left leg asleep, but I clenched my teeth and didn't show it hurt. "*Podorozhnik*," I said, nodding toward the plant. Not looking at the man directly, I could still see him, big and powerful, gazing at me, making me feel important and almost grown-up.

"Do you want to take a walk in the field with me?" he asked, tilting his head toward the forest.

I knew it was an adult offer, not usually proffered to a twelve-year-old, and I felt grateful for his attention. I felt I'd been chosen, and it made my heart beat fast and hard. Too bad there was no one around, no one to see me walking with this handsome man. He stood there waiting, now smiling a little, his eyes crinkled, and that made him even more attractive. But then something tightened inside me. There appeared a strange expression in his eyes, making his gaze oily and uncomfortable, as if he could see something in me I didn't know about, something shameful and illicit my father would've hated.

I didn't want to offend him, but something made me shake my head and step back. He stopped smiling. I turned and started walking toward our house, although I knew that twenty minutes later, when my mother arrived, there would be no one there to meet her. I could sense the man's eyes on my back, and his stare made me feel sordid, as if I'd done something I could never tell anyone about, something that must be wrapped up tightly and hidden out of sight, on the lowest shelf of my heart.

THEY ALL KNOW SOMETHING I don't—my sister, handsome Volodya who works in the morgue, Zina the lab assistant who giggles when she is around him, and all those people on the streets and buses, elbowing each other on their way to work. They are all privy to a secret, deep and disgraceful, a secret they don't talk about. It is only revealed in slanted glances and smirks, in a raised shoulder, in a bitten lip.

There is nowhere I can find out what this secret is about. Some of the girls from my grade behave as if they know what it is, as if they belong to this club of wisdom and experience. They stretch their mouths in all-knowing smiles or narrow their eyes in little smirks, but I have my suspicions. My friend Masha, for example, the girl whom I see less and less frequently although she lives in my courtyard, announced recently that when blood begins to trickle down your thighs, you must pull on long underwear with rubber bands above your knees to catch it before it falls to the ground. Masha said this with the utmost confidence, throwing back her head with perfectly cut hair to underscore her scholarship; yet I knew she was even more ignorant than I. The rubber-banded underwear seemed just as efficient a measure as the instruction of our civil defense teacher to hide under our desks if America hit us with an atomic bomb.

I try to find the answer in books. Not in Russian books, because they all avoid talking about the secret. Indecent and shameful, it is consigned entirely to the books of the rotting capitalist West. In my English literature class we are reading A. J. Cronin's *The Citadel*, which exposes the ulcers of capitalism, but in a socialist, sterile way. I leaf through the collected works of Guy de Maupassant because a girl in my school, one of those who pretend they are in the know, said there is racy stuff in his books. I skim through the pages in search of the raunchy, but find nothing more than two people sleeping in one bed.

Then help seems to come from the most unlikely place. My school is taking us to see an American film called *Men in Her Life*. I am so excited I can hardly wait for the day, a week away. Men in her life—what can be more straightforward and titillating? I imagine a string of American men, all debonair and provocative, fighting for one woman, who is, without doubt, privy to all the facets of life. But when the lights in the theater turn off and grainy black-and-white images appear on the screen, the men of the title do nothing but walk around in white shirts with smoking jackets and bow ties and speak in long, undecipherable harangues of American English. What's even more disappointing is that there are only two of them. They look alike, bony and unsmiling, and from the little I can understand, they seem to appear in the woman's life successively rather than concurrently. The film drags on for two hours, and I cannot sneak out early because our teacher is sitting in my row. When the lights finally come on, I am exhausted from understanding so little English and disheartened because the knowledge was denied, again.

WHEN MY MOTHER AND I return from the anatomy department, we bring the formaldehyde smell back home, where it lingers in the hallway, around our coats and shoes.

"Where do babies come from?" I say casually as she is thrashing around the kitchen, throwing together a quick dinner. I watch her grab a piece of meat out of the refrigerator and force it down the throat of a meat grinder. A few vigorous cranks of the metal handle, and the face of the meat grinder erupts in red twists squeezing out into a bowl underneath. Of course, I have a general idea about babies, but I want to hear my mother, an anatomy teacher, give me her straightforward version of an answer.

"Babies come when a female sex cell is connected with a male sex cell," my mother says, patting the mixture of meat and bread into palm-size *kotlety*. "Then a fetus is developed in a uterus, and nine months later a woman gives birth to a baby."

I am grateful to her for this direct and daring explanation sprinkled with the words "male," "female," and "sex," which I can bet are not used so nonchalantly in other apartments facing the courtyard. Chewing on my *kotlety*, I contemplate the weight and abstraction of my new knowledge. I am enlightened by adult anatomical vocabulary, yet still completely ignorant.

ON OUR WAY TO the medical school we pass a maternity hospital, a four-story building overlooking a little square with streetcar tracks crossing in the middle.

"This is where you were born," says my mother.

In the summer, the hospital windows are opened, and young women lean out shouting details about their condition to their husbands, who are not allowed past the reception desk. "The water broke, but I'm still here," one woman yells. "There hasn't been any water, hot or cold, for three days," screams another one. I am not sure they are talking about the same water, but I have no one to ask.

Like every maternity patient, my mother stayed in the hospital for a week. Husbands came in the evening, after work, to stand on the streetcar tracks in front of the hospital and shout questions to their wives who were hanging out of the windows.

"What color eyes?" They wanted to know, cupping their hands around their mouths so their voices could reach all the way up.

"Blue," yelled the women, leaning out precariously. "All infants have blue eyes."

"And hair?" The men persisted as streetcars jingled a warning for them to get off the tracks. "What color hair?"

Had my father been standing on those tracks instead of sulking in a friend's dacha about becoming a father of a girl at fifty-five, I know what my mother would have shouted down. I've seen my pictures as an infant. "No hair," she would've said. "Bald. Just like Khrushchev."

Amid all this clamor, waiting for my father, she stood in the window to show me to the other women's husbands, to the people peering out of the open streetcar windows.

Still, seeing the maternity hospital does nothing to get me closer to understanding. Like the inside of the hospital wards, the secret is still just that, a secret.

I STAND UNDER A poster for a movie, *Love Under the Elms,* hanging in our local House of Culture, which bears the name of the First Five-Year Plan. The poster shows a tree with heavy, sprawled branches that must convey the weighty and complicated nature of that love. It is an American movie, but it stars Sophia Loren, who everybody knows is Italian. I don't understand how an Italian actress can star in an American film, how the borders between countries can be so unprotected and so easily crossed. But there is even a bigger question looming in my head, the question about the title. It is based on a play by an American playwright, Eugene O'Neill, as my friend Masha, whose mother teaches college English, informed me, and its real title is *Desire Under the Elms.* So what does this mean? Are desire and love the same? Or did the translator take too broad a license? Or—the more likely possibility—was the change in translation deliberate, a metamorphosis from the bodily and the sensual toward the soulful and the more lofty? None of us is surprised, for example, when during rehearsals Marina's theater removes whole passages from Western plays. After all, as everyone knows, the capitalist West with its economy and art can produce nothing but vulgarity and shame.

I'm afraid I will never learn the answer to any of these questions. Under the film title there is a warning: forbidden for children under sixteen. This means there is a kiss on the screen, a real kiss where you can see the lips, not where all they show is the back of the head. The warning is written in small, but deliberate letters, and it means that for four more years I won't be able to see robust Sophia Loren— in love, or desire—who undoubtedly knows more about the secret than the skinny, black-and-white heroine of *Men in Her Life*.

I think of wasp-waisted Sophia Loren in a flaring skirt, as I recently saw her in our movie magazine, *Screen*. She was walking on twiggy heels past some baroque buildings on an Italian street, which looked like any of our streets, except for the absence of flags and slogans stretched over the façades. Looking at the poster, I try to imagine her in America, but there is nothing concrete to anchor the image. We never see America on television; it's a fictitious place, too foreign and too far away.

There is no man on the poster, so I imagine Sophia Loren and the tall, enticing Volodya from my mother's anatomy department lying under the elms, immersed in their desire. They are experienced and urbane: Sophia Loren because she is from a capitalist country, and Volodya because he is eighteen and has a real job. I envy them both, but I envy Sophia Loren more.

I wonder if other countries have the secret, and if it is as well-guarded as it is here. I can decipher nothing from A. J. Cronin or even the supposedly raunchy Guy de Maupassant. Maybe in sultry Italy, or stately England, or mythical America, they are all born with some inherent knowledge. Maybe the secret is like their borders—unprotected and easily permeable.

IT IS THE LAST day of my vacation, and I must say good-bye to the museum, Aunt Klava, and human anatomy. I won't be back until next fall, another revolution anniversary when schools close for a recess. The diagram I have been copying for days is finished and propped on a museum desk. It is perfect in the precision of its red arteries and blue veins, a splash of color among jars of monochromatic organs.

I pace along the corridor, past the doors with squares of glass in the middle. Professors stand in front of charts where human bodies are reduced to clusters of threads in primary colors, and behind one of the doors I see my mother pointing to a red clump inside a paper chest. I wonder if she loved my father with that hot, sweaty love that the poster for the Sophia Loren American movie promises. I wonder if my mother, with her need for order and marching in step with the collective, even knows about that kind of love. Or maybe she knew when she was young; maybe she used to know and then forgot.

I walk down to the basement and saunter past Zina's lab and Volodya's morgue. Both doors are closed, but I hear a giggle behind the lab door. I know it's Zina's giggle, the little laugh she lets out when Volodya is close. I stop by the door and stand there, although I don't know what it is I'm waiting to find out. Then there are muted sounds of Volodya's voice, more like bursts of whisper, then Zina's babble, then rustling and stirring and breathing. I know I should leave, but I stand there, as if the soles of my shoes have become glued to the cement floor. I know I should leave, but the secret is right here, behind this door, so I stand and listen. There is a creaking noise, and the sound of a chair scraping the floor, and more breathing. There is more whispering and stirring and clanking. I don't know how long the secret lasts and when it ends, so I can't estimate when I should plan a safe retreat. It would be embarrassing, it occurs to me, if that door suddenly flew open and revealed me to the eyes of Volodya and Zina, an ignorant twelve-year-old standing in the hallway, spying on their adult ways.

Again, I feel disappointed. I'm angry that handsome Volodya is choosing to do the adult things with stringy-haired Zina, who ignores me, pretending to stare into her microscope when he is not around. But most important, I'm frustrated because this dangerous eavesdropping has not divulged anything new about the secret.

There is a door between us, as always, and that's where all important things are kept, behind closed doors.

So I unglue my feet from the floor and go up to the dissection room. My mother's class is just over, and her white-gowned students are tiptoeing away from the table on which lies the Man, now a scavenged body, a black skeletal frame with occasional flaps of muscle tissue hanging on dry bones between the joints.

"Go find Aunt Klava," says my mother when she sees me. "And turn in your white coat."

I don't know that Aunt Klava is standing right behind me, so when I turn, I stumble straight into her sharp body. She opens her arms and holds my cheek to hers, her wiry hair prickling my face. She pats me on the back with her hand, so little and dry it could be a claw of a bird, rasping tobacco-smelling words into my ear. I can't make out what she is saying, but it must be a good-bye wish, and we stand like this for a few moments, exposed to the gaze of the whole class of freshmen who have just reduced a human body to the anatomical museum display of its parts.

I wish live bodies were as logical and scientific as cadavers. I wish they didn't contain any secrets, thrilling and shameful, protected by those who know them with the same zeal we use to protect our borders from foreign intervention. I wish I were sixteen so I could see *Love Under the Elms*, in color, with real American men, and real passions, and a real mouth-to-mouth kiss as big as the screen of our local House of Culture, which bears the name of the First Five-Year Plan.

I wish I could ask my mother—the one that is gone, the one in the portrait—about the secret, about life, about love and desire. I wish I could ask her about my father.

My mother—the real one— takes off her white coat and her cloth hat and folds them up neatly for Aunt Klava. "The dissection is over," she says and smiles a teacher's smile. "It's time to go home."

# CHAPTER II

# Dangers of Big Rivers

IN JULY, JUST BEFORE I turn thirteen and when Marina is on tour with her theater, my mother and I go to visit our family in Stankovo. It is a small town on the banks of the Volga, a hundred kilometers from Ivanovo, where she was born.

I look forward to the ride on an overnight train as much as I do to visiting my aunt and my three cousins. The cardboard tickets my mother bought three weeks ago give us admission into a train car, and when the whistle blows and the platform begins to sail away, we leave behind, in a cloud of smoke, some vigorously waving women with handkerchiefs clutched in their fists. The wheels, tentative at first, gradually get into a steady rhythm; the locomotive sighs and begins its droning pull, and the first suburban stations flicker past, surrounded by rows of tiny dachas.

We are traveling in a more expensive four-berth compartment, separated from the narrow hallway by a mirrored door that slides open when pulled by a metal handle. I am on the upper berth, with my mother underneath me on the lower. There is another passenger, Luda, from the small town of Kaluga, which we will pass later this evening. She is staring out the window, her elbows planted on the table, her fists squashing up against her cheeks. Her heavy arms bulge out of a short-sleeved dress, and the braids of her thick wheaten hair, crisscrossed on the back of her head, sag like a hammock under their own weight.

A man appears in the doorway of our compartment and, peering at his ticket, pushes in his suitcase. Luda turns her head, a flicker of interest brightening her face as she examines the new passenger. A plaid shirt stretches over his belly, pants bunch around his hips, and his hair, parted just above his left ear, is slicked over his balding head. He hoists a suitcase onto the upper shelf, sweat beading on his forehead. I know his ticket probably indicates that he has a lower berth, but according to train etiquette, lower berths always go to women. Before bedtime, following another unwritten rule, he will leave the compartment to let the women undress and go to bed and then, by the light of a blue bulb, climb onto his bed, carefully stepping on top of the table to lift himself up.

"Luda," says the woman, stretching her hand toward him when he finishes with the suitcase and wipes his face with a handkerchief.

"A pleasure," he says. "Semyon."

He then acknowledges me with a glance and smiles politely at my mother.

Luda invites Semyon to sit on her lower berth and we all stare out the window. Outside, fields of potatoes and buckwheat sway on the horizon and clouds begin to boil in the anticipation of evening. Fields soon give way to a wall of forest. Black fir trees and white birches flicker by in a checkered pattern fringed by purple and yellow stalks of Ivan-da-Marya flowers, their colors as inseparable as the two lovers who, according to a folk legend, gave the plant its name.

We soon find out that Luda came to Leningrad to hunt for food. An aluminum bucket with eight kilos of meat is tucked under her seat, along with string bags full of logs of bologna, wheels of cheese, and pot-bellied mayonnaise jars. "Look for a line," she says, explaining her strategy, which is the same strategy my mother explained to me a year earlier. "The longer the better. If there's a line, there's something at the other end of it."

Semyon agrees with this tactic in principle, but adds an opinion. "I hate lines," he says. "Never stood on one."

"Your wife does, right?" smirks Luda.

Semyon smiles a guilty smile. "You women are stronger than us."

Luda, as we quickly learn, lives with her parents, her brother, his wife, and their two "bratty" children. Most of the food from the Leningrad trip will probably be snatched and hoarded by her "shameless" sister-in-law, who manipulated Luda's "simpleton" brother into marrying her despite the family's objections.

"Do you know why it's so easy to supply this huge country with food?" she asks, patting the bench full of string bags and buckets, reciting an old joke. "Because they only have to supply Moscow and Leningrad. The rest of the country hops on the train, grabs what's left, and delivers it home."

At dusk Luda unwraps her dinner—half a loaf of black bread, four tomatoes, two hard-boiled eggs, and a half of a roasted chicken. Semyon pulls a bottle of vodka out of a newspaper cocoon and triumphantly installs it on the table next to the chicken. Then he runs to the conductor and returns with three ribbed tea glasses, which he says he promised to bring back before she started evening tea service.

My mother gives the bottle a disdainful look and proceeds with unwrapping our own dinner. There are more hard-boiled eggs, two hefty pieces of cabbage pie she baked three days ago, and two thick slices of bologna glued with butter to chunks of black bread.

Semyon yanks off the silver bottle cap and measures out vodka, half a glass each, for Luda and himself. Then he turns to my mother, who puts her hand over the top of the third glass under Luda's gaze, first disbelieving, then sneering. I know my mother despises vodka and feels suspicious of those who drink it.

"Too bad we have no salted herring for a chaser," says Semyon, using the diminutive *selyodochka*.

"No *selyodochka*, what a shame," pipes in Luda, shifting from ridicule of my mother's refusal to drink to anticipation of a feast. Her nimble hands cut the chicken and slice the bread. Suddenly she slaps herself on the hip and shrieks, "Fool! What a fool I am! I completely forgot!"

She lifts her berth and roots inside. Triumphantly, she pulls out and unwraps a jar of pickles with chunks of garlic and stalks of dill floating inside. "This'll do as well," she says, putting it on the table next to the bottle. "I was bringing it to compare with our own pickles, but what the hell." She nudges the metal lid with a knife and it obediently pops open. "There's nothing you'll spare for good company."

"To good company," says Semyon, raising his glass to click with Luda's. He drinks in three big gulps, pats his lips on his sleeve, and grunts. Then he squeezes his eyes shut for a second and his whole face ripples in wrinkles of exhilaration. He grabs a pickle and bites half of it off as his features smooth back into place.

"To good vodka and good food," says Luda. She exhales and, after finishing half of her vodka, starts making squealing noises, waving her hand in front of her face. Then she curses under her breath, drinks the rest, and finishes Semyon's pickle.

For a second, my mother looks at them scornfully, then turns and peers out the window. Drinking vodka is as low as one can get, as far as she is concerned. At celebrations, she sips a little cognac and the sweet wine my grandfather brews in twenty-five-liter jars out of piles of sugar and black currants from his garden.

I see that Luda is now staring at my mother with the same scorn my mother had in her eyes seconds earlier.

My mother senses the stare and meets her gaze. "Vodka from tea glasses," she says in her teaching voice and didactically shakes her head.

"Vodka from tea glasses," mimics Luda, curling her mouth. "And what do you prefer, Madame Leningrad, champagne?"

My mother purses her lips. "What I prefer is none of your business," she says in a voice she uses to admonish.

"Leave her alone," Semyon tells Luda and grins apologetically at my mother. "You're from different places, you're used to different things." He doesn't say my mother is *kulturnaya*, cultured, and Luda isn't, but I know that's what he means.

"I can see that," Luda retorts. "She refuses to drink vodka, so maybe she's not even Russian."

I think of Masha Mironova, whose mother is Russian, like mine, but whose father isn't, wondering how being Russian makes life easier if any vodka-sloshing woman on the train can still hurl any accusation she wants straight into your face.

My mother gets up and props her fist on her hip. "I'm as Russian as you are," she says. "I just don't drink as much."

"*Touché*," says Semyon, extending his arm as if holding a rapier.

"I don't know *touché*," says Luda, her cheeks flaming like autumn apples. "What I do know is that she's calling me an alcoholic."

My mother did not say the word, but I know that she thought it. It is the word she hurls into Marina's face when, on such occasions as an opening night or an actor's birthday, my sister's key fumbles in the lock of our apartment and fails to find the keyhole. On these nights my mother deliberately unlocks the door and yells that Marina takes after her father in drinking the same way I take after mine in obstinacy.

"Why are we arguing?" says Semyon, positioning himself between the two berths. "We have good food, good drink, and good company. Let's make the best of our trip."

Luda pounds her empty glass on the table. "You and my sister-in-law, the one married to my idiot brother." She glares at my mother. "Always pointing a finger at me. Always telling me I drink too much."

"Who drinks too much?" Semyon looks around in mock bewilderment. "A bottle for two, normal stuff."

"Just wait." Luda gets up and takes a step toward my mother, nudging Semyon out of the way with her weight. "One day soon you'll crawl out to the countryside looking for bread and then I'll spit on you. The way you spit on me when I stock up in Leningrad."

This is ironic because the berth I am sitting on is full of string bags with the same provisions Luda is bringing back: cheese, mayonnaise, and bologna my mother has stored up for my aunt's family. In the corner of the trunk underneath me is a bucket, the same as Luda's, the same bucket we always see in our stores, its contents covered with several layers of plastic—eight kilos of meat, a glorious harvest from two hours in a butcher line. Leningrad provisions, as Luda's joke goes, being delivered to the faraway corners of our country by the people themselves, one shopper at a time.

"Kaluga next!" the conductor's voice rings out from the corridor. Our door rattles on its hinges and slides open, and the conductor's henna-colored head pops into the doorway.

I'm glad the conductor showed up when she did. I'm scared of Luda, of her thick forearms and her braids, so strange on an adult head. She reminds me of Aunt Polya, and I'm certain that if we were in an open space and she had a chance to shriek at the top of her lungs she would reveal the same kitchen voice.

"How long is the stopover?" asks my mother.

"Fifteen minutes," the conductor yells back, bustling down the corridor in her black uniform with brass buttons on the front.

Luda now feverishly turns her attention to lifting her string bags out of the trunk. Semyon is helping her with the bucket, and she joins a line of passengers getting off that has stretched down the corridor to our door.

"Such a *nekulturnaya*," my mother mumbles into Luda's receding back. "Culture hasn't been anywhere close to this woman."

If we are fast, my mother and I, we can jump down the three metal steps of the train and check out the local offerings peddled by kerchiefed women: strawberries sold by the cup; jars of home-marinated mushrooms, their slippery caps glistening through glass; and fried *pirozhki* filled with cabbage, mouth-watering and greasy. At the end of the platform, a freckled girl holds up a tiny basket of wild strawberries.

"Let's buy them all," I whisper to my mother, who hands a ruble note to the girl as I take the basket, the tangy forest smell tickling my nostrils.

"Tea!" rings the conductor's voice back in our car. "Who wants tea?"

A minute later, three steaming glasses nestled in metal glass-holders—the same glasses used earlier for the vodka—are lowered onto our table. We drink strong tea with wild strawberries, gazing out at the stars that appear one by one, tangled in the freshly crocheted spread of darkness.

For less than a day, my mother, Semyon, and I are united by the rattle of the wheels, by the changing frames of landscape. We speed through blackness in the cloister of our compartment, where reality is measured by the intensity of amber tea, by the scent of wild strawberries.

The magic will last until noon tomorrow, when the train will arrive at its final destination, Stankovo, and we will step into the bustle of the station, into the arms of my aunt, uncle, and cousins. But for now we are still here, looking out the window into black emptiness to the lullaby of clattering wheels.

MY AUNT MUZA MEETS us at the train station with my three cousins, Kostya, Fedya, and Kolya. The reason she has three, she jokes, when they crowd around us in the elbowing turmoil of the train arrival, is that she has always wanted a girl. After her third son, Kolya, was born, she realized that girls were my mother's destiny, not hers, and gave up.

*Muza* in Russian means "Muse," which was, perhaps, my grandma's attempt to memorialize her own unrealized opera singing career. Her father, a factory owner and a man of strict morals, banned her from studying at a conservatory, where she'd won a scholarship, because no decent woman, in his view, should appear onstage.

My aunt is short and round, fifteen years younger than my mother, and looks nothing like a Muse. Keeping with the family tradition, Aunt Muza is a doctor, an obstetrician at the town's only hospital. Round-faced and stocky, she made it her priority to beef me up, to infuse color into my cheeks, which she calls "city pity." Every afternoon she installs herself in the kitchen, whose walls are adorned with braids of garlic and onion, first in front of the table where she chops, mixes, and kneads, and then before a gas stove, which makes her face even more rosy and shiny. From under her dancing fingers flow sheets of cabbage pie, pans full of potatoes fried with onions, and steaming pots of a sauerkraut soup with beef bones called *schi*.

Aunt Muza gets beef from her patients, women who work in stores or meat-packing houses. She likes to repeat a joke that outlines the scarcity of Stankovo's food supplies: *A man comes to a butcher shop. Do you have any fish? he asks. Here we don't have meat, says the saleswoman. Fish they don't have across the street.*

The lack of fish in Stankovo is a dark mystery to my mother, who cannot comprehend how a town sitting on the bank of the greatest Russian river can be devoid of its most indigenous product. "*Blat*," mutters Aunt Muza—you must have connections. Muza's own *blat* weaves through the fabric of the town's female population, and in addition to beef shanks, she sometimes lumbers home with a whole snapper carefully wrapped in newspaper, its slippery tail sticking out the top of her string bag.

Those few things the shops do have are placed inside near-empty glass cases, their solitude raising them to the status of delicacies. In grocery stores permeated with the smell of the sawdust that covers their floors, I stumble upon foods different from what I can find at home, and that alone makes them tantalizing. In an echoey bakery I beg my mother to buy a cake covered with a mysterious brown glaze, which is the store's only ware. I find a dairy, two bus stops away, and although it is usually out of milk by noon, it sells delicious, raisin-studded ice cream packed into a waffle cone by a big morose woman, nine kopeks for as much as she decides to scoop in.

In the afternoons we all go to the Volga. My cousins Kostya, Fedya, and I race as far as we can into the brown vastness of the river. Kolya skips stones on the far side of the narrow beach, away from the rock where we pile our clothes. My mother, Aunt Muza, and Uncle Fedya come with us.

"We're so lucky to live close to the Volga!" my aunt exclaims. "Look at this natural beauty. Where else could you find such vistas?" Muza seems to find beauty or luck in almost everything, and this time she's lucky to live on the riverbank because hot water in their apartment building has recently been turned off.

During the bathing-in-the-Volga ritual, Aunt Muza tells us stories about the hospital. So far they have all been short and funny and have nothing to do with illness. But I sense that what she does at work is daunting and dangerous compared to my mother's job of teaching anatomy.

Aunt Muza is putting on a huge two-piece bathing suit, green with yellow flowers, while my uncle, thin and already balding, is staring through a pair of binoculars in the direction of some girls giggling and cavorting further down the riverbank.

"She keeps running a high fever, this woman," says Aunt Muza, carefully folding her dress and placing it on a rock. "Three days

after the surgery, and she's burning like a stove." *Gorit i gorit*—
burning and burning—she stresses the *o*'s the same way Kolya
does, which still sounds strange to my Leningrad ears.

"The usual remedies don't work, the antibiotics are still rotting
in some warehouse, and the department chief has just flown off
to a convention of honorary communists in Moscow." Aunt Muza
cannot fasten the clasp on the back of her bathing suit brassiere,
and it takes my mother a minute or two of vigorous pulls to make
the two ends meet.

"I wheel her back and open her up again, and what do I find?"
continues Aunt Muza, testing the water with her toe. Her stomach
is so round, even more than my mother's. I wonder at what stage
in life women's stomachs undergo the miraculous transformation
from flat like mine to barrel-shaped like Aunt Muza's.

"A surgical napkin left in her gut," announces Muza. "A napkin
in the belly, with peritonitis brewing, no antibiotics, and the
department chief receiving an award in Moscow."

I don't know what a surgical napkin looks like, but I imagine
one of those huge linen squares that appear on the table for major
holidays. A napkin that big, I decide, could only fit into a belly
the size of my aunt's. But the conversation makes unpleasant
thoughts pop into my mind, and I strain to listen to groans in
my stomach, attaching each one to the possible presence of a
foreign object.

"Who left the napkin?" asks my mother in the voice she uses
when she demands to pin down responsibility and dispense
appropriate punishment.

Aunt Muza shakes her head and flips her wrist in a gesture
that seems out of character with her plump features, her cheerful
roundness. She gazes into the darkness of the river for a minute, her
eyes wide open, as if straining to make out something deep below
its brown water. "It was the nurse's aide," she finally says, shifting
her gaze back to the land. "The aide got drunk on surgical alcohol."

"She should be put on trial," glowers my mother, her voice ringing with satisfaction at having located the culprit. "Tried and convicted. The patient could have died."

Aunt Muza starts wading into the water, pushing it sideways with her hands as if clearing some unseen debris from the surface. When it gets up to her thighs, she stops.

"It's not that simple. The aide, Alya Svetlova, has worked there her whole life. Scrubbing and washing since the war. She should be peacefully collecting her pension and growing potatoes like everyone else, but she has to work double shifts to support her thirty-year-old idiot-of-a-son who beats her up."

"A firing squad. It would have been quick under Stalin—no investigation and it's over," proclaims my uncle, who has stopped staring at the girls and is now sitting on the rock rubbing the lenses of his binoculars with a sleeve of his shirt. "They used to shoot people for lesser crimes than that."

"For being two minutes late to work they used to throw you in jail," says my mother. "You overslept and missed the bell and the next thing you know they're banging on your door in the middle of the night. I saw people disappear for missing the bell. There was order then."

"Order!" erupts Uncle Fedya and spits on the ground. "Look around. Gangs of hooligans on every corner, nurses drunk in operating rooms. Where has the order gone?" His arms fly up in the air. "A hand of steel—that's what the people need. They understand strength and that's the only thing they listen to. Put someone strong in charge and even the worst bum will shape up overnight."

"That's absolutely right," says my mother, and she drives her fists into her hips, which makes her look like a teapot.

I am glad I wasn't born when Stalin was in charge. It's unclear to me why my mother, my uncle, or anyone else would lament the era of throwing people in jail for being late to work. Did they also throw students in jail for being late for school?

"I had a surgery case during the war," says my mother, who cannot offer an equally dangerous story from her present teaching experience, so she has to dredge it out of her surgical past. Only now her voice isn't as firm and she doesn't sound as certain as she did a few minutes earlier when she argued for a hand of steel. "A nine-year-old boy got blown up on a mine, in the spring of 1942, when the Volga ice began to shift. His dead friend's mother brought him in." I'd heard the story before—three boys with buckets wading into the river to collect the fish floating belly up among chunks of ice from a mine explosion, setting off another one by mistake. I know that what impressed my mother most was that woman, who had left her own dead son on the riverbank to carry his only surviving friend to the hospital two kilometers away.

"I began to prepare him for surgery," my mother says. "The boy was already on the table when the Commissar stormed in, shouting I had no right to operate on civilians in a military hospital."

"What did you do?" asks Uncle Fedya, tossing a rock in the water, and I see Aunt Muza look at him the way Vera Pavlovna looked at Dimka the hooligan when he asked why the Great October Socialist Revolution is celebrated in November.

"I did what I had to do, operate," says my mother. "He ordered me to ship the boy to a civilian hospital as soon as I was finished. 'We'll see about that,' I said." She folds her arms across her chest, just as she probably did twenty-five years ago.

"So what happened?" asks Uncle Fedya, who stopped tossing rocks and is now looking at my mother, interested in the story.

"After I was done, I went to talk to Dr. Kremer, the head of the hospital. He was also a surgeon and he understood. He turned out to be *intelligentny*. We agreed that the boy would stay for three days so I could make sure the stitches worked and there was no infection. On the fourth day we transferred him to a civilian hospital."

*Intelligentny* is a multi-faceted adjective my mother likes to use to characterize people. It is a salad mix of education, culture, intelligence, and manners, plus a certain view of the world that allows an alternative. The Commissar, who yelled at my mother for breaking a military rule, was obviously not *intelligentny*. The head of the hospital, who colluded with her in rule-breaking, certainly was.

By this standard, Uncle Fedya, with his myopic views and a love for hands of steel, is not at all *intelligentny*, whereas Aunt Muza, with her compassion and common wisdom, could stand a chance. I try to divide the people I know into *intelligentny* vs. not *intelligentny* categories, but the list of the former comes out much shorter than the latter. Not *intelligentny*: Aunt Polya from my nursery school, my third-grade teacher Vera Pavlovna, Luda on the train, every saleswoman in every grocery store. *Intelligentny*: my English tutor Irina Petrovna.

Then what about my mother and Marina? They are educated but not terribly cultured. My mother didn't bring her bathing suit to Stankovo, so she goes swimming in her white bra and pink underpants. Marina licks plates. Most important, they both yell, at me and at each other, which automatically disqualifies them from the *intelligentny* category.

But do you have to be *intelligentny* yourself in order to decide if others are? Am I *intelligentny*?

I watch the sun heave toward the jagged line of forest on the other bank of the river. My uncle tests the water with his foot and a shiver runs through his skinny body. "*Holod sobachii*"—"dog's freezing cold," his favorite expression, except the *o*'s don't roll down his tongue because he is originally from around Moscow.

From Aunt Muza's movements in the water, from her cautious stroke, I sense that she, too, isn't so sure about the advantages of a hand of steel or the benefits of jailing and shooting. I sense that she, like Kolya, believes in whirlpools, in the might of the river, in its silent menace, so I give her the benefit of doubt and add her to my short *intelligentny* list.

WE ARE BOUNCING ON a bus over gouged roads to a nearby village to stock up on bread and milk, my mother, Aunt Muza, and my cousins, each carrying an empty basket. When the bus deposits us in the middle of a dirt road, we walk on a footpath through fields specked with blue stars of cornflowers and purple butterflies of wild sweet peas. I am glad I've brought a sweater because I am freezing, although the sun is beating down and my cousin Kostya has unbuttoned his shirt.

We walk along a footpath through a patch of weeds to an *izba*, a log cabin with a straw roof pressing down on two squatty windows, perched on the brink of the forest. A kerchiefed woman waddles down the two front steps.

"*Zahodite, zahodite*," she invites us in, her mouth stretched in a toothless smile. She is ageless, in a black canvas dress, with veins threading her suntanned hands. When my eyes get used to the semi-darkness of the entrance, I make out a goat lying on a bed of straw and a hen clucking around a litter of brown chicks. The chicks scurry away, the goat struggles up on its spindly legs, and the six of us, too many for the house's only room, crowd in front of a Russian stove, a brick wall with an opening in the middle for cooking and a ledge on top for sleeping.

I have never seen a real Russian stove. Everyone knows, from Russian folktales, what it is supposed to look like; you always find Ivan-the-Fool sleeping on top while more serious characters spend the day riding horses or planting wheat. But this Russian stove is blackened with soot, and I can't imagine anyone lying on the narrow brick ledge.

The ageless woman wants us to taste her cottage cheese and yellow sour cream and the black bread she baked in the Russian stove. To demonstrate the thickness of her sour cream she sticks a big spoon in the middle of the bowl, filled to the brim, and the spoon remains standing, like a proud flagpole, a testament to the virtue of homemade food. She brings in a pitcher of goat's milk, steam rising from its surface.

I don't drink the milk because it has a pungent smell, and the sour cream melts into a puddle of fat on my tongue. While I pick at the bread, my cousins wolf down bowls of cottage cheese and bread hunks loaded with butter. "Eat, eat," nudges my mother, her elbow in my side, although the spinning sensation in my stomach nauseates me and I don't feel like eating.

At last, we leave the *izba*, having paid eight rubles for our baskets filled with loaves of bread, jars of sour cream and cottage cheese, and a hefty chunk of butter wrapped in a plastic bag. Kostya, the oldest cousin, treads carefully because he is clutching a three-liter jar of goat's milk to his chest. While we wait for the bus, I'm so cold that Aunt Muza wraps her shawl around me, but I still shiver. She puts her palm on my forehead, shakes her head, and says that I'm getting sick.

AT NIGHT, I BURN and sweat and have strange dreams. I dream about my cousin Kolya, who is afraid to swim in the Volga because there are whirlpools there. The *o*'s in the Russian word for whirlpool, *vodovorot,* rolled down his tongue like a handful of peas when he told me about his fear by the foot of the steep Volga bank, where brown water, bottomless after the first few steps, licked the dirt in lazy ripples.

In the dream, Kolya and I wade in, our bodies cutting through the water. An undercurrent tingles my ankles and makes me stop for a moment. Kolya is walking in up to his chest, then to his neck, until I see only his ears sticking out of the sides of his round head. I've never seen Kolya so deep in the river. I try to yell to him, but no sound comes out, no matter how hard I strain. He keeps walking slowly, as if remembering his fear, and I know he is walking straight into the whirlpool. One more step and he is embraced by the power underneath, and all I can see is his head spinning on the surface of the water as he is pulled further and further away from the shore.

I stumble back to the narrow beach, where my uncle in bathing trunks is staring through the binoculars at my school friend Masha doing a cartwheel in her leotard. I don't understand how Masha got to Stankovo from Leningrad, where she should be spending her summer vacation, but I'm glad she did because I can tell her about Kolya and the whirlpool. It is no use telling my uncle, who is glued to his binoculars, fascinated by Masha's cartwheels.

To get to Masha I must climb the slope of the riverbank, so steep that when I approach, it rises like a wall. The wall closes on me like the top of a trunk, and I know that now I will not be able to save Kolya from the whirlpool no matter how hard I try.

A cool weight presses on my forehead, and the top of the trunk opens a crack. I see a hand straightening something white and wet on my head. "A compress for your fever," says my aunt's voice. But I know immediately it's a surgical napkin, so I yank it off because I don't want it to end up sewn into my belly. The hand struggles, shoving the compress back onto my forehead, but I scream, and when the hand recoils I am free to run back to the shore, where the whirlpool is spinning around Kolya.

As I careen down the riverbank, small rocks tumbling in my wake, a question is pounding in my head in sync with my steps: Why of all the kids who swim in the river was it Kolya who stepped into the whirlpool? Why not the girls cavorting in their bikinis on the beach, or Igor from across the street who wobbles to the river on his rusty bicycle, or my cousin Kostya, who refuses to even acknowledge the danger? Why not me?

Not me, not me, not me, a little hammer bangs in my temple as they try to push a wet napkin in my face again, and again I scream it off my head. The hand then rests on my forehead, pleasant in its cold heaviness, soothing. For a moment, I pause in my flight down the riverbank trying to understand why it was Kolya who was pulled away by the undercurrent. The water below is black as oil, glistening under the last strokes of the sun; no insects glide over its surface, no boats cut into its heft. Through the haze of heavy air the answer sinks in like a rock through water: the whirlpool singled out Kolya precisely because Kolya knew about its existence.

I look down on the Volga, on the stillness that belies its danger, on its beckoning silence. Masha with her cartwheels is gone, and my uncle, who for some reason never ventures to look through his binoculars at the river itself, is focusing on several specks of people etched against the evening sky on the rim of the far riverbank. Stepping out of my shoes, I walk across the hardened dirt of the beach to the waiting water. The river, lukewarm and soothing, envelops my feet, kisses my legs, strokes my back. Its blackness is entrancing, spellbinding, impossible to resist. As I walk deeper, the bottom slides away from under my feet, leaving me to spin slowly in the tender embrace of the whirlpool.

ONCE MY FEVER BREAKS, Aunt Muza doubles her efforts to not only add new pounds to my waist but also replace several lost during my illness. A bad flu, she says when I ask her what it was. She sings while she kneads and chops—old ballads and songs from the radio and films. She must have inherited my grandma's unused opera talent: her voice soars in sophisticated roulades that quickly get trapped in her little kitchen. I obediently sip her *schi* and chew on her *pirozhki*, grateful to my three cousins who, without much effort, can sweep clean a table full of food in a matter of minutes.

I watch her dance in front of the stove, her thick hands surprisingly graceful, her whole body submitting to the food-making ritual and yet presiding over it. I want to ask her what has happened to the patient with the napkin in her belly. I want to ask her about the vague perils that seem to lurk in the most mundane places, but it somehow seems both dangerous and foolish to validate verbally something that is so murky, nothing more than images floating in a feverish head.

I'm surprised I remember this dream at all. There is only one other dream that didn't evaporate the moment I opened my eyes, and it probably stayed in my memory because it was so odd. In the dream, my father was sitting in his boat, speaking about what happens a minute before the curtain goes up, as if he were an actor. The people in the audience hold their breath and all the noise stops, he said, just before the magic is about to begin. Don't let the magic slip away, he warned me. Don't sink into the quicksand of the ordinary.

Did he recognize the magic in real life? Or do I remember this dream so well because I wished he had?

I wonder if Aunt Muza's napkin incident could have happened in the past, when my father was alive, when there was order, according to Uncle Fedya and my mother. I wonder how orderly it must have been, that order, if my uncle considers our present marching in step with the collective a state close to anarchy. And yet, even in that order, there were *intelligentny* people in charge like Dr. Kremer in my mother's war hospital, who chose not to follow military rules. Was life easier then? Were there fewer dangers, or more? Would my friend Masha's parents still have chosen to give her the mother's Russian name instead of the father's Jewish one?

Reluctantly I think of what my uncle might say if he knew that Masha's parents made that decision because they wanted her to have an easier life.

Jews, he would say. You can't trust them. They were cowards during the war, hiding from bullets at the front. Hiding in cellars and attics, while our Russian boys spilled their blood.

I don't know how Uncle Fedya, who was a private during the war, can be privy to such a global view. So I remain skeptical about his opinions, and I don't mention my friend Masha to him even once, finding it ironic that it was the two of them, Uncle Fedya and Masha, who crossed paths in my fever dream.

"Can we go for a swim?" I ask Aunt Muza, who has just wrapped several kitchen towels around a pot of freshly made dough.

"No swimming for you, my sweet," she says, wiping her flour-powdered hands on her apron. "After the fever you've had you can just about forget swimming until you get back home. But you can walk with us to the river—fresh air is good for you." I am not sure my mother would approve of such an early outing, but since permission has been granted, I rush to the door, where my street shoes, my little orphans that are now almost ruined by Stankovo's dust, have been patiently waiting this whole week.

We take the familiar path, my cousins flying down, my mother, aunt, and uncle trotting in careful little steps. I am at the end of this procession, every step echoing in my head, and my muscles, unused for a week, shaking inside my skin.

Down on the hard, narrow beach Aunt Muza changes into her green and yellow two-piece bathing suit, carefully folding her huge white bra and underpants. I wait for her to say something about her patient, but she stands at the line where the dark water sighs softly at her feet, gazing into the distance where Kostya's noisy splashes rip open the oilskin of the river.

My mother and Uncle Fedya are sitting on the rock talking. From her body language I know she is telling the story of her uncle Volya. I've heard the story several times, when she told it to my father and to our neighbors from the third floor. In 1937 her uncle, who worked in a propaganda bureau, took a stranger from Moscow to a restaurant, where he told a joke.

"The night they came to arrest him, he said to his wife, Aunt Lilya, and to his fifteen-year-old daughter Anya that it was all a mistake, a misunderstanding, and he'll surely be back soon."

"Was he?" asks Uncle Fedya.

If Uncle Fedya knows what was happening at the front during

the war, if he knows where the Jews were hiding, he should know the answer to this question. Were I in my mother's place, I wouldn't bother telling him what seems to be obvious. But my mother obliges because she likes telling stories about her life.

"We were told he was shot trying to escape," she says. "He was later rehabilitated posthumously, after Aunt Lilya and his daughter Anya were already dead. Anya took a nursing course when the war started, volunteered for the front to avenge her father, and got killed in 1942. Found a bullet, just as she wished, though she didn't have to look far."

I am not sure that Uncle Volya's posthumous rehabilitation benefited anyone since neither his wife nor his daughter lived long enough to appreciate it.

After all, this past order heralded so by Uncle Fedya does not seem to have made life any easier or safer. Shooting someone for telling a joke hardly seems any better than leaving a surgical napkin in a patient's gut.

My legs give out and I sit down on the grass, next to my cousin Kolya, who is engrossed in searching for something between his toes. Aunt Muza was right when she didn't let me go swimming because my head pounds like a drum and a million golden dots flash before my eyes. As the sun glides toward the river, Kolya and I gaze at the black water, which I am now certain is full of invisible whirlpools.

# CHAPTER 12

# A Lesson in Russian Classics

THE MORAL CONFLICT OF Turgenev's *A Nest of Nobles* is between personal happiness and duty," says our teacher, Nina Sergeevna, peering above her glasses to make sure we are listening. We are pretending to listen.

Nina Sergeevna, her graying hair pinned up around a squirrel face, is teaching us about *lishnie lyudi*, or useless people. There is a whole gallery of such people in our literature. *Galereya lishnih lyudei*, says Nina Sergeevna, and a roll of fat quivers under her chinless jaw. In the sixth grade, it was Pushkin's Onegin and Lermontov's Pechorin from *The Hero of Our Time*. Corrupted by their noble birth and family wealth, they galloped across Russia and Europe, doing nothing but dueling, gambling, and breaking the hearts of innocent women, not giving a bit of thought to the fate of the serfs or the oppressed masses in general. Then it was Goncharov's Oblomov, who spent his life sleeping on a divan, refusing to get up even when a woman he fancied knocked on the door of his estate. Now it is Turgenev's Lavretsky, who failed to challenge the serf-owning nobility because he couldn't find enough willpower to tear himself away from the spoiled society that produced him.

I imagine myself as Lisa and Andrei, the only boy in my class who can distinguish a participle from a gerund, as Lavretsky. It's nighttime, and we are in the orchard—all our classical novels have an orchard as vast and dense as a forest—and Andrei is kneeling at my feet. My shoulders begin to twitch and the fingers of my pale hands press even closer to my face. Andrei, of course, understands what these twitching shoulders and these tears mean. Is it possible that you love me, he whispers. I am frightened, I keep saying, looking at him with moist eyes. I love you, he says, I'm ready to give my whole life to you. I tremble and lower my eyes; he quietly pulls me toward him, and my head falls on his shoulder. He moves his head away a little and touches my pale lips.

Of course, I know that Andrei is my age and way too young to be Lavretsky, who is married and has a child, but this isn't important as long as he is in love with me, Lisa. At the end of *A Nest of Nobles*, Lavretsky's wife, who had been unfaithful and conveniently out of the picture for the first hundred pages, shows up unexpectedly, repentant, at the most unfortunate time, wreaking havoc and driving Lisa to a nunnery. The last scene is tragic. In the eight years between the end of the novel and the epilogue (there is always an epilogue), Lavretsky has turned into an old man with gray hair and a cane. I see Andrei visiting me at the monastery, and I pass close to him, without looking up, with the docile gait of a nun, and only my eyelashes tremble, only the fingers of my clasped hands laced with rosary beads press even harder together.

Despite all these scenes unfolding in my head, I know I would never retreat to a monastery if Andrei, for instance, turned out to be married to my classmate Katya. I can think of a number of things I would do: I could snatch the book he is reading out of his lap and thwack it over his head. I could scramble out of my desk and flee the classroom in despair, leaving behind an unfinished composition on the struggle of common people against the yoke of serfdom in tsarist Russia, ignoring Nina Sergeevna, who would thrash down the aisle in her felt boots, shouting for me to come back. I could even go as far as announcing to Katya that we are no longer on speaking terms. But I can't see burying myself in a monastery so that Andrei, at the end of his life, stooped and defeated, could see my eyelashes tremble and my hands clasp around rosary beads. I am obviously not as strong and pure as Turgenev's heroines, unable to resolve the moral conflict of personal happiness vs. duty in the correct, classic way, and this may be the reason why the leggy, green-eyed Andrei, the boy who makes my insides melt, does not turn to look in my direction.

At home, I don't talk about Andrei. My practical mother thinks that romantic infatuation is improper and wasteful unless it ends in marriage. From her occasional raised eyebrow and slant-eyed look toward my sister, who is twenty-seven and still single, I know she wouldn't approve. Twenty-seven is a dangerous age for a woman not to be married, only two years shy of Natalia from Turgenev's *A Month in the Country*, who, as everyone knows, is described as middle-aged.

My sister doesn't have time to get married. In the morning she goes to rehearsals, and at night she goes onstage, activities far more enviable and meaningful than standing in lines for bologna or stooping over a pot of borsch. My mother, however, doesn't see it the same way. She blames the theater, with its late hours and irregular workday, for Marina's lack of proper suitors, her single status, and, possibly, her future lonely and childless life.

At home, my mother talks about canned tuna fish that has all but disappeared from stores and about our neighbor Olga from the fifth floor who bleaches her hair with peroxide, making it look like straw. But instead of disappearing tuna and our neighbor's yellow hair, I would like to talk about personal happiness and duty. Are they always mutually exclusive so that you are only able to achieve one or the other? Turgenev, who stares at us from the wall of our literature classroom with melancholy eyes, seems to think so. With a white beard and mustache, his hair sadly curling on his forehead, he looks like Lavretsky in the epilogue of *A Nest of Nobles*, disillusioned and old.

MY SISTER IS AT the kitchen table, slurping soup before an evening performance. Her hair is in a ponytail, bangs reaching down to perfectly arched eyebrows. I wish I had my sister's features, her big eyes and high cheeks, instead of my own face, dotted with freckles and beginning to erupt with pimples. Maybe then Andrei would look at me the same way he looks at my friend Katya.

"Eat your soup with bread," says my mother, who never misses a chance to fill us with more food.

"I don't want any bread," snaps Marina, and she glances at her watch because she has to be backstage forty-five minutes before the curtain. I see my mother fold her mouth for a harangue on the nutritional value of grain, and I make a preemptive strike.

"We have a composition contest at school," I say. At the end of today's class, after Nina Sergeevna declared the lives of Turgenev's nobility to be without direction and meaning, she announced the seventh-grade essay competition.

"What's the topic?" asks Marina, tilting the bowl and spooning out the last drops of soup.

"Anything we want. Describe and analyze a novel, a story, or a play." I pause after "play," letting the weight of the word sink in.

Marina gets up and rinses her plate under the kitchen faucet. "I have to go."

I know that there is a new play at her theater, with the intriguing, foreign title *We Bombed in New Haven*. An American play in a Leningrad theater, a phenomenon as next to impossible as dinner without soup. I saw a poster on Nevsky Prospekt of a man in a black flight suit with a skull in his hand, despondent and Hamlet-like. This is what I'm going to write about, I've decided: this play, this foreign, undoubtedly sold-out wonder, which I'll somehow manage to see whether Marina agrees to take me or not. She doesn't yet know of my scheme. She doesn't know many things about me, things I keep inside because they are too brittle to be exposed. She doesn't know, for instance, that a dark envy curdles my heart every time she walks through the stage door where the baked-apple-faced babushka sits on guard, every time she stares into a three-way mirror and makes up her face until someone new and intriguing emerges from under her fingers. She doesn't know and she doesn't care because theater for her is just a job, just as dispensing milk is for a paunchy saleswoman with a ladle, just as shoveling fish skeletons and bones and apple cores was for the garbageman from the cellar of our apartment building. If I could sing like she can, I would stay in the theater and never bother to come home, where wet laundry hangs on ropes stretched across the room and where the air is permeated with the smell of mothballs and yesterday's soup. I wouldn't waste my stage voice, if I had one, on arguing with my mother about a figure skating score that a Bulgarian judge gave some dancer from Finland, or about whom we should not invite to Marina's upcoming birthday—Irina the stage hairdresser because she is only a hairdresser, or Slava the actor because he has an affection for *zelyoniy zmei*.

The discussion of *zelyonyi zmei* makes my mother drive her fists into her hips. Marina, always ready for a fight, takes her position in front of the stove, sharpens her voice, and stabs the words at my mother's face.

"Slava is the best actor we have," she yells. "He can play any role in any performance, even if the head of our local party cell directs it himself."

"He's in love with the bottle," says my mother, "and he has let

*zelyonyi zmei*, the green serpent, wring its coils around his neck."
She bangs the lid over the pot of soup to punctuate her statement
because this is just what she's predicted would happen to anyone
who has come under the corrosive influence of theater.

I know it's not Slava my mother is so worried about. He is
*chuzhoi*, not part of the family, and that means he doesn't deserve
any sympathy or compassion. The opposite of *chuzhoi* is *svoi*, and
we can count *svoi* on the palm of our hand—my grandparents, my
uncle Vova, who lives in the small town of Ryazan, and my aunt
and three cousins, who live in the provinces.

The person my mother really worries about is my sister. She
worries about her proximity to all this theatrical chaos; she worries
that the green serpent will finally overpower Marina. "There are
so many normal jobs," says my mother, making sure I'm within
earshot. "Look at Valya from the fourth floor—she's just been
assigned to the district library around the corner. Look at Irina
Petrovna's daughter. Your former classmate and already a chief
engineer." These are the jobs my mother understands; they are
practical and safe, unlike acting or speaking English.

I wonder if my mother would be considered *intelligentsiya* by
the previous century's standards. She is educated, and she's read
Turgenev and other classics. She's heard Tchaikovsky's *Eugene
Onegin* at the Kirov and dragged me to see its multiple productions
of *Sleeping Beauty* and *Swan Lake*. Yet it is difficult to imagine a
Pushkin or Turgenev heroine grumbling about an uneaten slice
of bread or a tuna shortage. Those corseted women, both young
and old, with pale fingers and chestnut curls, seemed to have other
things weighing upon their consciences, things that provoked
multi-page discussions and often conflicted with one another,
things like love and honor, or happiness and duty. They sighed a
lot, pressed their children to their bosoms, and peered from their
aging cabriolets as wooden church steeples and small villages
sailed by amidst the fields of wheat. They didn't seem to think

about salads and pies ending up in *chuzhoi* stomachs any more than they worried about *zelyonyi zmei.*

FROM OUR SEATS IN the seventh row I see the open stage perfectly, and the fact that there is no curtain immediately signals to everyone but my mother that the play is modern, not at all like Gorky's dusty *Lower Depths,* which we saw here two months earlier. My mother glances at the stage and utters one word, *besporyadok,* disorder, which is what she says when I leave my uniform dress hanging on a chair, or when radiators in our apartment turn off on New Year's Eve without warning, or when there is no janitor in sight to break apart a slope of ice in front of the entrance to our building. My mother doesn't like the gray cubes piled on top of one another on the stage or the silhouettes of landmarks from foreign cities in the back. She doesn't like the fact that Slava's name is in the program next to that of the main character, Sergeant Henderson.

While she sits there, disliking everything, the music starts, so now she can hate the music, too. After the first ten minutes it's clear that it is a play within a play, and the actors onstage are pretending to be American actors pretending to be American pilots. They strut around in black flight suits that aren't like any uniform of any Russian soldier, the suits so slick that even our House of Fashion on Nevsky Prospekt, with its single window of clothes outside the Five-Year Plan, would have trouble conjuring them up.

Slava-Henderson walks around with the script so the American actors played by Marina's theater actors know the plot. According to the script, he is about to be killed in the second act, but he isn't worried. It's Theater, after all, and the script is fiction, having nothing to do with what happens for real. It's Theater, a place of thrilling, magic make-believe, so unlike the numbing make-believe of our day-to-day life.

But then a corporal gets killed, and the actor who played him disappears. Maybe it's not all make-believe, thinks Slava-

Henderson. Maybe the actor really did get killed; it was, after all, in the script. Slava holds the actor's helmet, smeared with blood, and my palms sweat in admiration at how his whisper floats to the highest box where a lighting man wields metal handles behind two huge projector lights. I skew my eyes at my mother, but her face is the usual mask of seriousness, and I can't tell if she is also, on some hidden level, appreciating Slava's acting gift.

Slava-Henderson's monologue makes me think about the essay I'm going to write for my literature class. Since Nina Sergeevna warned us that the moral of the work we select must transcend time and reverberate in our present, everyday life, I couldn't have chosen better material. As far as I can see, this play is about the dangers of make-believe and thus about us and our *vranyo* game. We all know we have to pretend, just as the characters in this play. In school, Andrei and I pretend to be obedient Pioneers worthy of a young Lenin, whose profile is pinned to our uniformed chests. My mother pretends that her uncle Volya was arrested in 1937 because he was *vrag naroda*, an enemy of the people, and not because he was simply out of luck when he told a joke in a crowded restaurant. My friend and classmate Katya, whose father, a colonel, has access to an exclusive library full of rare books on literary criticism, pretends her father's rank has nothing to do with her exemplary essays that score perfect fives.

The least pretender of us all is my sister, the actress. Maybe she is simply tired of pretending onstage, so she says what she thinks, at least when she is home. "Those cretins in the Ministry of Culture are closing another play," she says every year, at least once. "It's too controversial. Too many jabs at our bright future."

During the intermission, I don't stampede to the buffet, like everyone else. I silently pace around the lobby, thinking. My mother paces next to me, like a guard. She looks worn out, as though she's just sat through an execution, and as much as I wish for her to go home, I know that according to the rules of correct behavior, one never leaves the theater before the end of a performance. I think about *We Bombed in New Haven* and about Slava. I think it's curious that this play has found its way into Marina's theater, that an American playwright was able to pinpoint such an indigenous Russian quandary. My mother sighs as we pass Slava's portrait in the lobby: a sharp nose and intense eyes, a little like the portrait of Pushkin on the cover of our literature textbook. Slava, I repeat in my mind, Slava, Slava, what a perfect name for you, because *slava* means "glory." He stares from the wall with the concentration of Sergeant Henderson, his eyes like guided missiles aimed directly at my heart.

THE ESSAY I WRITE is perfect. I even quote Lenin: "One cannot live in a society and be free from that society." In America or anywhere else. It is dangerous to live a life of make-believe, I write. Just as Henderson and his actor-pilots, you may check the script one day and discover you've been written off. Just like my mother, you can look at your young portrait and not recognize yourself.

I marvel at my own sentences that shimmer on the page, so philosophical and compelling, imagining the squirrel face of Nina Sergeevna melting in awe as she reads them.

MY SISTER IS IN the kitchen pointing a ladle at my mother, who has planted herself by the garbage bucket. They're arguing about how many bottles of liquor to buy for Marina's birthday party. The standard calculation is a half-liter bottle of vodka for two guests, so Marina is insisting on six bottles since she has invited ten people. No, my mother protests, we have two bottles of Hungarian wine called Bull's Blood, so four bottles will do. Five at the most.

"It's my birthday and I am the one to decide," shouts Marina in her stage voice.

My mother grabs at the chipped enamel lip of the sink, staking her territory. "Is this what these alcoholic actors need?" she shouts back. "Is this why they come to a birthday party?"

I know this argument is not only about the number of bottles. My mother is upset that among the expected guests is Slava with his drinking affliction, which she thinks is so toxic that my sister will instantly begin to slur her words and fall down simply by breathing the same air.

The prospect of seeing Slava in person, in our own apartment, gives me a tingle as if my blood had suddenly frothed into champagne.

"What actors need is a little understanding," my sister yells. "A touch of empathy. It's a damned profession, and we are damned."

"Why?" I ask, perplexed by how "damned" could be paired with acting.

"We twist our souls to live other people's lives," says Marina. She lowers the ladle and turns in my direction. "Did you know actors couldn't even be buried in Christian cemeteries before the Revolution?"

"Where were they buried?" I ask stupidly.

"Behind the cemetery walls," my sister enunciates as if she were talking to an audience. "Away from the good, sinless souls."

I know nothing about Christian habits, and it's a mystery to me where my sister could have learned this bit of information. Maybe this is what they teach in drama school. Maybe Marina doesn't, after all, perceive her job to be as uncomplicated as a saleswoman's or garbageman's. It's a job that requires imagination and audacity, something I could never muster. When she was in secondary school, she used to alter her grades in the journal that teachers require our parents to sign at the end of every week. With a pen and a razor blade, she changed satisfactory 3's to perfect 5's on Saturday afternoon and then, after my mother signed the journal, she would turn 5's back to 3's on Sunday night so that the teachers wouldn't notice the difference.

Maybe my sister understands more than I give her credit for. I can even concede that she is as infected by Theater as I am, or almost. But why does she ignore me so completely, why does she keep me away from that little side door that leads backstage, to the heart of all conceivable happiness? Is it possible that she is trying to protect me because she can see something in me, or rather the absence of something, that I cannot yet see myself?

ON SUNDAY, WE COOK for Marina's birthday. The guests are invited for Monday, the theater's day off. We make a huge platter of herring-in-a-fur-coat—grated potatoes, carrots, and beets swathing the chunks of herring on the bottom in colorful, fluffy layers. My mother bakes pans of *pirozhki* and, when they're out of the oven, glistening and tanned, glazes them with three rubber-banded bird feathers dipped in egg. Marina goes on a hunt to meat stores and returns with chunks of pork she puts in the oven to roast. Everything is ready, transferred from pots into the crystal bowls.

On Monday morning, Nina Sergeevna waddles into the classroom with a string bag full of our essays on her arm. She dumps the string bag on her desk as if it were full of turnips, demonstrating her disdain for our pitiful efforts to enter our voices into the sanctuary of literature and the arts.

I glance sideways at Andrei, who is staring across the classroom at Katya. In the streak of morning sun his hair has a copper glint and, if he weren't turned in Katya's direction, I'd see the fuzz on his cheeks and that glow that only the ten-o'clock light can give to his face. As Nina Sergeevna pulls our essays out of the net of her bag, I scribble on the wooden surface of my desk with a pen. *Andrei*, I doodle and then, underneath, I write *Slava*, in careful, big, calligraphic letters, as though this deliberate effort could reveal some meaning behind the names, something deeper beneath the surface, where all those un-Pioneer yearnings burrow in their shameful caves.

Before she turns to the results of the competition, Nina Sergeevna, who never lets a moment be unproductive, has to teach us something. This distraction makes me squirm because I've been waiting for this since I finished my essay, anxious to hear about its outstanding qualities. As I count the minutes, she compares Turgenev's *A Nest of Nobles* and his story "Mu-mu," which in the fifth grade gave me a night of weeping for the dog of the title, drowned by its owner at the order of his heartless landlady. I wish Nina Sergeevna could stay quiet and simply stand there and listen, or stare at something in amazement, as Andrei is staring at Katya, as I am staring at Andrei.

When she is done with the aristocracy's lack of will and purpose, she finally shuffles through our skinny notebooks, pulls out one, and looks at Katya. "Excellent criticism of the noble classes," she says. "You state correctly that Turgenev was optimistic about the future by expressing his faith in the new generation that will be able to solve the tragic contradictions of his time." I know that this idea comes from a shelf in the Military Library, where Katya's father found it. She has written about Turgenev's *On the Eve*, a later novella in which Elena, the heroine, chooses personal happiness over family duty by marrying a destitute foreign revolutionary. Yet somehow, in the end, after Elena's beloved husband dies and she is stranded alone in Turkey, she is completely drained of happiness and instead saddled with duty. Although it doesn't seem to be a fair resolution of the conflict, I know Katya had no trouble, as our teacher instructed, making it reverberate in our present-day lives.

I watch Nina Sergeevna's hand hover over my notebook, and I shift at my desk, ready for praise.

"Some of you, however," begins Nina Sergeevna ominously, "have chosen to write about foreign literature." She picks up my essay and holds it with two fingers as if it were a worm. "We must not have enough Russian classics." She stares at me with her beady rodent eyes, and I look down at the desk surface ruined by my indelible purple pen. "Our writers," she lifts her gaze to the portraits on the wall, "have not created enough volumes of poetry and prose for one of you not to feel an urge to turn to a foreign piece." She returns her gaze to me so that everyone in the class can know who exactly felt the urge. "An American play. *Amerikanskii spectacle.*" The word *Americanskii* rasps out of her mouth like an indictment.

With the whole class gawking at me, I wish I could fall through the floor. No, first murder Nina Sergeevna and then fall through the floor. I wish I'd thought this project through, remembered who was going to judge it, and if I had to write about a play, written about Gorky's *Lower Depths*, which I saw in September. I wish the American air force, instant and lethal, would descend from the sky and sweep everyone out of the room so I could stay alone with Andrei and explain to him all about *We Bombed in New Haven* and my new love Slava, its dazzling star.

Now Nina Sergeevna is pointing at me like Lenin in the statue at the Finland Railroad Station. "What you wrote is chaotic and convoluted. More than that, it advertises your ignorance and your arrogance. Look how smug I am!" Nina Sergeevna flaps her arms as though trying to take off, a huge bat with jagged front teeth. "First read our own classics and then and only then look to the West. Our own, *svoi,*" hisses Nina Sergeevna, spit flying across her desk. *Svoi,* the opposite of all that foreign *chuzhoi* undeserving of our attention and our ink.

I feel hollow and sick. I feel as if someone has ripped me open and turned everything inside out, so that instead of my brown uniform, shiny at the elbows, what everyone sees is a bloody porridge of vessels and nerves crushed around a dark, bruised heart.

I stagger home from school in the gauzy twilight of the end of November. I unbutton my coat, I lean into the wind—anything to expurgate the words of Nina Sergeevna.

If I were a Turgenev heroine, would I, after this embarrassment, have to lock myself up in a nunnery, or marry a destitute foreign revolutionary? I don't know the answer. It is November, the time of floods, when wind heaves water from the Baltic Sea, swelling the canals and closing schools. The water underneath is still at least a meter below the street level, but to make this day even more dramatic I wish for the canal to spill into the streets so that I would have to flail my way through churning water, succumbing, in the end, to its cold raging might, like Evgeniy in Pushkin's *Bronze Horseman*. Then, learning about my untimely death, Nina Sergeevna would lament her failure to recognize the brilliance of my essay, all too late.

Even if it's true that I am deficient in my knowledge of Russian classics, I don't want to think about them any more. Instead, I decide to think about tonight, and the happy prospect of my sister's birthday party rises up inside me and mercifully nudges other thoughts aside.

I AM ON THE stair landing, one flight above our apartment—where the guests are still raising toasts to Marina—gagging on a cigarette stolen from my sister's purse. I fumbled through her bag in the toilet, under the rusty tank with a chain, after realizing that the probability of Slava looking in my direction is even less than that of Andrei, after deciding that if I cannot get the attention of the men I like and if I am accused of a lack of humility toward the Russian classics and life in general, I may as well start smoking.

I hear our apartment door groan open, and I stand very quietly in the dark, squeezing my back into the wall, waiting for whoever it is to go back in. But when the door shuts, I sense that the person is on the wrong side of it, my side. There is a crinkle of cellophane and the sound of a lighted match. I breathe noiselessly, strangling a cough. Footsteps start up the stairs, up toward where I stand. By the sound I know, at least, that it isn't my mother; they're fast, less calculated, breathless steps.

It is Slava, with a cigarette between his teeth and an opened bottle of Bull's Blood.

He doesn't seem at all surprised to see me pressing into the wall, trying to stub out a cigarette against a sewer pipe. "Come," he says and makes an upward movement with his arm, as if inviting me to fly. In the light of a match is another flight of stairs, a short one, leading up to a squatty door to the attic, upholstered in black vinyl. "Here," says Slava, who in the dark has the sharp, weighted movements of my father, and he gives me his hand. "Come." He smells of cigarettes and of our apartment, the smell of too many people and burned sunflower oil.

I obediently follow him, step after step, to the black door. What's happening is so surreal that I feel nothing but a hollow in my chest and the sting of tobacco on my tongue. He gives the door a shake and it scrapes open, releasing a little cloud of dust and an odor of mildew and mice. He lights another match, which plucks out of the darkness a beam and a wall of pocked cement and something as gritty as gravel on the floor. It's an eerie place, a place I didn't know existed all this time right above my head, a place no one knew existed but Slava, who is privy to all the mysteries and secrets and the answers to questions we don't want to ask.

We creep slowly, match after match, until we get to a wooden ladder. Slava climbs up, jiggles a metal latch, and above us opens a night sky, paled by the city lights, wide and still. He crawls out, takes my hand, and pulls me onto the roof. I crouch and sit on the cold metal, awed by the sudden vast openness, by the smallness of the life beneath.

Below, in the tar of a November night, a trolleybus, like an awkward insect, crawls past a shuttered newspaper kiosk where the news has all grown old since this morning. Two amber squares of windows glow on the black façade of the building across the street, revealing a toy-size figure waiting for a streetcar; an open truck packed with shaved-headed soldiers bumps across the tracks and rattles through the red light.

"Are you cold, kid?" says Slava, and I realize I'm so cold that I can't even answer right away because my teeth are chattering. He pulls off his sweater, tugs it down over my head, and hands me the bottle of Bull's Blood. "Take a swig," he says, "it'll warm you up."

I upturn the bottle over my mouth, but in the dark I underestimate how much is left, so the wine spills out and pours down my face. Now I've ruined Slava's sweater, making him think that I am a fool who has never tasted alcohol before, proving that he should've left me standing where he found me, by the sewer pipe, hacking after my first cigarette. I hold the bottle at arm's length and try to wipe the wine off my face and neck with the back of my other hand while Slava, laughing a tipsy laugh, tries to scramble to his feet to get a better view of a canal glistening in the distance. He is oblivious to my streaked face and his ruined sweater. He doesn't care that according to my mother, we are *chuzhoi* to each other and he shouldn't be sharing with me this climb through the attic, this diminished life below, these waves of roofs that rise before us like a tide churned by the undertow of the sleeping city.

I feel like laughing, too, because this view from the night roof, which I haven't even known existed, is so real and so exclusively mine. This view, it suddenly becomes clear, trumps everything else: today's public humiliation in literature class, the impeccable Katya and her nauseating perfection, even my sister and the Theater she keeps all to herself. The thought makes me dizzy and elated. It fills me, like the wine, making me progressively drunker. It is I, not Katya, standing here next to god-like Slava, I, who would selfishly choose personal happiness over duty and a foreign play over a Russian classic, who would have to think twice about retreating to a nunnery like the virtuous heroine at the end of *A Nest of Nobles*.

"Look at this," says Slava, who has just finished off what was left of the Bull's Blood, and he pulls me closer so I can see the gray dome of the city's silent synagogue poking in the distance from behind the roofs. I'm not sure if he wants me to see the building or he badly needs support to stand straight, but it doesn't matter. I lick the last drops of wine off my lips and fit myself into his arms, pretending we're in the novel's love scene I've so often imagined, the scene with pale fingers, moist eyes, and twitching shoulders. Again, I am Lisa; only now I am not so brittle and somber. Now I'm giggling. There is no orchard and no bench, but Slava, even in his green-serpent state, is a highly superior Lavretsky, worthy of the classic Turgenev with his sad eyes and a noble wave of white hair. In a few hours, all this tar above us will start to dissolve into streaks of gray and then pink, but we aren't looking up. Trying to keep our balance, we are holding on to each other in an awkward embrace, just like the two characters in *A Nest of Nobles*, both of us so unclassically drained of duty, so dizzyingly high over the treetops and rows of dark windows, so drunk on Bull's Blood and personal happiness.

# CHAPTER 13

# A Tour of Leningrad

THE FATE OF THE October Revolution was decided on the streets of Petrograd. Here, the first regiments of the Red Army were formed to defend the new freedom and to vanquish the old world once and for all."

Maria Mikhailovna pauses and tells us to close the quotation marks. Now she is going to dictate a Mayakovsky verse, she says, which we must also write as a quote. I am not sure about the meaning of the English word "vanquish," so I skew my eyes in the direction of Tanya Puchkova's notebook. But Maria Mikhailovna is already reciting:

*They blew as always, October's winds,*
*As cold as capitalism their icy blast.*
*Over Troitsky bridge sped cars and trams,*
*Snaking along the rails of the past.*

The Mayakovsky poem, which we all know by heart, sounds stilted and pompous in English, and I can't imagine repeating these lines with a serious face to a busload of touring high school students from Britain.

We are sitting around a long oval table in the House of Friendship and Peace on the Fontanka Embankment. Maria Mikhailovna, in a short, stylish jacket and scarlet lipstick, reads the text of a historical tour of Leningrad from a thick notebook she holds in her well-manicured hands. There are about thirty of us, and we sit very quietly and scribble down every word that falls from her lips because we know we are lucky and privileged to be here. A few months ago, the English schools from the whole city of Leningrad nominated their best students to be trained as tour guides for groups of English-speaking high school students. When the principal called Tanya Puchkova and me into her office to tell us we'd been selected, she talked about the great honor and responsibility. These are students from a capitalist society, she said; we will be the ones to represent our city and embody our superior way of life.

Although I have trouble seeing myself as such a large-scale embodiment of our culture, I am thrilled to be part of this program because it is my only chance to practice English with someone who didn't learn it from textbooks.

So far we haven't seen any English students. We are still at the end of the lecture period, coming here twice a week to write down every word Maria Mikhailovna dictates about the history of Leningrad and its architectural landmarks. When all ten lectures have been copied and memorized, we will take an exam: each of us will stand in the front of a bus filled with the rest of our group and recite a part of the tour chosen at random by Maria Mikhailovna. Those of us who pass will be allowed to be tour guides; those who don't will sit in the back of the buses with British students, making sure order is maintained.

To me, it seems better in all respects to sit in the back of a bus than to stand in the front. Instead of clutching a microphone in sweaty hands, raking the memory for every minute historical detail and every rule of English grammar, I can gaze at the city's landmarks from the back of the bus, possibly even exchanging a phrase or two with someone who speaks English better than red-nailed Maria Mikhailovna.

I furtively look around, at the marble columns and gilded moldings, at the curves of the fireplace mantel under a huge mirror in an elaborate frame of curly bronze. The house of Friendship and Peace occupies the former Shuvalov Palace, which means that before the Revolution this whole building, with its four floors, elaborate chandeliers suspended from six-meter ceilings, and gilded doorknobs, belonged to one family. I try to imagine what one family could have done with a space big enough for a hundred, or how they could've possibly used this grand room, where the table for the thirty of us on the gleaming parquet floor seems like a speck of dust.

Almost every architectural landmark Maria Mikhailovna has so far dictated to us is prefaced with the word "former." The museum of the history of Leningrad is in the former Cathedral of the former Smolny Convent, the Naval Museum is in the former Stock Exchange building, and the Central Historical Archives are in the former Senate building. The former Kazan Cathedral is now the Museum of Religion and Atheism. The former Mariinsky Opera and Ballet Theatre is now called the Kirov. The Executive Committee of the Leningrad City Soviet occupies the former Sheremetyev Palace, and the former Estate of Counts Beloselsky-Belozersky is now a District Committee of the Communist Party.

"The request to rename the city of Petrograd after Lenin, put forward by the Petrograd workers, peasants, and Red Army soldiers, is hereby granted," dictates Maria Mikhailovna. "Let this largest center of proletarian revolution be hereafter forever linked with the name of the greatest leader of the proletariat—Vladimir Ilyich Lenin." Close the quotation marks, she says, finishing a citation from the resolution of the Second Congress of Soviets in 1924, the year of Lenin's death.

This is our last lecture, the history of the Lenin Museum, located in the former Marble Palace. Maria Mikhailovna has covered everything from 1703, when Peter the Great laid a stone in the foundation of the Peter and Paul Fortress, to 1917, when the former Winter Palace, the residence of the tsar and then the Provisional Government, was stormed by workers and peasants. There seem to be very few architectural monuments built after 1917 that are worthy of foreign eyes.

Reflected in gilded-framed mirrors, Tanya and I descend the marble staircase, and the heavy entrance doors of the former Shuvalov Palace slam behind us. The waters of the Fontanka River are like lead, the same color as the sky, and we walk to the bus stop through the April dusk, past a dock for tour boats abandoned now and until the end of May.

Tanya lives two buildings away from me, so we get off at the same stop. "Maklin Prospekt," announces the driver as the bus turns to our street and screeches to a halt. Our English teacher told us yesterday that Comrade Maklin, whose name our street bears, was not Russian, as I've always assumed from the name's "-in" ending, but an Irishman named McLean. I don't know why they would name a Leningrad street after an Irishman, unless he was a revolutionary and somehow made his way here from Ireland in 1917 to assist in overthrowing the tsar.

I am in the eighth grade, and I am cynical. I no longer believe in the cause of the Young Pioneers, the organization we parted with last year, when we all turned fourteen, to become members of the Young Communist League, or Komsomol. I had strong doubts about joining the Komsomol, which I'd expressed at home prior to our exchanging the red Pioneer kerchiefs for pins with a bonfire and a profile of Lenin.

"It's all a bunch of *vranyo*," said my sister. "All this hypocrisy and mendacity." Marina likes big, theatrical words she's learned from plays. "All this Communist delirium about paradise on

Earth and equal labor. They pretend they pay us, and we pretend we work."

"Do you want to go to college?" asked my mother.

I don't know a single person who hasn't gone to college, except our school janitor Aunt Lusya, so I knew my mother had asked that question to make a point.

"You won't get into college without a Komsomol pin," said my sister. "It's the third question on the application, after your name and ethnicity."

Now Tanya and I both wear our Komsomol pins on a black uniform apron cinched at the waist around a brown dress. Despite our cynicism and our doubts, we both want to go to college.

WE ALL PASSED THE exam, said Maria Mikhailovna, all thirty of us. This means that when school is over and the first bus tour comes from England, we must take turns being tour guides.

The first group of British high school students, our age, arrives in the middle of June and stays in a hotel away from the city center. The hotel building looks as if it belongs in the new districts at the end of the metro line, so I am not even sure it is a hotel for foreigners. It could be a notch below that, a hotel for high-ranking Russians, with white corridors and peeling paint, yet with rooms that boast a towel and a bar of soap.

This, of course, is all speculation. We are not allowed to enter the hotel doors, as Maria Mikhailovna has warned us, reciting a litany of rules. We must arrive early and wait outside. We must wear clean clothes and have our hair washed. It's better if we don't accept any gifts, and under no circumstances can we accept foreign money.

The law is clear on the possession of foreign currency—punishment by imprisonment. But some other tenets of Maria Mikhailovna's rules aren't so unequivocal. What's the definition of clean clothes and washed hair, for example? I wash my hair once a week, like most others, on Saturday. Tanya, I know, washes it on Sunday, when she goes with her mother to a public bathhouse because they don't have a tub at home. So if the British arrive on a Tuesday, is my hair considered washed or already dirty? I wish someone would explain how this dilemma would be resolved in England, but the only person privy to Western life is Maria Mikhailovna, and there is no way I'm going to ask her.

Tanya and I arrive early and wait outside. I watch the sun glint in her blonde, shiny hair, which means that she washed it under the kitchen faucet last night. We stand by the six tour buses lined up across from the hotel. Maria Mikhailovna comes out of its doors with a sheaf of papers in her hands and assigns us to the buses. We've both been assigned to sit in the back.

I say to myself I should be relieved, but I am disappointed. How is Sveta Kurdina, who blinks nervously in the front of the bus as she tries to adjust a microphone, a better tour guide than me? What criteria did the House of Friendship and Peace apply to separate the front from the back?

Even before Sveta starts to breathe into the microphone, I study the occupants of the bus, those capitalist high school students who warrant so many rules. No doubt, they are different: they're wearing blue jeans, they have washed hair, they chew gum, and they all speak English. It is their English that lifts them above everything I've seen before. It is their English that fills me with both euphoria and melancholy. Although the sounds of this language are intoxicating, like New Year's champagne, I know that no matter how hard I study, I will never be able to speak like these students. My own English will forever be confined to Maria Mikhailovna's lectures on the history of former palaces. So the best I can do is sit quietly and humbly, inhaling the sweet smell of exhaust fumes, in the midst of this linguistic heaven. The best I can do is listen and, if I dare, maybe even speak.

As the bus begins to move and Sveta launches into her rendition of Peter the Great's plan for the city, Tanya aims a conspiratorial smile at me. "We're like two spies," she whispers in Russian so no one will understand, "like two paratroopers in the Nazi rear." Of course Tanya and I both know that what she said is ironic, that the British fought on our side in the war, but we still can't help feeling surrounded by the enemy, by a species alien to our own, by creatures from a different universe.

Half-turned toward Tanya, I realize that I'm sitting with my back to the boy next to me, that I'm breaking one of Maria Mikhailovna's rules: don't turn your back on a visiting Brit. "Excuse my back," I say, as Maria Mikhailovna taught us. I'm astonished at my own voice, at the English words leaving my mouth, exposed to someone who can immediately detect their lack of phonetic accuracy.

"Never mind," says the boy and smiles. "It's lovely." *Lahvly,* he says, showing his white teeth, looking straight into my face with his dark Western eyes.

I've been put here to maintain order, I remind myself, so I must act responsibly and suppress a foolish giggle. I must pull together all my resources and arrange the words I know into the correct sequence of English morphology and syntax. "How do you do," I say, like a character in a dialogue from our textbook. "My name is Lena. What's yours?"

"Kevin," says the boy. Or did he say Calvin? The sounds bubble in his mouth and stick together, like overdone buckwheat *kasha.* I'm hopeless, and Maria Mikhailovna was right not to allow me in front of the microphone. I shoot Tanya a glance of desperation, but she is now busy talking to a girl on her other side.

Besides introducing myself, I don't know what else to say, so I feel grateful that Sveta announces our first stop. We must all get off the bus, she commands, and stand in a semicircle opposite the entrance to St. Isaac's Cathedral to have a proper view of the massive granite columns in the front.

To Sveta's frustration, the English students don't want to form a semicircle as she told them to do. They stand as they please, in a small crowd, listening politely as she gives the exact number of kilograms of gold used to gild the cathedral's dome. One hundred kilograms, she says, and some of the students whistle, and some make a noise as if they exhale.

I think this piece of information about the amount of gold is in questionable taste because what we have been told to convey on this tour is a sense of the city's artistic, inner beauty. But perhaps Maria Mikhailovna included it precisely because she thinks people from capitalist countries are materialistic, uninterested in the lofty and the ideal.

I pretend to examine the sculptures on the portal of the cathedral, but I am really looking at Kevin, or Calvin. He is a bit taller than I am, with black hair longer than any boy in my school is allowed, a thick neck and a big, craggy chin. He looks like a rugby player, whatever rugby is. I watch him poke in his ear, then scuff the asphalt with the side of his shoe. Then he suddenly looks up, and our eyes meet for a second before I turn away and pretend to stare at the monument to Tsar Nicholas I, which is still allowed to stand in the middle of the square only because of its unique artistic value.

I can't wait to get back into the bus to sit next to the boy again. He asks if all our churches are covered with so much gold. Our former churches, I correct him in my mind. Goold, he says, suh moch goold. The simplest words in his mouth seem to tangle into alien shapes, so hard to decipher I strain my ears. Maybe he doesn't have the pronunciation I expected because he is from Scotland or Northern Ireland. Maybe I should ask him about the revolutionary McLean, whose name hangs on the corner of my street.

After a stop in Palace Square, the boy turns to visual aids. He empties his wallet into my hands: two cardboard stubs (tickets for something?), a blue plastic rectangle with numbers, a picture of a girl (his sister?), a card with his own picture and his name (Kevin!).

The tickets, he explains, are for a movie he saw just before the trip (movie? Does he mean cinema?); the piece of plastic is a Visa (a visa for what? To enter the Soviet Union?); the girl is his girlfriend (girl friend?); and the card with his picture is his *ay-dee*.

I am not sure the visual aids are helping much. "What's an *ay-dee?*" I ask, starting with the most incomprehensible.

"It's an *ay-dee*," Kevin says, throwing his head back, trying to find the words to explain the obvious. "A document to get into a school. A paper to show the police."

The word "police" helps. "Like a passport?" I ask.

"No," says Kevin. "A passport is to come here. An *ay-dee* is for England."

I smile, letting him know that I understand. But I don't. Not completely. Here, when I turn sixteen, I'll get a passport at a local militia office. But I won't need it to get into a school. I'll keep it in my mother's drawer, along with her own passport and her war medals until I am twenty-one and it will be time to get a new one. Right now I don't have any document certifying that I am me. Everyone in my school knows who I am, and why would our militia, out of the blue, ask me for a document to confirm my identity? They are busy cordoning off the streets for official motorcades or standing in big intersections with zebra-colored batons in their hands making sure we don't cross against the light. It is odd to carry such a document around, but maybe it's one of the characteristics of capitalism, in addition to homelessness and unemployment.

We bump over the tram tracks, to the other side of the Neva to look at the Peter and Paul Fortress, where Dostoyevsky and Lenin were imprisoned for their revolutionary activities. The day, sunny in the morning, has crumbled into the usual leaden Leningrad day, with sheets of clouds and blasts of wind tearing through the red banners lined along the embankment. Sveta herds us into the fortress's prison yard and then into a solitary stone cell with a narrow iron bed and no windows, exemplifying, according to Maria Mikhailovna's lectures, the injustice and cruelty of the tsarist regime. We don't all fit into the cell, so Kevin and I stand in the cobblestone corridor, next to a life-size figure dressed as a tsarist prison warden.

"I wonder if this works," says Kevin and wraps his hand around the warden's gun. I'm glad that the museum babushka is busy watching the group inside the cell because one of the worst things you can do, as everyone knows, is touch a museum exhibit. "*Rukami ne trogat*," says a sign in big letters. "Do not touch with hands." But what if Kevin had touched the gun with his elbow? I wonder about the possible repercussions of our language differences. Whereas the Russian word *ruka* includes everything from fingers to shoulder, the English *hand* only goes as far as the wrist. Does the sign, in its English version, really mean "Do not touch with hands or arms?" Or are the English-speaking tourists exempt from the elbow-touching prohibition?

I would like to share this linguistic inquiry with Kevin, but I'm afraid I wouldn't be able to pull together enough grammar and vocabulary. I'm so glad I understood completely Kevin's phrase about the gun that I don't want to risk another language embarrassment.

Kevin isn't very talkative, and I am grateful. As we walk back to our bus, he kicks pebbles and whistles, not even bothering to look at the spire of the Fortress, which is probably covered with no fewer kilograms of gold than the dome of St. Isaac's Cathedral.

I don't know what I would do if the impossible happened and I could go on a similar tour of London. Without doubt, I wouldn't whistle, or kick pebbles, or grab museum guns. I don't even know if I would recognize the real Trafalgar Square from a dusty picture in our English textbook or have the nerve to open my mouth and speak.

From Peter and Paul Fortress we drive past the cruiser *Aurora*, which shot a blank in October 1917 to start the storming of the

Winter Palace. It is an ancient ship, with black smokestacks and fake-looking cannons on the deck. Not interested in the cruiser *Aurora* or Sveta's story, Kevin is counting the money he's pulled out of his pocket because we are approaching the end of our route, a *Beriozka* shop. I watch him casually handle the pound bills, so strange-looking and infused with such dangerous power if they somehow should migrate into my hands, or Tanya's hands, or even the hands of Maria Mikhailovna. One of many statutes of the Criminal Code forbids possession of foreign currency.

Entering a *Beriozka* shop, like speaking English, lifts us above the crowd. We are among the select few Russians who are allowed to go in. *Beriozka* means birch tree, a symbol of Russia. It is a store exclusively for Westerners, selling items only for hard currency, that of capitalist countries. I don't know why the Eastern European socialist countries, with their more reliable, planned economies, do not have currencies as trustworthy as those of the unstable, dying, capitalist West.

Or perhaps I do know. Perhaps it's part of the same old game, *vranyo*. The game we all play: my mother, my sister, my teachers at school, my friend Tanya, who is talking to a girl in Reebok sneakers, and even Maria Mikhailovna—or maybe especially Maria Mikhailovna—with her well-tailored suits and lectures on Leningrad, the cradle of the Great October Socialist Revolution. The rules are simple: they lie to us, we know they're lying, they know we know they're lying but they keep lying anyway, and we keep pretending to believe them.

The store's windows are shuttered so that no one from the street is able to see what's inside. If they could see, they would storm in, through the steel turnstile, past the bored cashier, to the shelves with instant coffee, Polish ham, French cognac, and poems by Pasternak.

I follow Kevin to a display with souvenirs: rows of *matryoshka* dolls, bears carved out of wood, hand-painted, lacquered boxes from

Palekh, busts of Lenin. He doesn't seem to be interested in cans of something called shrimp, or bottles of liqueur with floating golden specks, or skinny logs of hard salami I haven't seen since elementary school. He isn't interested in the shelf with Russian books, volumes with semi-banned Tsvetayeva and Mandelstam, with Bulgakov's *Master and Margarita*, which my sister says is the epitome of Russian twentieth-century literature, as underground as Solzhenitsyn. I pick up each book, hold it, then put it back. While the British students are gawking at samovars and wooden spoons, I stand next to the shelf with these book treasures, so close and so out of reach.

"WUDJA LIKE TGO FOR a waak?" asks Kevin when we get off the bus back near his hotel. The British students are crowding around Sveta, who has an embarrassed look on her face, not knowing what to do with packages of pantyhose and ballpoint pens they are handing to her. I don't know what I would do, either. Although Sveta has never seen Western pantyhose, she hesitates to take them. I wish these jean-clad students would be a little more insightful and give her a book of poetry from *Berioʒka* or, at least, a can of something called shrimp.

Would I like to go for a walk with Kevin? This is a rhetorical question, but I don't answer right away because I'm thinking about Maria Mikhailovna, with her laundry list of rules. Is walking outside as gross a violation as going inside a hotel? Is it a violation at all if a British tourist initiates the invitation? I'd like to ask my friend Tanya, but she is busy scribbling her address on a piece of paper for the girl in Reebok sneakers. I look at Kevin, who is staring at me with his dark Western eyes, waiting for an answer, and something tells me—a little sly voice—that in the official game of *vranyo*, it would be a legitimate move to take a walk with this boy, despite the fact that he is a capitalist, the worst kind of foreigner of all.

The wind has ripped holes in the sheets of clouds, and the sun has revealed some interesting things: the outside of our bus is covered with a layer of dirt, the puddles in the sidewalk sparkle with a rainbow film of gasoline, and Kevin's eyes are hazel, not black. I look around: the British students have gone inside the hotel, and there is no Maria Mikhailovna in sight. Tanya makes big eyes when I tell her I'm going for a walk with Kevin, but I can see she is envious.

We take the metro to the city center, to places worth parading in front of a visitor. As we glide down an escalator, down and down, underneath all that swamp Peter the Great decided to turn into a city, Kevin's eyes widen in surprise and his mouth drops open to expose straight English teeth. "It's a mile deep!" he exclaims with the same glee I saw in his face when he grabbed the museum gun in the prison of the Peter and Paul Fortress. Down at the metro platform, he stands stunned, gaping at the crystal chandeliers, marble columns, and mosaic walls. "This is a bloody palace," he says, turning around to examine every piece of granite and inlaid marble that spells the station name.

I know that "bloody" doesn't mean "bloody." I know it's a curse, and I promptly file the word into the English compartment of my head, a corner where I am no longer a law-abiding tour guide for the House of Friendship and Peace but someone completely different, someone whose vowels are called diphthongs, whose *l*'s lilt and *r*'s roll, and whose sentences, unlike those in our docile Russian, soar at the end.

I like the English compartment of my head because it feels like Theater. It feels like I'm playing a role, pretending to be someone confident and bold. That's what my sister must feel like when she is onstage—liberated from everyday drudgery and imbued with the power to be someone else. It is thrilling and a little dangerous.

This thrill, to my surprise, makes English words spring from memory and align themselves into grammatically correct sentences. I tell Kevin all about the construction of the Leningrad metro, about pushing and drilling through the marsh of the Neva delta. I tell him about the granite slabs hauled from the north, just as they had been dragged by serfs for the construction of St. Isaac's Cathedral. Pointing guide-like to the chandeliers and the marble, I see that the people around us, loaded with string bags on their way from work, turn around to look. They look at Kevin because he is obviously a foreigner and at me because I'm speaking English—in the way they look at actors when they come out of the stage door after a performance, in a way I can only call deferential.

Kevin marvels at the digital clock, which clicks off seconds between trains, and at the train, which arrives before the clock registers one minute. It's rush hour, I explain. Ordinarily, the intervals between trains are up to two minutes. I know I sound formal and stilted, with words like "intervals" and "ordinarily," but Kevin nods vigorously, letting me know he understands.

We are carried up another mile-long escalator and spat out the glass doors onto Nevsky Prospekt.

"D'ya wanna have a cup of coffee?" asks Kevin.

I don't know where he thinks he can find a cup of coffee on the main avenue of Leningrad, but I don't flinch. That is another thing Maria Mikhailovna has taught us: never show you're surprised, no matter how improbable or far-fetched a question may seem. Do we have bears roaming the streets? No. What percentage of the population is unemployed? Zero. Are there places to have a cup of coffee? I don't know of any. We must pretend we are sophisticated and erudite, above the naïve or materialistic questions of British high school students, above drinking coffee on Nevsky Prospekt.

I see a line snaking around the corner, and Kevin sees it, too. The House of Friendship and Peace can't do anything about the lines. There are a couple of feeble strategies Maria Mikhailovna suggested during our practice tours. You can distract the tourists' attention by pointing to a former church or palace. You can make a joke. When Maria Mikhailovna took us to the Hermitage to practice her museum lectures, she demonstrated what to say if your group asks to use a bathroom. These toilets are museum pieces, too, she said. Preserved from the time of Catherine the Great.

The line Kevin is now gawking at is for toilet paper. It stretches around the corner into the side street, three or four rows thick, elbowing under a banner that reads, "Thanks to the party for the people's welfare." I hope Kevin doesn't insist on turning into that street because the location of the slogan is just too pathetic, as if someone deliberately put it there to make a point so obvious it's not worth translating. But he isn't interested in the slogan. He is staring at two women approaching from the front of the line, both wearing necklaces of toilet-paper rolls they've threaded on a rope for easy carrying.

"Can I take a picture?" he whispers, lifting his camera, a glee in his hazel eyes.

I don't think the two women in toilet-paper necklaces would like it. I don't think the babushka behind an ice cream cart, who is already eyeing us with a frown, would like it. I don't think the militiaman directing traffic would like it. No one would appreciate having this picture taken, but Kevin is daring: he lowers the camera and snaps shots from his hip, pretending to examine the colonnade of the former Kazan Cathedral. He thinks he is a genius, having come up with such a brilliantly distracting maneuver, but in the area of pretense no British student can compete with our decades of daily practice. All of us—the ice cream seller, the toilet-paper-bedecked women, and the militiaman, if he were to drop his zebra baton and look in our direction—would, in a blink of an eye, see right through Kevin's trick.

I have to think fast, and do something, because the babushka has planted her fists on her hips and is getting ready to start shouting while one of the women with toilet paper around her neck is pointing in our direction. Another minute, and the militiaman will turn around to investigate who is creating all this commotion, yelling in the middle of the city's historical center. I grab Kevin by the elbow and tell him to walk fast, very fast, tell him to run, run until we are a block away, lost in the human current of Nevsky Prospekt.

"That was close!" he says, catching a breath, beaming from his adventure. I can hardly share his excitement: the thought of unrealized possibilities involving the militiaman makes my blood run cold. Maria Mikhailovna and my mother would cringe at the headline—"Detained: A Foreigner and His Unauthorized Guide." We march briskly, hidden inside the crowd, for another block. I am horrified at what could have happened. I am horrified at being horrified, at my own cowardice and fear.

But none of this can I show to Kevin. He lives in London, where there are no yelling babushkas, no militia, and no shortage of toilet paper. I have to pretend to be a guide again. I show him the Moika Embankment as we walk past the House of Books with a turret and a glass globe on top, and past Pushkin's apartment, where the poet lay dying after the duel he'd fought to protect his wife's honor.

Kevin likes the House of Books, but he has never heard of Pushkin.

Along Trade Union Boulevard and past the Palace of Labor, we make our way to Decembrists' Square on the Neva, where Peter the Great, on a rearing horse, in a laurel wreath and with royal grandeur, reaches toward the water. Two and a half centuries ago, he willed the city into existence, hammering pilings into the marsh, transforming the islands of the windy Neva delta into a port with only one goal in mind: to open a window on Europe. It is appropriate, I think, to come to this monument with Kevin, who, by standing here, provides irrefutable evidence that this thoroughfare still functions, even if only in one direction.

As Kevin snaps pictures, completely legitimate, of the Tsar and the Admiralty's golden spire, I lean on the parapet and look into

My mother during the Soviet-Finnish War, 1939

My father during the Great
Patriotic War (World War II)
reading *Pravda*, 1943

My father after
my birth, 1955

My grandmother, my mother, and Marina, 1950, Ivanovo

Lunch at my Leningrad nursery school
(I am second from the right), 1959

Third grade: Vera Pavlovna in the center; Dimka the hooligan next to her
on the left, second row; Zoya the diamond in the last row, second from
right; I am in the third row, fifth from left, 1965

With my grandmother
and grandfather at the
dacha, 1964

Lunch in our dacha veranda, early 1960s. From left: my
cousin Kostya, my grandfather and grandmother, Aunt
Muza, my mother and father

Doing garden work
in front of the dacha
veranda, 1968

Marina (center) in her first film role: Dunyasha in Rimsky-Korsakov's
*The Tsar's Bride*, 1963

My mother (first row, center) with her students at a dissection class, late 1960s

Visiting my mother in Leningrad
after I had been in the U.S. for five years, 1985

My mother and Marina in New Orleans, 1998

With my daughter in
Nutley, New Jersey, 1989

With my husband and daughter on a trip to San Francisco, 1993

the churning, zinc-colored water. If my mother hadn't decided to marry my father in 1950, which involved moving here from the provincial town of Ivanovo, I wouldn't be parading all this architectural beauty in front of a boy from England. I wouldn't be standing here, surrounded by the wide bridges spanning the granite embankments, by the lace of iron banisters and fences, by spires, domes, and the robust curves of Italian baroque.

What prompted my mother to accept my father's proposal, I wonder, while Kevin is looking for an angle from which to photograph the Bronze Horseman across the street. Was it a search for a better life, as practical as she is: giving my sister a father, having another child, moving to a capital city? Or was it rather that she was running away from something? After all, as I know from one of her stories, she was summoned to the Ivanovo NKVD headquarters after the war, after her uncle Volya had already been arrested and shot, and forced to spy on the chairman of the anatomy department where she worked. Dr. Zlotnikov, Moisey Davidovich, her PhD adviser and a Jew. Every month she was ordered to come to a certain address (an empty apartment that could be used to house a whole family, she thought bitterly), where an NKVD officer was waiting for her with a pen and a stack of blank paper. She couldn't refuse, she said, so every month she came to this secret place and wrote about the most mundane, innocuous things that involved Dr. Zlotnikov: a conversation about the percentage of enlarged thyroids at the Ivanovo textile factory for her dissertation in progress, a shortage of scalpels at a dissection class, a lab assistant's alcoholic son. But a fear always clawed in the back of her mind that even those benign things would be twisted and mauled, just like Uncle Volya's joke, and then Dr. Zlotnikov's arrest would weigh on her conscience forever.

For a year she came to that apartment once a month, as though to an illicit, sordid rendezvous that had to be kept secret from the honest world and, under the gaze of the young, plain-clothed

NKVD man, filled scores of pages with her squared handwriting. So when my father proposed marriage and said they'd have to move to Leningrad, she not only saw it as an escape from her harsh, provincial past, but also as a return to decency and peace of mind.

Two years after she moved, Stalin was dead. Once again, the future bled on the horizon, another hint at the bright dawn promised by the Revolution. Her move to Leningrad worked out the way she'd envisioned: Dr. Zlotnikov retired without having been arrested; she had a baby and a teaching job.

Would I ever be able to move away from here—the only place I've ever known—as my mother moved away from Ivanovo? It is one thing to exchange a provincial town for the second biggest city in the country. But what place could possibly trump Leningrad?

Kevin, finished with photography, wants to walk along the Neva, past the Hermitage, past the arch of the Winter Canal, where Pushkin's desperate Lisa jumped from the stone staircase into the black water. We walk by the wrought-iron fence of the Summer Gardens, another Pushkin landmark, a favorite strolling place of Onegin and the poet himself. But Kevin doesn't know Pushkin, so he tells me something about rugby and then something about driving, although it's hard to understand why at fifteen he would even bother thinking about such an impossible thing.

"I'm saving to buy a car," he says.

That's funny, the notion of being able to save enough in one's lifetime to buy a car. I chuckle, but Kevin's eyebrows mash together in a frown. Now I need to explain that I'm not laughing at him for saving money to buy a car. I'm laughing because I think of a joke my sister told me. Even in Russian telling a joke is tricky, and I pull all my linguistic resources together to help Kevin understand.

*Three drivers—an Englishman, a Hungarian, and a Russian—all drive down the same road. The Englishman wrecks his car on a tree, gets out, and shouts, "Damn, this car was six months' salary!"*

*The Hungarian hits the same tree and yells, "This car was five years' salary!" The Russian crashes into still the same tree and wails, "This car is thirty years' salary!" The Brit turns to the Russian and asks, "Why do you buy such expensive cars?"*

Kevin narrows his eyes, and I can almost see him thinking. I must have translated the joke so badly that I should probably explain to him it isn't about expensive cars. But after a few moments of silence he slaps himself on the forehead and grins, although I'm still not sure he understands or just pretends to.

We take the metro back. It's seven-thirty and I don't want him to be late for supper. From the metro station to the hotel we walk in the sun, which, since we are in the period of white nights, will stay up for another four hours before it dips below the horizon, only to re-emerge an hour later. Deprived of the architectural prompts the city center offers, we no longer know what to say to each other.

"Can I take your picture?" he asks finally, and I stand blushing in front of an archway where another babushka, a street cleaner, is hitting the pavement with a bunch of twigs attached to a stick.

When we do the compulsory address exchange—pen-pal friendship, as Maria Mikhailovna calls it—Kevin fumbles in his jeans pocket and produces a bracelet, real silver, with intricate burnished flowers stamped into the metal. I've only ever seen real silver in my grandparents' set of teaspoons my mother takes out of a silk-lined box twice a year for holidays. I know Kevin bought the bracelet in the *Beriozka*, while I was staring at the books.

"It's for you," he says, and then adds, "Please, take it."

I've never owned any jewelry, especially something made from silver. It is an insanely generous gift, my first gift from a boy, if I don't count the mandatory pocket erasers and combs I've received in my eight years of school for International Women's Day. I feel my face turn red, and I can do little not to look dumbstruck.

Sparkling on my palm, the bracelet is a reminder of the exclusive status that permits me to enter a *Beriozka* shop with all its forbidden treasures. But is it really a privilege to stand next to shelves with foods I can't eat and books I can't read? I don't know the answer. I don't know if it is better to learn about Kevin's hometown from my text called *London: The City of Contrasts* or spend a day there, riding the underground and taking pictures. What I do know is that all this thinking is just that, thinking. It changes nothing. No matter how many jokes I tell, no matter how cynical I've become, this is the way things are here. Contrary to my mother's hopes for a better future, I will never travel to London, or save for a car, or taste shrimp.

The British students, with their *Beriozka* souvenirs and clean hair, are going to pack into buses tomorrow and leave. Despite a postcard I'll receive from Kevin in response to my long letter, elegantly composed and meticulously copied onto a pretty piece of paper, I will never see him again. Tomorrow morning he'll walk through Peter the Great's "window on Europe" guarded by the armed border patrol of Pulkovo International Airport. Tomorrow afternoon he'll cross over to the other side—London, the city of contrasts.

I thank Kevin with all the expressions of appreciation I know in English, but there is an embarrassing question scratching in the back of my mind like an ungrateful cat. Would I rather have a silver bracelet or Bulgakov's *Master and Margarita*? I wiggle my wrist, now shackled in cold silver. "Exquisite," I say to Kevin, who thinks I am sincere, who doesn't know this is just a little instance of *vranyo*.

# CHAPTER 14

# *Work*

I AM SEVENTEEN AND JUST got accepted to the Leningrad University's English department, evening division. The day program where I applied did not admit me because my parents were professionals and because my family lacked connections. This made me think of my mother, who had to wait for a milkmaid's daughter to drop out to be accepted to the Ivanovo medical school because my grandfather by then was an engineer and no longer a peasant. It was interesting, I thought, that with our incomparable leaps toward a better future in other areas, nothing has changed in the college admission process since 1930.

"*Nyet huda bez dobra:* there is no evil without good," my mother recited, when I repeated what my English professor said at our first class. "The evening program is much better because all of you are qualified," she told us. "You got in because you know English, not because your mother drives a tractor or because your father sits in a Smolny office." It made me feel good to be so qualified, yet still resentful toward the university's admission board.

But now I need a job, immediately: the evening division requires its students to work during the day. By the end of September I must bring to the dean a letter, signed and stamped, certifying my full-time employment.

. The prospect of having a job is thrilling. It plucks me out of the wading pool of my classmates and drops me into the sea of adults, instantly making me a grown citizen imbued with real, paid-for responsibility. But it's not the responsibility that sounds so attractive, it's the status and the rights that working brings. It's the feeling that I've finally reached real life, quivering on the horizon like a promise, that everything before this was mere expectation, a string of landmarks on the way to that horizon.

"I'm going to work," I'll utter casually as I pass handsome Vitya from the fourth floor, who will blink his usually disinterested eyes and stare after me in stunned admiration.

I don't know how one finds a job, but I don't need to: my mother is in charge. As a result of her commandeering, a neighbor from the third floor, Alec, offers me a position.

"You'll be a draftsman," my mother says.

"But I don't know how to draft," I object, instantly imagining how I will embarrass our generous neighbor on the very first day of the job.

"You don't need to know anything. They'll tell you what to do. As I understand it, you'll copy some blueprints."

"Blueprints of what?"

My mother pauses, pretending she's sorting out the silverware in a drawer. "It's a secret factory," she says. "They make ships."

"Ships?" I giggle. "What kind of ships? Atomic submarines? They have to make atomic submarines, otherwise why would it be such a secret?"

"I don't know," my mother says. "All Alec told me is you need to get clearance."

Clearance will take two months, Alec says, but in the meantime I can still work copying drafts. Maybe these are drafts of outdated submarines, those that are no longer classified and can be safely exposed to my unvetted eyes. I sit in a huge room with long tables, next to a boring girl with thin lips and dusty-looking hair, arrogant because she's just received her clearance. Sometimes we draw blue lines on translucent drafting paper, but mostly we carry rolls of drafts to the production department, hot rooms the size of my school gym with rows of forges managed by bawdy men. I walk fast and look straight ahead, but my heels click on the metal floor no matter how hard I try to step softly, and the men leer from behind their enormous machines and smile and yell things I don't want to hear.

So far I haven't seen any boats, or any parts that could belong to a boat. To my relief, I haven't seen Alec, either.

Every morning at eight I pass through a checkpoint. This is the time when the whole factory files in through one turnstile, so we often stand outside in a small crowd, in the morning dusk, waiting our turn to show our IDs to a woman on duty. From her perch near the door, she silently peers at each one of us and angrily presses the button to open the turnstile. Once in a while she starts screaming when someone has forgotten or lost his card. I don't know why she has to be so angry. She's not the one who will have to stay behind the factory wall until five, when it will be dusk again, when we will have to walk through the same turnstile back into the unclassified world.

Every morning at eight a question buzzes in my head, persistent as a fly: is this all there is to work? What has happened to the spirit of adulthood and independence, to that promise quivering on the horizon? I try to ask the girl with dusty-looking hair, but she doesn't understand what I'm trying to say. She keeps drawing thin lines and carrying the rolls of blueprints to the production area, ignoring leering men and their catcalls. Or maybe the men can sense how boring she is and don't even bother to look up and yell after her.

At the end of October, a frightening thought begins to stir in my head, especially on those dark mornings when freezing half-rain/half-fog congeals the air into globs of icy aspic as we stand outside the checkpoint. Everything I've done so far has always been the eve of something else. Eighth grade was the eve of an academic path, when a few of my classmates left to go to vocational school; the all-night walk around the city after graduation was the curtain call of childhood and the eve of the next morning, when boys suddenly grew tall and brazen; the marathon of university entrance exams was the eve of self-sufficiency and freedom—all these things, although nerve-wrecking and difficult, have led to something else. This waiting at the checkpoint, replayed every morning with slight variations of a different angry woman on duty shouting at a different man who forgot his card, only leads to the pocked cement of the factory yard, to the cafeteria with more surly women ladling cabbage soup, to production lines with no hint of any boats.

I quit on the first day of November, just a few days before they approve my clearance.

FOR THE NEXT EIGHT months I am a lab assistant at my mother's anatomy department. I've grown up in its formaldehyde-saturated walls, so this job doesn't even feel like a job. I sit in a small room across from another assistant, Luba, creating micro-scope slides professors use in their research. Right now the predominant research project has to do with space travel and weightlessness. Every year or so we watch on television a time-delayed broadcast of another space crew parachuting down somewhere in Kazakhstan after another successful mission, and our anatomy department provides its contribution to animal research. Luba and I pull lab rabbits out of their cages in the basement, strap them to a centrifuge, and spin them at a cosmic speed that blurs the rabbits into circles of gray and white. If they are still alive after the centrifuge stops, we have to kill them with ether, because what the researchers need is the rabbits' spine. We have to carefully break the vertebrae, remove the soft cord of spine in one piece, freeze it, and then create slides by slicing it into thin translucent chips that will fit onto a microscope glass. I hate holding a rag full of ether to the rabbits' faces, to their clotted and damp fur, whereas Luba hates breaking the vertebrae, so we delineate the labor in a mutually agreeable way.

When there are enough slides stacked up, we sit on top of our desks and chat with Sasha, who is short and square-jawed and always wears a white doctor's coat. Sasha is an *aspirant*, a graduate student working on his dissertation, which presumably tackles the question of organic spine changes in space, so he spends more time in our lab than anyone else, always telling jokes, always laughing.

"There is a Russian, a German, and a Jew," says Sasha, and I wonder if I've already heard this one since all Sasha's jokes include an international trio roughly representing our view of the world hierarchy. "And God says to them, I'll grant you one wish each, any wish you like. Kill all the Germans, yells the Russian. Kill all the Russians, screams the German. And what do you want, God asks the Jew. Grant them both their wishes, says the Jew, and I'll have a cup of coffee."

I giggle, but Sasha is watching Luba's reaction. I know he likes Luba, who is twenty-four and has black eyes bigger than a microscope lens.

Luba obligingly smiles at his jokes, but when Sasha leaves, she isn't so charitable. "He's married," she smirks and disdainfully bends her wrist. "Plus he's short and looks like an ape."

Luba likes Professor Rodionov, who is also married but is the tallest man in the department and from a distance resembles the French actor Alain Delon. She times her cigarette breaks to the end of his classes so she can casually ask him for a light when he leaves the dissection room. He behaves politely but never goes beyond lighting her cigarette. I don't think she stands a chance because everyone knows that Professor Rodionov is a class system snob and would never pay attention to someone who, like Luba, can boast nothing past a secondary school diploma.

Although according to our history books, social classes were eradicated in 1917, along with the tsar, Professor Rodionov takes great pride in belonging to what he calls "the erudite elite."

"A classless society," smirks my sister, "means that the classes never acknowledge each other's existence."

At noon, a curly-haired woman named Valya comes around with a crate of milk. Since we work in a hazardous formaldehyde environment, all of us in the anatomy department are entitled to a free daily bottle of milk. Valya always has medical questions for Sasha, who is eager to answer and who, like most *aspirants*, knows everything. Yesterday she wanted to know if a gallbladder actually contained gall, and the day before she needed a cure for warts. Today Valya is interested in the most reliable method of contraception. Luba shakes her head and leaves the room, outraged by this shamelessness. I am curious, so I stay.

"Cement," says Sasha. "Cement all orifices and nothing will get through, I guarantee."

Valya bursts into loud laughter and slaps Sasha on the back with her broad palm. I go back to pasting rabbit spinal cord onto slides, disappointed. Frankly, I was hoping for something more informative.

When I get home, I find turmoil: Marina is looking for a birthday present for the musical director of her theater. The birthday party is next Monday, and she is desperate. "Men are impossible to find presents for," she proclaims. "Vodka is too pedestrian and decent cognac impossible to get."

"Give him a book," says my mother in her teacher's voice.

"He already has a book," says Marina with a straight face although we all know it's an old joke, so old that my mother's posthumously rehabilitated Uncle Volya was telling it back in 1937. "The only thing I can think of is something to add to his collection."

"What does he collect?" I ask.

"Rabbits," says Marina. "All kinds of rabbits—glass, porcelain, wood. All sizes."

It's instantly obvious what the present must be. It cannot be a coincidence that the music director collects rabbits and in the anatomy department where I work tons of rabbits sit in rusty cages, waiting to become statistics for Sasha's quantitative study. I'm certain my idea is brilliant and unbeatable. I'm bursting with my own genius; I can no longer keep it in. "A live rabbit!" I shout. "Give him a rabbit from our lab!"

My mother looks at me with a quizzical expression, not sure if I am serious, not sure if removing a rabbit from the anatomy lab is a proper thing to do.

"Yes, yes, a live rabbit!" I babble, choking on my own words. "You'll have a unique birthday gift—and we'll save a rabbit from being centrifuged, smothered with ether, and sliced."

I see my mother hesitate and I trot out my last argument. "We have too many rabbits right now anyway; we've just had an inventory," I say. The inventory bit is a fib. "Sasha said yesterday," I add, "we should start stewing them for lunch."

Now my sister's eyes are burning with excitement, too. With the combined forces of both of us, my mother doesn't stand a chance.

On Monday, my sister and I go to the basement of the anatomy department with rows of dark, smelly cages and pick a tri-colored rabbit—black, white, and yellow—a sign of luck, according to my sister. The rabbit rustles inside folded newspaper as Marina fits it into a string bag to take on the bus across the city.

I imagine Marina arriving at the birthday party with a rabbit in a string bag. I see the whirl of shock and excitement; the petrified rabbit pressed to the parquet floor; the flurry of rabbit-related toasts; the hands that pet and cradle the rabbit until, in utter panic, it pees on someone's dress; the empty apartment with clouds of cigarette smoke over the ruins of dinner and the semiconscious rabbit gasping in the corner of a dark hallway.

"Are you sure he can handle a live rabbit?" I say, but all I see is Marina's back disappear behind a closing door.

IN THE BEGINNING OF my second year, my English professor Natalia Borisovna pulls me aside and says there is an opening in the House of Friendship and Peace, where I used to work as a tour guide in the ninth grade. The job is the director's secretary and has nothing to do with speaking English, but with time and luck, the professor points out, it may evolve into something else. At any rate, she adds, it is an impressive and prestigious place to work.

My job is to sit behind an enormous desk in front of the director's office and answer the phone. The director, Viktor Nikolaevich, a party member like every functionary, doesn't seem to be interested in the calls that come through me; the only calls that make him excited come on a red phone without a dial that sits on the desk of his office. When the red phone rings, he puts his feet up on a coffee table, laughs into the receiver, and leaves shortly afterward, always in a good mood. Viktor Nikolaevich often seems to be in a good mood. A smile starts from the corners of his eyes, dimples his cheeks, and stretches his large lips when every morning he crosses the waiting room in confident steps at the civilized hour of ten o'clock.

"*Hozyain*," deferentially mutters Ludmila the bookkeeper as he saunters by, the word that means "master." He is tall and broad-shouldered and looks like a master. He looks as if the House of Friendship and Peace, with its marble stairways, bronze chandeliers, gilded moldings, and thirty people hunkered down in their first-floor offices, belong exclusively to him and not to the state.

The echoey waiting room where I sit behind a vast desk makes me feel both humble and important. It is the social center of the first-floor offices, where people make arrangements for foreign delegations visiting our city. It draws coordinators from both the socialist and capitalist departments to exchange the latest gossip and parade their clothes. The socialist women are usually dressed in brighter colors. The tall and reedy Olya, coordinator for the German Democratic Republic, wears sky-blue suits with short skirts, while the doughy Galina, coordinator for Czechoslovakia, favors spiky heels and heavy makeup. Sergei, the handsome, sad-eyed coordinator for Bulgaria, comes to complain about a hangover and the fact that he has to arrange hotel reservations for groups of Polish Soviet deputies because Sveta, who is responsible for Poland, is on a yearlong maternity leave.

The capitalist coordinators wear more subdued beiges, grays, and dark greens. Rita, who ten years ago graduated from my department of the university, appears hand-in-hand with the hooded-eyed, theatrical Tatiana Vasilievna, the coordinator for all the English-speaking countries. Tatiana Vasilievna makes me feel even more inferior than I normally do in this exclusive environment of such important and well-dressed people. She likes to give advice to everyone below her in rank, and that's pretty much everyone except Viktor Nikolaevich, who sits behind an oak door next to my desk.

"Use a little bit of makeup, darling," she murmurs into the ear of Anna, a typist in the corner of the waiting room hunched over a typewriter in her perennial gray suit shiny from wear. Anna, who is twice my age and excruciatingly shy, forces her lips to smile, wishing she could compress herself into a wall, away from Tatiana Vasilievna's ringed fingers, which clutch a thick batch of papers to be typed. Darling, *dushenka*, is what she calls all younger women before she insults them or overwhelms them with work.

"*Dushenka*, don't call me Mrs. in front of those British gentlemen," she coos to Rita, embracing her. "I'm not married anymore, am I?"

Everyone in the House of Friendship and Peace knows that Tatiana Vasilievna's husband packed up and fled three months after the wedding, nine years ago, just as she turned thirty-five. It's a wonder he stayed so long, said Ludmila the bookkeeper, who told me the story.

"Otherwise they'll think I'm a housewife with a bunch of runny-nosed children," whispers Tatiana Vasilievna to Rita. "Just like you."

Rita smiles an embarrassed smile and apologizes. I don't know how she is able to squeeze a smile out of her scrunched face, but I suspect she must be thinking about the future, about ten years from now when Tatiana Vasilievna reaches fifty-five, a retirement age for women, the moment that will put Rita in command of all English-speaking countries. Although I realize it's a formidable prospect to be in charge of the whole English-speaking world, it hardly seems worth ten more years of Tatiana Vasilievna's reign. I imagine myself in Rita's place, coming back with witty, powerful responses I'd need days to think up, responses that would disarm Tatiana Vasilievna and turn her into a kind, sensitive person.

Tatiana Vasilievna spends a lot of time in the waiting room because she likes the director, my boss. He has a wife, of course, and like all functionaries, must serve as an example of a proper society cell, but this trifle is irrelevant to Tatiana Vasilievna. She thinks up projects and explains them at length to Anna the typist, who shrinks like a turtle into her worn-out suit every time Tatiana Vasilievna sails into the room. She moves papers around my desk, pretending she's reading each one, waiting for the oak door to open. If it doesn't, she clutches at her chest and starts to vigorously fan herself. She breathes hard; she calls for Rita in a barely audible voice. When Rita comes running, Tatiana Vasilievna puts the back of her hand over her forehead and implores her to call for a doctor. This is the time when Viktor Nikolaevich, who can usually sense this turmoil, comes out of his office to bring her back to life. One time, when he was away at a meeting, she fainted onto the floor in front of the fireplace, her legs neatly crossed at the ankles.

From my boss's squinted eyes I think he sees right through Tatiana Vasilievna and her theatrical hysterics, taking her for what she is—a neurotic, lonely woman. But she is a high-ranking coordinator for a hefty chunk of the capitalist world, so we have to pretend we're concerned about her shallow breathing and her chest-clutching, rushing to the bathroom for cold water and to the café for wedges of lemon, unbuttoning her blouse just enough to expose a hint of lace from her brassiere.

Although I don't know where our coordinators shop for their lace underwear, web-thin pantyhose, and well-fitted suits, I know where they don't. Maybe owning hard-to-get decent clothes is another perk for being a coordinator at the House of Friendship and Peace, along with a food package containing a kilo of beef, a jar of instant coffee, and a stick of hard salami they can pick up at a special distributor before major holidays. What I wear to work comes from elbowing in line at a local store or from the artistic hands of my sister—a Hungarian shirt with small purple flowers and a brown skirt resewn from Marina's old pants. My sister has lately been in a good mood, so she's making me a little black dress from a piece of fabric I found rolled up in our armoire, a number just like the one I saw in the *England* magazine left open on Rita's desk.

Aside from Tatiana Vasilievna and her nervous fits, there isn't much at work to pay attention to. I sit at the desk, do my homework, and stare at the grandfather clock in the corner whose hands don't seem to move. At around one-thirty I go to the House of Friendship café, an exclusive place with waitresses and a printed menu, which is open for lunch for employees and members of the select public involved in foreign affairs and which stays open on those nights when there is an art or culture festival in the ballroom on the second floor.

It's those nights that intrigue me. Days are predictable and boring, all work, coordinators trekking through with their reports, Ludmila the bookkeeper offering her latest gossip, Viktor Nikolaevich cackling into his red phone, Anna hitting the typewriter keys with the speed of a machine gun. But what happens here at night? Who sits at these tables in the café when we're all safely tucked into university classrooms or our apartments, and what kinds of transformations occur to the soup and meatballs and pastries with pink roses after the clock strikes six?

So the next time there is an evening affair celebrating an anniversary of the British composer Benjamin Britten, I don't leave at five-thirty. It's a Wednesday, the only weekday with no university classes scheduled, and my conscience is clear. I walk up the marble staircase with wrought-iron banisters to the main ballroom, vast as a stadium and made even bigger by floor-to-ceiling mirrors in gilded frames. Of course, I immediately see Tatiana Vasilievna—it is, after all, an English-speaking affair—directing Rita in how to arrange the chairs for musicians and where to place the podium.

"I have to face the audience directly," she instructs. "You don't want me to twist my head off, do you?"

As Rita tries to push the podium, Tatiana Vasilievna clasps her head and closes her eyes. "*Dushenka*, you're scratching the parquet, don't you see?" she hisses.

I step back because I don't want to take part in moving the podium or the chairs, especially under the commandeering of Tatiana Vasilievna. I also don't want to explain to her what I'm doing here, way past my working hours, at a concert of capitalist music, exposed without her approval to a very real possibility of communicating with people from English-speaking countries.

I see them filing in through the front door as I walk back downstairs: a group of women who look youthful and ageless, all with rich, blondish hair and real leather shoes, and men in blue jeans, whose movements are unhurried, as if they'd never had to squeeze into a rush-hour bus. They are now gawking at the gold, marble, and crystal that belonged to Count Shuvalov, who owned all this voluptuous excess before 1917, when the Bolsheviks handed it down to the people.

Tatiana Vasilievna appears on the top of the stairs and stands there magnanimously, as if this opulence belonged to her, waiting for the group to ascend to her height. They walk past me, sending in my direction a whiff of the West, an odor of perpetual cleanliness and good clothes, and knowing that Tatiana Vasilievna is going to be occupied for a while, I retreat into the café in the hope of rubbing shoulders with the select members of the public invited to such exclusive affairs.

The truth is I don't know if I really want to retreat to the café. I'm petrified. I'm afraid that the moment I walk in everyone will take one look at me and realize that I've never been to a restaurant at night. Aside from my sister, who sometimes goes to the Actors' Club, I don't know anyone who has. There are a few restaurants in the city, so someone must eat there, but they're always guarded by stone-faced doormen who can only be bribed by things we don't have. The interiors, I've always imagined, were sets from old movies: a piano next to a potted palm, a starched napkin in a circle of light cast by a table lamp, a bent waiter with a white towel over his arm. As I stand in the doorway of the House of Friendship café, I feel as exposed as if I were entering my boss's office having forgotten to put my clothes on.

The lunch room with neon lights has metamorphosed into a dark cave gauzy with cigarette smoke. At the far end I can still make out the counter with pastries, and I gather all my courage and walk straight toward the shelves with familiar éclairs, focusing on the beacons of tarts crowned with pink roses. I pretend I belong here, and although I do belong here, I feel as if I were walking across a minefield, ready to make a mistake that will shatter my disguise and expose me for what I am: clumsy, ill-mannered, and unworldly.

By the pastry counter, like a savior, sits Natasha from my university English class. I lunge forward and greet her as if she were a best friend I haven't seen in years, despite the fact that I sat next to her in my phonetics class only yesterday. She tells me how she ended up here, at this concert and in this restaurant, but her words sail past my ears. I'm so relieved I order a Napoleon and a coffee and a bottle of lemonade for both of us, although I'm not even sure I have any money in my purse.

"So who do you think all these people are?" I ask Natasha, nodding toward the crowd smoking in the dusk. There is no food served, I notice, only sweets and drinks.

"I was going to ask you," says Natasha. "You're the one who works here."

She is right; I should know. Everyone who works here probably knows, with the exception of our typist Anna, who sees nothing but the typewriter keys because she's mortified to oblivion by Tatiana Vasilievna. All my co-workers, I bet, have sat at these tables at night, ordering platefuls of éclairs and perhaps even glasses of the cognac and champagne whose golden labels gleam behind the counter.

To be decadent, Natasha pulls a pack of cigarettes out of her purse. We light up and lean back, feeling relaxed and hedonistic now, lazily poking into our plates as though our parents forced us to eat Napoleons every day for breakfast, lunch, and dinner. This pretense makes me feel like everyone else, makes me feel I belong in a dark corner of this restaurant where no one questions my presence.

Then, with her imperial gait, Tatiana Vasilievna walks through the door and marches straight to the pastry display. She sees me sitting at the table and her face congeals into the expression she wore when Rita failed to procure her a first-class ticket on the same-day train to Moscow to accompany a group of American businessmen.

"May I have a word with you?" she says ominously as I obediently get up because that's what primary school and our mothers taught us to do when we speak to a person older than ourselves.

"Your work ends at five-thirty," she says, deliberately glancing at her gold watch. "There's no need for you to be in this restaurant at night." In her high heels she is taller than I, or maybe it is my curled shoulders that make her tower over me.

I can't think of anything to say. I don't know if Tatiana Vasilievna can prohibit me from entering this restaurant, but judging by her lifted chin and narrowed eyes, she's certain she can. And it is this certainty, this authority leaking from every pore of her heavily made-up face that makes me stoop even lower. I'm too docile and cowardly to belong here, after all, and I hate Tatiana Vasilievna for driving this point home.

"*Dushenka*," she says in an injured tone because I wounded her senses by eating a Napoleon in a place I am not permitted to enter at night. "You should remember: What's allowed for Jupiter is not allowed for the bull."

Although I've never heard this saying before, I can imagine that Tatiana Vasilievna has made it up so that she could compare herself to the most powerful Roman god. But why am I the bull? In addition to barging into restaurants without permission and generally not knowing my place, I must also be ignorant of Roman mythology and the idioms that employ it. I glance at Natasha, who is sitting very quietly wedged between the table and the wall, not knowing if this exchange somehow applies to her, too.

With Tatiana Vasilievna leading the way, I leave the restaurant and all its dusky decadence. Still stooped and utterly defeated, I walk through the double oak doors out of the House of Friendship and Peace, which, as it has just become clear, offers neither of the two solaces it was named for.

*

THERE IS A RUMOR that my boss, Viktor Nikolaevich, is being transferred to Czechoslovakia. People say this with respect: Ludmila the bookkeeper deferentially lowers her voice while Olya the coordinator of the German Democratic Republic rounds her eyes and her mouth into perfect *o*'s. Since the transfer is to a foreign country, it is definitely a promotion. How big a promotion? Bigger than Bulgaria or Vietnam but smaller than, say, France. At any rate, Viktor Nikolaevich now spends less and less time behind his door, which triggers an injured expression on Tatiana Vasilievna's face every time she sails into the waiting room only to find his office empty, only to become so despondent she doesn't even try to pretend to faint because he isn't there to see her exposed cleavage or her knee sheathed in shimmering nylon and carefully bent on the floor right next to my desk.

I like Viktor Nikolaevich and dread the day when he has to leave. He is easygoing, he makes jokes, he never gets upset with me, and he protects me like a father would, although he looks nothing like my father. He doesn't smoke, he is broad-waisted and fair-skinned, and he has a mouth full of real teeth.

According to Ludmila the bookkeeper, he has a soft spot for the waitresses at our café. He loves them, she says, especially Maya, who has ash-blonde hair and likes to wear a tight uniform and red lipstick. For some reason I dislike Maya; strangely, it almost feels like jealousy. He is my boss and I want him to like me, only me. The other day, when I was leaving his office with a shuffle of papers to type, Viktor Nikolaevich took my hand, the one without the papers, and held it and stared into my eyes so intensely that I had to look down. When he let it go, I went back to my desk in the waiting room, and a few minutes later he left, having answered the red phone.

Since the Jupiter and the bull incident Tatiana Vasilievna hasn't spoken to me directly. Maybe she wishes she hadn't humiliated me in the restaurant because, as it turns out, I could be useful in detecting Viktor Nikolaevich's whereabouts when she feels like fainting again. Or maybe she expected an apology for my inappropriate behavior and, when she didn't receive one, decided that I was hopeless, worthy of the only possible course of action on her part—to ostracize and ignore me. Whatever the reason, she no longer addresses me, which is a great relief.

It's April, two months from the end of my second year at the university, and I'm busy thinking up ways to take my history final early. The course is compulsory, the history of the Communist Party of the Soviet Union, and taking it early solves the two problems inherent in the class. It will save me from sitting through the rest of the seminars, listening to made-up history, and according to those innovative minds who've done it before, it is much easier to get a good grade early since the professors haven't yet entered the mind-set of the two merciless final semester weeks. I have composed a letter, on the House letterhead and with the House stamp I keep in my drawer, requesting the university dean to grant me permission to take the finals early because in June we are so swamped with foreign delegations from all over the world that it's impossible for me, a House of Friendship employee, to find time to study.

In reality, of course, June is the month when things slow down and people start taking vacations, but the dean and the communist history department are used to the twisted truth. The letter is immaculately typed and has everything but the director's signature. I time the crucial moment for Monday, the last day before Viktor Nikolaevich leaves for his new position in Czechoslovakia.

On Sunday I lean on Marina to finish the little black dress she is sewing according to the picture in Rita's *England* magazine. On Monday morning, at ten, I stand by my desk to greet my boss, wearing the dress. It's short, very short, with a deep V-neck too low for work, and Viktor Nikolaevich immediately sees that. He opens his large lips to say something but doesn't. The blue of his eyes softens and melts as he gazes at me—at the whole me, for the first time since I started working there. The unexpected part is that it feels good, this look. It feels edifying. And maybe part of this edification is the fact that it is I being granted this stare of admiration—not Maya with her tight uniforms and red lips, and certainly not Tatiana Vasilievna, who could faint a thousand times, deftly exposing her nylon and her lace, and still fail to attract this look.

Viktor Nikolaevich goes into his office, and I follow him with a bunch of mail and a typed letter in my hand. He sits at his desk, puts on his glasses, and starts shuffling through the papers, pretending he hadn't just drilled me with a stare, pretending he no longer sees the little black dress I'm wearing.

"Could you possibly sign this for me?" I ask in a timid and submissive way that makes directors feel even more powerful. "To take my final early. The history of the Communist Party of the Soviet Union."

He takes my letter, reads it, then squints at me from above his glasses. "Overwhelmed with foreign delegations in June," he reads. "Impossible to find time to study, eh?"

I nod and squeeze out a little smile, showing that I know that he knows it's a lie.

He pulls a pen out of an enormous writing set presiding over his desk, signs, and hands the letter back to me. "It's my last day here," he says as I mumble my thanks. "We're going to celebrate after work."

It is obviously no use telling him that I have classes at seven.

The day drags on because Viktor Nikolaevich is mostly out of the office. First the red phone rings and he promptly leaves; then he reappears only to vanish again toward the café and its waitresses. Several times Tatiana Vasilievna whiffs in, followed by a trail of perfume, and on one of her attempts she gets lucky and bumps into Viktor Nikolaevich, who is also just walking in.

"Well, well, well, it's your last day, I hear," she coos and lifts her hand as if expecting him to kiss it. "Old friends must say good-bye."

Viktor Nikolaevich motions her into his office, and she throws her head back as she walks in so that her hair flips away to expose gold hearts drooping from her ears.

Five minutes later she is back in the waiting room, looking utterly disappointed. I stand by the desk, pretending to be engrossed in a bunch of work orders, but out of the corner of my eye I see her wiggle her shoulders as if shaking off embarrassment. Then she glances at me and notices my dress. I keep shuffling paper, but by her expression, even from this skewed angle, I know she is furious. I know she knows that Viktor Nikolaevich is going to spend more time saying good-bye to me than he did to her. And that knowledge tingles in my throat like champagne as she tosses her head back again and clicks out on her skinny heels.

Champagne is opened at six. Viktor Nikolaevich, who has already had some earlier during his multiple absences, waves me into his office and shuts the door. From across his desk, he pours two glasses; we drink; he pours more.

"To you," I say, and he says the same. The wine fizzles down my throat into my empty stomach—I was too nervous to eat lunch, or maybe I didn't want to parade my black dress around the café—and makes me instantly drunk.

"Will you visit me in Prague?" he asks, and I giggle because it's a silly question. We both know that I can't go to Prague, or any other foreign capital, that the few people who go must have the right connections or belong to the top bureaucratic layer, like him.

"Send me a visa and I'll visit you anywhere," I say and giggle. "Anywhere abroad," I add prudently.

Viktor Nikolaevich moves from his side of the desk to mine. He sits down in a swivel chair across from me, reaches out and pulls me in, then wraps his big lips around mine, tongue and all, definitely too long for a good-bye kiss. I knew something like this was going to happen, so I act as though I'm used to being pulled into my boss's lap, especially since it feels like I'm flying. Or maybe it is he who is spinning, I can't tell, or maybe it's the chairs that are dancing around the room. His taste is now in my mouth, cognac and champagne, and his smell is all over my face—a smell of cologne, or maybe it's the perfume Maya the waitress wore when he said good-bye to her.

Then he stops spinning, lifts me off his knees, and gets up. "Nice dress," he says putting on his suit jacket. "Go get your things. We're going to my farewell party."

Obediently I get up and amble toward the door, puzzled that we are going somewhere else, that draining a bottle of champagne and smooching in his office did not qualify as a farewell. Things around me are no longer flying, and I'm able to take my coat off the hook in one swoop. I don't doubt that Viktor Nikolaevich knows a lot of places to hold a farewell party, but there is a dark thought thumping in my head like a brewing headache, a dizzy feeling of to-be-continued. After all, he is forty-five and I'm his eighteen-year-old secretary in a minidress drunk on champagne, a situation so tattered and predictable everyone knows how it usually ends. But I'm also the only one from the whole collective of the House of Friendship and Peace he's taking to his farewell party. He isn't taking the sophisticated Tatiana Vasilievna, who's mad about him, or the lanky pretty Olya, who manages the East German delegation, or any other woman who works here and whose clothes are not resewn from her older sister's. He's taking me, who isn't supposed to drink lemonade at a café after working hours and who is now, full of champagne, meandering toward his black Volga.

His chauffeur, Borya, a kind old man with a puffed-up face, waves at me and smiles as if I'd been riding in this Volga all the time instead of merely handing him envelopes to deliver to important addresses at the Smolny, the headquarters of the Leningrad

Communist Party. Inside the car it smells of gasoline and old leather, and I'm glad that Viktor Nikolaevich, when he ambles out, plops down into his usual seat in the front. As soon as he slams the door shut, Borya cranks the car into gear and we rattle off.

The car flies along dark streets as I crane my neck out the rolled-down window to try to determine where we're going. I feel thrilled to be in this luxury car with Viktor Nikolaevich, seduced by all this exclusivity and attention. I also feel mortified about what he may want from me and to which I will, undoubtedly, submit. We zip along, until the building of the Smolny Cathedral sails into view, its pearly cupolas glinting softly against the black sky. Next to it is the yellow building of Smolny, the Leningrad Communist Party itself.

"Go straight to the entrance," commands Viktor Nikolaevich. "Grisha's office is just down the hallway."

Grisha, he says, is his friend who calls him on the red phone.

The car bounces through the main gate and pulls around the circular driveway to the entrance. I can walk straight now, whipped by the cold wind of an April night. Borya and I get out, propelled by the broad waving gesture from our boss, to face the two soldiers standing guard at both sides of the door, holding guns as big as I remember my father's hunting gun to be when I was eight. Their eyes diligently stare into the distance, but when they see Viktor Nikolaevich, they silently step aside and let us in. We walk along a corridor that smells of fresh paint, toward one of the doors with golden signs on the front. Inside, a man in his forties sits behind the desk, his wide-jawed face gleaming in the light of a table lamp, his forearms laid on the leather top. When we creep in, the man takes off his glasses and leans his chest on the desk to help himself up.

"Vitya, come in, buddy, come in," he roars, stretching out his hand, heavily patting Viktor Nikolaevich on the shoulder. "He's abandoning us, imagine that." He turns to me, and I make a sad face, a quite genuine one because I wish he weren't going to

Prague and leaving me with a new director I haven't yet met, who probably won't sign a phony letter or tell jokes and make everyone laugh.

Grisha invites us to sit in armchairs as he produces a small key out of the top drawer of his desk. "Celebration time," he announces and walks toward a safe in the corner of the room, an intimidating-looking cabinet of steel, a perfect place for top official secrets. This is where they must keep dissident files and plans for nuclear attacks on the West. This is where Pasternak's *Doctor Zhivago* and all of Solzhenitsyn's works must be stacked up in neat, forbidden piles. Borya and I sit very quietly, with our eyes on the key and what it is about to reveal, silently marveling at our privileged and exclusive vantage point.

In a precise, frequently performed movement, Grisha clicks the key in the lock, and the heavy door noiselessly opens. Inside, in the empty iron murk, presides a round bottle of cognac surrounded by six shot glasses.

As Grisha starts to pour, Borya waves his arms in front of his face, telling him he is at the wheel, responsible for delivering us home.

"Have one," says Viktor Nikolaevich. "You must drink to me. And don't worry about the rest."

Borya stops waving. I'm sure he is dying to try the cognac in a bottle marked "highest quality" that we have never seen in stores, knowing that no militiaman would dare arrest anyone who has just been to Smolny and seen the contents of one of its safes.

I sip the honey-colored cognac much more carefully than the champagne a few hours earlier. It has a strong taste, but it doesn't have the odor of regular cognac, which, according to my mother, smells of bedbugs.

I wonder what my mother would say if she saw me drinking cognac with three men at the Leningrad headquarters of the Communist Party. I know she would frown at the men and the drinking part, but what would she think about the highest-quality cognac, hidden inside a party safe? Or about all those kilograms of beef, and the well-fitting suits, and the trips to Czechoslovakia that Viktor Nikolaevich and his friend Grisha have access to because they can enter the building of Smolny, the seat of the party of which my father had been a member longer than either one of them?

Grisha reminisces about old times. He tells a story of him and Viktor Nikolaevich going fishing when they were on assignment in the German Democratic Republic. They dug the worms and got into a rowboat and caught the biggest pike Grisha had ever seen.

"You can't catch a pike with a worm," Borya interferes. "You need a lure."

"Forget a worm, forget a lure," laughs Viktor Nikolaevich loudly. "We didn't catch any pike, you old cheat. I'll tell you what we caught if you don't remember."

I wonder how I am going to explain my late arrival at home. I am supposed to be in class, English phonetics and then the history seminar, the one I'll soon be out of because in my bag I have a letter to the dean signed by the director of the House of Friendship and Peace. I wonder if my boss's friend Grisha is powerful enough to exempt me altogether from the final in scientific communism next year.

Grisha pours another round of cognac. I shake my head and cover the glass with my palm.

Grisha and Viktor Nikolaevich drink, and then my boss gets up, indicating that the party is over. He embraces Grisha, then motions for Borya and me to follow him back to the car. Borya shakes Grisha's hand, and I smile and say good-bye.

"How do you feel?" asks Viktor Nikolaevich, swiveling to me from the front seat of his Volga.

I feel like throwing up. The empty stomach, the champagne, the "highest-quality" contents of the Smolny safe. The expectation that in a second or two or five Viktor Nikolaevich will take my hand and, this time, will not let it go. The gnawing feeling in my guts that I'll have to do something I don't want to do yet, certainly not with my departing boss. The muted, cobweb feeling of being empty of protest, something my mother must have felt when she made her monthly visits to the secret Ivanovo apartment.

Viktor Nikolaevich stares into my face with his directorial blue eyes, his face so close I can smell cognac on his breath. At this close range he looks completely unfamiliar. I realize how little I know about this man, although we've worked together for almost a year. I don't know, for example, how old his children are. I don't even know if he has any children.

"Borya will drive you home," he says. "I'm the first one on the route."

I nod, stick my head out the window, and let the wind scour my face.

A few minutes later, the car stops at the building where he lives, somewhere in the center. My boss, who is now my former boss, gets out, comes around, and leans into my window. "Remember me," he says and smiles with his big lips and gives me a real good-bye kiss, short and dry.

"I will," I say, and I know that he knows that I mean it. I'll remember him. I'll remember that he was funny and generous, that he protected me, that he didn't do what he could have done. And sometimes it is not doing things that edifies a Communist Party boss and gives him a little bit of soul.

Borya and I watch him saunter toward his door as drizzle falls onto the windshield and smudges his contours, as though he were already beginning to be erased from memory.

I feel old, as old as Borya. I feel I no longer want to work, at least not in the House of Friendship and Peace. I don't want to wait years for a promotion that will allow me to move chairs and arrange train tickets; I don't want to wait for Tatiana Vasilievna to retire, for Rita to take her place and abuse me the same way Tatiana Vasilievna abused her. I don't want to squeeze into a bus twice a day at dusk, at eight in the morning and at six at night, for twenty or thirty years, before I may be allowed to coordinate the entire English-speaking world.

# CHAPTER 15

# *White Night*

"THE PRESENT PERFECT TENSE is not really present," I say to my private student Svetlana, who is focusing on my mouth with such intensity that my ears begin to burn. "It is really past, but you feel its consequences in the present. Like what happens in life—you *have left* a good job, one that would have made you coordinator for all capitalist countries, and yet you still feel uncertain about whether you've done the right thing." I write the auxiliary *have* in her notebook followed by the past participle *left*. "Give me an example," I say.

"I have already read *Crime and Punishment*," says Svetlana eagerly, a seventeen-year-old with the pimply face of a diligent student who has most likely finished the curriculum-prescribed novel well ahead of her teacher's assignment schedule.

Svetlana tries very hard, pushed by her father, a senior engineer and a party member, who is embarrassed to use a private teacher not authorized by law. But he is also keen on his daughter passing a college entrance foreign language exam, so he *has hired* me (an example of present perfect: a past action with results in the present) and he is now "looking the other way." That was what he said when we met for the first lesson, "You were highly recommended, although this is a gray area. So I'm going to look the other way."

Instead of having lessons in an apartment, mine or Svetlana's, we meet in an empty university classroom, a condition set by her father. His face twitches when he hears the word "private" paired with "tutoring"—a little spasm that ripples through his cheek—and meeting on the university grounds legitimizes for him, if only in part, turning to the educational black market.

My friend Nina and I are recommended as private tutors through the university's elaborate network of word-of-mouth references and connections. We started tutoring at the end of our second year and are now referred to those in need of private lessons by our most prestigious English professors who, in their British-accented voices, describe us as "highly capable young girls."

Working three hours a day in the nonexistent private sector, we make more money than the head of our department. We make a lot of rubles, but the irony is that despite our "accumulation of wealth"—the plague of every capitalist country, as we know from our scientific communism textbook—there isn't much to spend our wealth on. The clothing stores are full of gray coats, the shoe stores overflow with black vinyl contraptions that mangle feet, and the cosmetic departments offer hand mirrors in red plastic frames and dry black mascara that cakes on eyelashes in toxic clumps.

The only exception is perfume. Not unlike our bakeries, which are somehow still able to produce excellent bread, our perfume factories have cracked the fragrance code, flooding the stores with whimsically shaped bottles of exquisite scents in silk-lined boxes that look like they should be lying on the counters in the Champs-Elysées. I try to imagine the Champs-Elysées, which is translated into Russian as Elysee Fields, but the image doesn't make sense. I see vast fields covered with grass, like the fields behind our dacha, with clumps of sorrel and a Gypsy bull tethered to a suspiciously flimsy stick. But how can such fields—with or without bulls or sorrel—also have the world's most decadent shops? I don't know the answer, but I am grateful to our chemists that a new, complicated fragrance called "White Night" is sloshing in its bottle at the bottom of my bag.

Every month I feel the uneasy presence of Svetlana's father in the fan of bank notes the girl awkwardly hands me at the end of the class, the same way I handed the money to my tutor Irina Petrovna when I was ten. The bright shreds of paper—red, blue, and purple—will provide me with a new bottle of perfume. I would rather buy a jar of mayonnaise or a pair of boots, but these hopes are as devoid of reality as my conversational English class at the university that teaches us how to book a hotel room for an impossible trip to London.

I bring my bottle of "White Night" to the next lesson with Svetlana. It is a beautiful bottle, a little trapezoid with a soaring glass neck that is meant to be touched to the delicate skin of elegant women. It evokes a lot of things we only know about from books: crinolines and curls and countesses' pale shoulders, fainting debutantes and their maids, decadence and turmoil, young noblemen brandishing swords to affirm their honor, reckless hussars in tight uniforms and mustaches, country estates with vast orchards as dense as forests, idleness and pleasure, an alley of oak trees with a bench in the laced shade of their leaves, a peasant boy with a secret letter, troikas and Gypsies with their guitars and flowing hair, churches with gold steeples piercing the winter sky, a messenger on horseback buried by a blizzard, a pack of borzois leaping across a meadow, duelists lowering their pistols, honor and duty, sophistication and grace, "private" and "privacy"—words that even Irina Petrovna didn't know, that are so alien to us that the Russian language of today does not codify them as linguistic entities.

I lift the glass top out of the "White Night" bottle and touch it to Svetlana's wrist, then to mine, so we can both pretend that we are elegant and worldly, that we belong in the previous century, that we know something about privacy.

I think of the film *War and Peace*, a four-part epic as grandiose as the novel, which filled our movie screens a few years earlier. That was the world into which the "White Night" perfume would fit perfectly, but Svetlana and I would not. In the lavish film version, for which a hefty part of our army had to be pulled out of their barracks, dressed in nineteenth-century uniforms, and ordered to march in front of cameras and smoke machines, there was no place for people like me, who eat borsch and *kotlety* out of the same plate, who wouldn't know what to say if a stranger—not a neighboring prince, but let's say a fellow university tutor —knocked on the door and introduced himself. I wouldn't have at my disposal any of those graceful empty phrases that effortlessly slipped from noble tongues. I come from peasant stock, and no prince or count from the long roster of Tolstoy's characters would have wasted his time looking in my direction.

My university friend Nina has deep aristocratic roots. I imagine her childhood passing in Chekhov's dachas behind white, gauzy curtains blowing in the summer breeze, her aunts teaching her how to use proper eating utensils, her grandmother instructing her in how to entertain guests and carry on a conversation, her mother reading poetry in French from an old leather-bound book, a family heirloom passed down from a great-grandmother who adored Verlaine.

I envy Nina's childhood with dark, seething envy. I wish my parents had come from nobility. I wish my dacha had white, gauzy curtains instead of peeling windowsills covered with dead flies; I wish we spent nights sitting around a table sheathed in crisp linen, not an oilcloth with a pattern of sunflowers smudged from wear; I wish we discussed etiquette instead of lugging buckets of water to the beds of tomatoes and dill. I wish my mother had been born in Leningrad, instead of being transplanted here middle-aged, too late to become one of its *intelligentsiya*.

Besides Nina, the only other person who wouldn't be banished from *War and Peace* is my aunt Mila. She is my mother's cousin once removed, so she isn't really my aunt, but whatever she is to me on the genealogical tree of our family, I look forward to her yearly visits in June, when she stays with us for about a month to partake of Leningrad's culture and its white nights.

Aunt Mila is about sixty and lives in Minsk, where the nights are black all year round. She wears elegant silky dresses, and she becomes serious and lifts her chin whenever she peers into a mirror, powdering her face with an old-fashioned puff that releases little white clouds of talc. Aunt Mila isn't married and lives in her brother's family apartment, in a room just big enough for her single bed. It might as well be a communal apartment, she says; the food she buys promptly disappears unless she takes it directly to her room and hides it. I've never lived in a communal apartment, but I know from friends and books about the motley world of cramped kitchens with four rickety stoves and a common washroom (if you're lucky enough to have a washroom) with a rusty bathtub marked by a stripe of grime, about neighbors spitting into each other's pots of soup and refrigerators towering next to beds because you can't risk leaving your food in the kitchen open to anyone's cravings. Aunt Mila doesn't have space for a refrigerator in her room, so she hides her food inside a nightstand. She doesn't like to talk about her life with her brother's family, about tiptoeing around and hiding food, so when my mother prods her for details or throws up her arms in indignation at her relatives' impudence, Aunt Mila changes the subject and talks about Pushkin.

"You can be a useful person and still think about the beauty of your nails," she recites from a poem that has never entered our school curriculum. I like Aunt Mila as much as I like Pushkin's wisdom. One can be as serious and accomplished as my mother and, at the same time, spend an hour teasing your thin, flat hair or applying a newly bought eye shadow, mixing the two available

colors so that you don't look like a corpse—all without feeling guilty that instead you should be weeding radishes or standing in line for milk.

But then it turns out that Pushkin, with his virtuous Tatiana, and Tolstoy, with his innocent Natasha, were not as righteous as our textbooks portray them to be, after all. Aunt Mila, who was a literary critic and a writer before she became eligible for a state pension at the age of fifty-five, tells me things you won't find in any textbook. Pushkin, who she says wouldn't let a woman pass by without conquering her, is responsible for writing not only *Eugene Onegin* but also a volume of poems so indecent they couldn't be printed anywhere, let alone a school textbook. Meanwhile, the official Pushkin, after excelling at an exclusive school thirty kilometers from Petersburg, went on, until he was shot in a duel at the age of thirty-seven, to become the paragon of literary virtue, busy revolutionizing Russian poetry and fighting against the tsar's oppression. Are they two different men, one a pillar of propriety who stares from a portrait, the other a debauchee and a rake? Is this new, shameless Pushkin the same poet who wrote the scene in which Tatiana says to her beloved Onegin that she has married another man and will be forever faithful to her husband? Aunt Mila shrugs and gives me a vague smile.

But she doesn't stop at Pushkin. She has stories to tell about half the classic authors who used to stare down from my literature classroom walls. The official, textbook Turgenev wrote about the moral conflict between personal happiness and duty and about *lishnie lyudi*, useless people. Like everyone else, I had to learn by heart the stories from his *Hunter's Notes*, descriptions of pale Russian birches and limpid smoke from peasants' huts that went on for pages of single-spaced print and could only have been written, as my teacher Nina Sergeevna insisted, by a true Russian writer with a deep connection to his motherland and its nature, by a man with a profoundly Russian soul. According to Aunt Mila, the real

Turgenev spent his whole adult life abroad, chasing a married opera singer across Europe, not giving a bit of thought to the fate of serfs, called *dushi*—the same word in Russian as "souls." My aunt's Turgenev had plenty of souls, all cowering out of sight in his estate back in the old country.

Aunt Mila loves white nights, and on the evenings when the usual Leningrad clouds are swept away toward Finland, we take a walk after my mother switches off the television and goes to bed. Aunt Mila cannot sleep anyway, she says, because even at midnight the light shines in her eyes, as bright as at midday. As we stroll past St. Isaac's Cathedral and the Admiralty, the sun melts into the roofs and disappears behind the Nevsky façades, only to rise again before she can even tell me all about Herzen. We are walking along Herzen Street, past the pedagogical institute that also bears his name. That Herzen, as everyone knows, subverted the tsarist government from Siberian exile while writing an endless memoir called *My Past and Thoughts*. He accomplished his historic destiny "to unleash revolutionary agitation" after the Decembrists' uprising of 1825 woke him up from aristocratic amnesia, a quote by Lenin we all had to memorize at the start of the eighth grade.

But Aunt Mila's Herzen, instead of unleashing revolutionary agitation, shuttles from Paris to London, first with his wife, Natasha, and then with his friend's wife, also named Natasha, having more and more children. We should feel sorry for Alexander Herzen, Aunt Mila says. He was an émigré, just like Turgenev and Bunin and all the rest, émigrés by choice or by decree. They all looked back, she adds with a sigh; they all missed Russia. Their souls (not to be confused with their serfs) were turned eastward.

I don't know why Aunt Mila, who has to hide food in a nightstand drawer in her own country, thinks that Russian émigrés were all miserable. Would I be miserable if I were forced to live in Paris or London? If, instead of lining up for bologna or cucumbers, I had to choose between something called an artichoke

and something called shrimp? If I could walk into a bookstore and find any book on its shelves—any book title one could dredge out of memory—even stories by Nabokov or poems by Mandelstam, even Pushkin's volume of shameless poetry?

But Aunt Mila isn't swayed by my questions. That's where the word "nostalgia" comes from, she insists. Looking back at your homeland. Looking back at those birch trees and peasant huts, commemorating them in stories that students in literature classes will have to learn by heart a century later. Looking back and remembering things that used to seem insignificant and small: a wisp of smoke curling from a chimney into the frosty sky, for example, or your mother's figure growing bigger on the dacha road until you find yourself burying your face in her soft belly under a polyester dress with a red apple print.

ALTHOUGH A PERMANENT JOB is still a condition for attending the university, I don't have to look for one. My friend Nina supplied us both with required papers falsely testifying that we had employment. Because of her family roots, Nina knows translators from the Union of Writers, one of the few Soviet organizations familiar with the word "private." Its members are officially allowed to employ private secretaries, and Nina, with the help of her mother, has located two members of the Writers' Union who agreed to produce the two phony letters.

With this arrangement, I can wake up late to sit in the kitchen with Aunt Mila, drink my mother's gray coffee, and talk about theater and books. In an elegant gesture—I'm not sure what makes it elegant, but it is the opposite of my mother's broad, authoritarian reach—Aunt Mila lifts a slice of bread out of the basket in the middle of the table and looks around, holding the bread between her fingers as if it were a brittle work of art.

"Galochka," she addresses my mother, who is pouring milk over her bowl of cottage cheese, "could I have a little plate?"

My mother, who doesn't understand why anyone would waste a plate for a dry slice of bread, stops by the cupboard and pulls out a saucer. I know what she is thinking: there will be one more dish to wash. She has a little frown curling her eyebrows, the same expression I see when every day Aunt Mila locks herself in the bathroom and lets the water run for what seems like an hour, at least to my mother.

"There is Mila again," she says, with reproach that makes her voice metallic and high, "splashing like a duck." My mother doesn't say this because she needs to use the occupied bathroom, but because Aunt Mila is doing something that my mother regards as decadent and unnecessary. Taking a bath every day, and now a plate for a slice of bread.

I am not sure I see the point of depositing bread on a separate plate either, when I can simply lean it against my cup, but if Aunt Mila is doing it, there must be one. She must have a whole stack of plates in her room in Minsk, I think, to hold all that food she keeps in her nightstand drawer.

When she doesn't talk about *War and Peace* or *Eugene Onegin*, she talks about fairy tales. She still does occasional work for the Minsk radio station overseeing children's programs; she has recorded stories about Tsarina the Frog and Ivan the Fool and only recently finished the tale about Emelya the Lazy Bones. As Aunt Mila praises the richness of Russian folklore, a question slithers into my mind and waits for Mila's melodious voice to pause. There is a whole brigade in our folktales of characters who are incapable, sick, ugly, dumb, hunchbacked, or otherwise challenged. Yet they are the ones who seem to get all the spoils at the end. A frog turns into a princess; Ivan the Fool snatches the Firebird; Emelya the Lazy Bones manages to show his brothers how to instantaneously harvest wheat—all without leaving his bed atop a Russian stove.

The question I have is this: Why is it always Ivan the Fool who gets the kingdom, and not the smart, learned princes or brave, sensible knights? Why—contrary to what is written in the Young Pioneer and Komsomol codes—is it always the lazy Emelya, not his hardworking brothers, who manages to catch the magic pike? I'm just about to open my mouth and ask Aunt Mila, but my mother enters the kitchen, a raincoat cinched around her hefty middle, to remind us that we shouldn't touch the *kotlety* she cooked last night and piled into a bowl on the refrigerator's lower shelf. "They're for dinner tomorrow," she says. "Today we must finish the macaroni in the red pot."

And though we've been eating the soggy macaroni for the last three days, and though Aunt Mila is a guest who, in my opinion, is worthy of the newly made meat *kotlety*, I don't say anything. This is how it has been in our house for as long as I can remember: you finish the old food first, even if in the meantime the freshly made *kotlety* grow stale. This is the way it is. This is the way we are here, with our unquestioned rules and ancient inertia as thick as Leningrad's swamps.

I think of my mother, the one in the portrait her brother painted before he died, wondering if that person with the ironic smile, my young mother, would have complained about a bread plate or insisted on finishing old macaroni first. Judging by her curled lips and the radiant eyes that give the portrait a strange incandescent glow, I don't think she would have. But what is it that wiped that smile off her face and dimmed the luster in her eyes? Was it the war, the wayward husbands, the two dead brothers? Or did it happen later, when my father got sick and needed a hospital and they refused to admit him? My mother knocked on the door of every party boss in Leningrad, until finally one issued an order to let him in for one week. A special *ukaz*, a personal decree for a special party member.

How resentful my mother must have felt on that summer day ten years ago, how powerless and humiliated. Yet she demanded and pressed and fought, in her usual way—the only way she'd learned to achieve anything in our country. "From a lousy sheep at least a wisp of wool," she said with a bitter smile when she told us the hospital story. So why is it that she still grows silent now, when Marina curses the Culture Ministry, which has closed another controversial play, or when I mock the absurd topics in our textbook called *English Conversation*? Why does she defend the party that has betrayed her?

I no longer feel like asking Aunt Mila about our fairy-tale characters. After all, I am no less lazy than Emelya the Lazy Bones. I pretend, like everyone else; I don't confront anyone with any questions. For keeping quiet, I collect my privately earned rubles and learn all I want about English. For finishing the old macaroni first, I get to eat real meat *kotlety* the next day. So when I hear my mother leave for work, the question about the dumb and lazy characters getting rewards for their stupidity and sloth freezes on my tongue and sinks back into my throat.

WHEN MY TUESDAY STUDENTS come for their lesson, Aunt Mila goes out for a walk. They are a married couple, Roman and Malvina, both doctors. Out of my six private students, they are the only ones who choose to come to my apartment, and that's because they are Jewish and are learning English in the hope that they will be allowed to emigrate. They cannot possibly have their twenty-nine-year-old daughter stumble onto our English lesson and discover that their minds are harboring such a subversive thought; if she does, they are afraid she may alert the authorities and report their desire to emigrate to their employers. A convulsion of panic twitches throughout Malvina's body when she mentions the possibility of being fired and disgraced even before they are allowed to file an application to leave. Her face trembles; her shoulders curl and tears surge to her eyes. Her husband covers her hand with his fleshy palm, her sigh the only display of their common despair.

Then Malvina shakes her head as though to shake off dark thoughts. Springs of her black hair quiver around her face; her slim body is once again erect in its defiance. In a blue dress and a silky bright scarf, she looks like an exotic bird that landed on a patch of dirt on its way to sunnier shores. Roman is big and language-deaf; his mouth does not want to contort to form alien sounds, and he lets Malvina speak for both of them. She memorizes vocabulary lists for herself and her husband, and he simply accepts it as another gift from her, laughing at his lack of language ability, the phlegmy laugh of a chain-smoker.

I teach them how to make a doctor's appointment, how to book a train ticket, one-way and round-trip, how to buy a coat and ask a preposterously polite salesperson from the chapter on shopping to show you to something called a fitting room to try it on. I teach them all I know, all I think they will need to know if they are fortunate enough to succeed. It's all pure chance from now on: they will be lucky if they don't lose their jobs; if the visa department accepts their applications; if their daughter, after she realizes that being related to traitors holds such advantages as being able to receive parcels from the West, signs away her objections to their leaving the country; and finally—what would be the greatest luck of all—if the visa department, after scrutinizing their papers and stripping them of Soviet citizenship, issues a permit allowing them to leave.

I wonder whether Malvina and her husband will miss this place with that intense nostalgia Aunt Mila insists was scratching inside the souls of our émigré literary classics. What will my students miss after they step out of the plane in an abstract foreign airport with the allowed forty kilograms of luggage comprising their entire life? After two years in lines in militia and visa offices, after they've been publicly humiliated and denounced here, will they miss anything at all? From the mystic avenues of the unfathomable West, will they ever look back at the worn gray pages of this silly conversation textbook in the middle of this table covered with oilcloth, at this milky evening light—the light Pushkin commemorated in verse—pouring through the open window? Will they ever look back at me?

# CHAPTER 16

# The Crimea

I AM TWENTY, A THIRD-YEAR university student, and my classmate Nina is still my best friend. She is tall and looks British, or what we think looks British: blonde springs of hair and glasses. Together we smoke Hungarian menthol cigarettes and make plans for the summer. We dare to fantasize about the faraway and nearly impossible, the pinnacle of every vacationer's dream. The word Crimea, Krym, sounds like "cream"—sumptuous, hedonistic, melting on my tongue, with a sweet aftertaste of decadence and longing. It is the opposite of everything we know: it has crumbling mountains, white sun, and a high sky stretching all the way to Turkey. It has vineyards producing champagne that never reaches our stores and trees called magnolias that we read about in Somerset Maugham novels. It is the opposite of Leningrad—a new world.

With the help of our classmate who works in the foreign tourism office and has powerful connections, we buy train tickets to Simferopol and, on August 1, step out of the train car—after two days clanging through the entire width of the country, north to south—into the dusty, soupy warmth of the Crimea.

I don't know how I expected this wonder, Krym, to turn out: maybe like the salty wind and brightly dressed crowd of Chekhov's "Lady with a Lapdog," or a row of tall fences cordoning off the high-ranking dachas, or the brown cliffs jutting into the sea I remember from an old painting on the wall of the Russian Museum.

The real Crimea smells of heated asphalt and warm apple juice just on the verge of turning. In the crowd of other passengers, we elbow past a kiosk with cone-shaped vats of fruit drinks and a counter crawling with wasps to get on a bus that will take us to the small town of Sudak, only seven kilometers away from our destination. We are headed for the village of Novy Svet, which literally means "new world." "Not too symbolic, is it?" says Nina.

The bus rumbles along a narrow road that snakes across fields of brown grass. The road climbs up, and gentle mountains begin to rise against the bleached sky. From Sudak, we walk on a path that wraps around the mountain with bushes and low pines clinging to the steep sides. We walk and walk, stooping under the weight of our backpacks, pushing forward through the hot air that smells like baked earth.

And then we see it. The road twists again and there is the sea, emerald and still, several hundred meters below.

"Look!" Nina yells as if I could've somehow missed it. I stop on the edge of a hairpin curve and stare, like a fool hypnotized by a charlatan, stupidly endangering my life. I blink several times, but the sea is still there, astonishing and real.

This staring feels exhausting; it empties me of words. I don't know how to react to blue-green water. The biggest body of water I've ever seen, the Gulf of Finland, is always gray. The Neva is sometimes zinc and sometimes charcoal. The lake near our dacha is muddy brown, the color of its clay bottom. All the water I've known is monochromatic, the colors you find in the sepia photographs of our family album. Water, like earth, does not have color.

Yet this is insanely bright, as bizarre as if the ground suddenly turned purple or the pine needles neon blue. It looks like a giant theater set stretched all the way to Turkey.

Now it feels impossible to walk another step. The sea is here, practically at our feet, so we take a downward footpath, barely visible in the covering of thin grass poking through yellow pine needles, and glide down, saved from a free fall only by the counterweight of our backpacks.

The path ends at the pebbly beach of a small cove hugged by cliffs. At the proximity of five meters, the width of the beach, the sea is different: it moves and makes sounds, lapping onto the rocks in lazy little waves. It is nothing but water, after all, salty and warm as soup.

I take off my sweaty shoes, wade in, and let the sea ripple around my ankles, the blue-green sea, refreshing and entirely mine. Or maybe not entirely: there is a group of young people sitting around a small camp stove, plucking black shells out of a pot, giving us sour looks as if we'd trespassed into their courtyard. They seem to occupy the part of the beach that's in the shade of brown cliffs, where backpacks and folded blankets lie in a pile, although there isn't much shade anywhere now, the sun pulsing with heat straight over our heads.

I wonder if those black shells they're plucking from the pot are *midiyi*—mussels—the exotic shell creatures northern people never see. I always fish for names of unknown foods in the few foreign-language translations that appear in our literary magazine *Inostrannaya Literatura*, stumbling over oysters in Françoise Sagan and a vegetable called asparagus in Iris Murdoch. But aside from their names, I don't know what they look like, let alone taste like. Is asparagus related to spinach if they're both dark green and both hiss with sibilant sounds? Even the word itself, "asparagus," sounds as decadent as "pineapple" and "quail" from a Mayakovsky poem, the two truly unsocialist foods eradicated in 1917 along with the tsar. How can oysters, whatever they are, be eaten raw? The Leningrad store called Okean does not provide much help. It is vast as an ocean, and just as forbidding, its glass display cases full of canned sardines in tomato sauce and smelts frozen into huge blocks of ice that saleswomen in white gowns shatter with crowbars on the wet, empty counters.

According to our plans, Nina and I were going to walk into the village and rent a room from a local babushka, a ruble a day, a cement-floored cell with two dusty mattresses, a communal outhouse, and chickens clucking in the owner's yard. But what we stumbled on in this cove has uncovered a new possibility: we could live on the beach, much closer to the sea than any babushka could fathom, breathing air scented with seaweed and pine, and use our rubles for more exciting ends. Besides, thanks to Nina's brother, who is partial to camping, we even have two small inflatable mattresses rolled up in our backpacks.

At about nine, when the sea and the cliffs and the pines that climb all the way to the paved road are instantly swallowed by heavy southern blackness, Nina and I lie still, listening to every rustle and every creak, petrified that someone from the group whose territory we've invaded will sneak up and dispose of us. Trying to peer into the night, I strain my eyes so hard that they finally close, and I don't even know when I fall asleep because the blackness on the outside of my eyelids is as thick as it is on the inside.

In the morning, the brightness is as intense as the dark of last night and, still alive, I plunge into the sea, letting my body float on cool, salty water. I stare into the thin-blue sky, water rippling around my eyes, green water with yellow sand underneath, which changes to gray pebbles as I turn my head, and then to brown cliffs and then back to thin-blue sky. Green water, transparent and sparkling, so inviting and so deep. I begin to understand why my provincial aunt Muza, who has been in the Crimea only once, has always reverentially spoken of it as the Sea.

The Sea is the heart here, and everything else, including the people, exists in relation to the Sea. The inhabitants of our adopted cove, young engineers from Kiev, are beach veterans: they've been coming here in August for the last three years, claiming this cove with their camp stove, their cans of meat and packets of dry soup, their blankets and guitars. They peel mussels off the rocks, rinse their tin bowls in sea water, lure crabs out of their crevices with crumbs of food, wade waist-deep and wash their hair with brown laundry soap, the only soap that lathers in this water. All day long they sit around in bathing suits, smoking and drinking, skin peeling off their noses and backs.

It takes a day for our camps to merge. It takes two more days for me to notice Boris, the oldest of the Kiev group, whose hair and eyebrows are so blond and bleached by the sun that they look almost white. Or rather it is Boris who notices me, and I simply notice him back.

"HE'S A DIFFERENT BLOOD group," says Nina. It's our turn for kitchen duty, and we're peeling potatoes and rinsing them in the gentle surf, talking about Boris.

I know exactly what this means, and I know she is right. A different blood group is someone who hasn't read Bulgakov's *Master and Margarita*, which was officially published two years ago, and who prefers a soccer match to a Tarkovsky film. All of our new Kiev friends seem to fall into this category, in which soccer takes precedence over avant-garde cinema. A different blood group is someone who thinks that Mikhail Baryshnikov, who has just defected to the West during one of the Kirov Theatre ballet tours, is a traitor and the enemy of the motherland. My sister, when she read the denouncing article in *Pravda*, said *molodets*—good for you. My mother said nothing. Nina said he should've done it earlier. The

Kiev engineers treat the topic with disapproving silence, staring at the green sea ripples or turning to more pressing issues, such as shaking sand and pebbles out of their bathing suits and towels.

But it is flattering that Boris dives deep into the sea to bring me conch shells and necks of two-thousand-year-old amphoras, which should sit in museums instead of the pockets of my backpack. It is flattering that it is I he takes snorkeling along the cliffs and not the curly-haired Natasha from his Kiev group, who chain-smokes, sighs, and pretends not to look in his direction.

The truth is that despite our differences, I'm drawn to Boris, to his blue eyes and steely arms and solid legs bristling with bleached-white hairs. He is six years older than I and very different from the mild-mannered Vitaly back in Leningrad, whose dissertation in psychology I agreed to type in April for sixty rubles. Vitaly pressed my hand between his clammy palms, awkwardly brought me roses, and spoke in the dim, careful voice of an inexperienced lecturer.

There is nothing careful about Boris's speech: words rattle out of his mouth, swift and definitive, sharpened by a trace of the Ukrainian pronunciation so alien to my northern ears.

In our conversation, we've somehow drifted to the Great Patriotic War, and Boris is adamant. He's talking about Kiev, which was occupied, unlike Leningrad.

"They walked there on their own will," he sputters, hitting a rock with the heel of his hand to accentuate his statement. He's telling us about Babi Yar, a ravine near Kiev, where Germans, with help from the local police, executed thirty-three thousand Jews. "They were ordered to walk and they walked, like sheep," he says. "All the way to their own graves."

Nina shakes her head and starts collecting the bowls. Her upbringing compels her to be wise and silent, not allowing her to show anger and condemn stupid statements that blame Kiev Jews for being shot and piled into a ravine.

Devoid of noble roots, I want to argue with Boris, to wipe this smirk of assurance from his lips, this arrogant flicker from his blue eyes. I want to tell him that what he is saying is as stale and wrong as the NKVD order that made my mother spy on her dissertation adviser or the sayings of my provincial uncle, who rants about Jews and their cowardice during the war. But I realize I don't know much about Babi Yar except what I read in the tenth-grade history book, two lines of official jargon denouncing the mass execution, not one word that the victims were all Jewish. I realize that Boris knows more than I do about our history, and although there is no doubt he is a different blood group, I don't know which is worse, his wrong conviction or my ignorance.

I am ignorant about a lot of things. I've never read all four volumes of *War and Peace*, for example. I leafed through the love scenes—pausing at infatuations, elopements, and breakups— but skipped all the battles. For my university exam in foreign literature, I never bothered to open Marlowe or Cervantes, instead regurgitating the professor's lectures about the impact of their works. All I know about the history of Russia—the real, pre-1917 history—comes from my high school textbook, in which the centuries of Russian monarchy are allotted less space than the fifty-eight years of Soviet power. I would never admit this to Nina, of course, or to anyone else, but the truth is I'm a dilettante. I pick up crumbs, never burdening myself with a whole.

ON THE MOUNTAIN ABOVE our cove there is a border patrol post, because on the other side of the Black Sea, a hundred kilometers away, lies a foreign country, Turkey. Due to this proximity, sleeping on the beach is against the law. When we look up, we sometimes see soldiers with German shepherds etched against the sky, as though they peer across the sea trying to decode the secrets of our capitalist neighbor.

It's evening, the sun just beginning to melt into the edge of the cliffs, and we are sitting around the camp stove, on which mussels boil in a pot with seawater, drinking local wine Boris brought from Sudak in a gallon-size gasoline canister. I see the silhouettes of two soldiers on the mountain, but this time they aren't standing still or milling around the post. They are beginning to walk down the mountain path. Maybe they've decided to take a trip to Sudak for a gallon of wine, too, but instead of getting smaller their figures grow, definitely approaching, so I nudge Boris, and now we're all staring at the two men in uniforms being pulled by their wolf-like dogs straight down to our cove.

We are all silent now, and even Yura stops strumming his guitar. Everyone remembers last Wednesday, when a boat coughed up to our beach at four in the morning, and two men with militia caps and a megaphone stepped out of the damp darkness, blinding us with flashlights. They demanded to see our internal passports, identifications we carry to get on a train. When we reluctantly pulled the documents out of our backpacks, they snatched them from our hands. I would've been petrified if Boris hadn't told me that the same thing had happened the previous year and the year before that. It must be an official ritual, he said. The militiamen shouted, pushed, and crunched around the beach, serious and self-important, as if our blankets strewn on the pebbles directly threatened the country's national security.

"How will we get our passports back?" Boris yelled.

"We'll talk tomorrow at the precinct," barked the man with the megaphone and kicked Boris's backpack.

The next day we all walked seven kilometers to Sudak and spent five hours sitting on the precinct's hallway floor waiting for our passports, which were released at six when the militiaman on duty had to go home. That was when we discovered the local wine, sold by the liter from milk cisterns.

So the first thought on everyone's mind now is that the militia has informed the border patrol to watch us through binoculars to make sure that we pack up and leave as we've been told. And now, seeing that instead of leaving we've taken to drinking wine from gasoline canisters, they have activated the military to evict us by force. Now they are coming for us with trained dogs and guns slung over their shoulders. We are lucky they aren't bringing tanks.

I try to imagine what this will do to Nina's and my standing at the philology department. We've been considered diligent and trustworthy, so responsible, in fact, that our senior English professor hinted recently about the possibility of our teaching at the University's summer Russian program for American students. It is the highest honor to be allowed to teach students from foreign countries, she said. Especially as foreign as the United States. And now, with the dogs clawing the dry earth of the slope, choking on their chains, the prospect seems as dim as the smoky horizon over the sea sloping toward Turkey.

The German shepherds pull; the soldiers yank them back. The dogs stop, sniff the air, and jerk in the direction of the pot on our camp stove, where the fat from a can of beef is just beginning to coat the freshly boiled potatoes. For a few minutes it looks like the soldiers are interested in the contents of the pot, too, because they trot after their dogs as if driven by a common purpose, their boots crunching the pebbles in unison.

"Don't hand anything over," Boris commands. "Say our passports are still in the militia precinct."

"Offer them some wine," says Nina. "It's a polite thing to do."

No one else, after the day spent walking all the way to Sudak and sitting on the militia precinct floors, thinks we should be polite with the law.

The soldiers stop and assess the situation: ten kids their age in bathing suits, swilling wine out of mugs; an empty can of stewed beef they haven't seen since they were twelve. It's just what they saw peering down into the cove, wine and meat; their binoculars didn't betray them.

"Join us," says Nina. "Would you like some wine?" she asks and rinses two mugs in the sea.

The soldiers, who look no older than nineteen or twenty, tell their dogs to lie down, and the shepherds, their noses sniffing the food smells out of the air, reluctantly obey. The soldiers wedge down into our circle, toasting with their filled mugs, and even Boris now has trouble believing they are here to arrest us.

Their names are Vitya and Serega. Vitya is bony and tall; Serega is as solid as if he'd been carved from the rock buttressing the side of this cove. They're both local, from Simferopol, where the train deposited Nina and me two weeks earlier, and they're fortunate they haven't been sent to Uzbekistan or Kamchatka for the two years of their draft. They've wanted to come visit earlier, but this is the first time their sergeant has taken off to get an order of new uniforms. "Look," says Vitya, bending his arm and pointing to his sharp elbow sticking out of his khaki shirt. "Yeah," confirms Serega, pulling off his boots to demonstrate their soles, worn down to holes. His feet are wrapped in *portyanki*, a square of fabric used instead of socks, which look and smell like they are in dire need of change, too.

They earn three rubles a month, the price of the rapidly emptying canister of wine that sits next to the camp stove.

We hand them bowls of potatoes and canned beef; we pour more wine. Yura tunes his guitar and sings Vladimir Vysotsky songs about war that everyone knows by heart. When darkness creeps behind us and pounces without warning, Vitya and Serega, full of wine and food for the first time since they were assigned here four months ago, trudge away, dogs following reluctantly, their chains dragging on the gravel behind them.

"Hey, you forgot your guns," yells Boris into their backs.

"That was a hell of a military force," says Nina. "I hope they don't attack us like that again."

We never find out if Vitya and Serega have received new uniforms. From now on, we only see them on top of the mountain, outlined against the sky, too far away to see the holes in their shirts or their boots, too far away to even wave hello.

IN RESPONSE TO MY postcard with a view of Novy Svet, my mother sends a letter to the local post office marked "general delivery." In my postcard I wrote: I'm all right here in the new world. Of course, I said nothing about Boris. It was shocking enough for my mother to find out I was living on a beach; I couldn't possibly say I was living on a beach with a man. Sex is a deep and shameful secret not meant to be discussed. In our books, printed by the state publishing house, Progress, a man and a woman may break steel-production records or risk their lives to protect a collective, but they'll never find themselves in the same bed. Western films are dubbed into a benign Russian version, racy scenes carved out. Sophia Loren and Marcello Mastroianni are allowed to kiss, but usually viewed from the back and only for two seconds.

My mother's anatomy charts of human reproductive systems, despite the unabashed names of their parts, fail to reveal a single crumb of insight into what makes sex such a dishonorable thing. Such a dark force that must be eviscerated from films and never mentioned in our books. "We don't have sex in the Soviet Union," said a stern woman from the Ministry of Culture in a recent TV interview, when a French reporter asked a provocative question about Lelouch's film *A Man and a Woman*, dubbed into Russian and recently released into our theaters. Is it possible that happy, shameless sex has been successfully eradicated by the Great October Socialist Revolution, along with social inequality and decent shoes?

I am not as ignorant about sex as I am about Babi Yar. In spite of my country's taboo and my mother's silence, or maybe because of it, I've taken the initiative to investigate the subject on my own. By the end of ninth grade, just before I turned sixteen, I had to know more. When my mother left for the provinces to visit Aunt Muza that April, my sister invited her actor friends to a party in our apartment. The actors brought wine, and I was drinking Riesling, sour and warm, out of a glass used only for special occasions. The sounds of the piano banged and warbled in the air, professional voices climbed the ladder of the scales, laughter floated on the clouds of smoke. The Riesling was making me happy and unafraid. I wiggled closer to big, dark-eyed Gennadii, who had recently made a film that was sending the girls in my class reaching for their handkerchiefs, and positioned myself on the divan next to his solid elbow. He poured me more wine; he suggested we go out to the stair landing for fresh air.

I leaned on the wall between the flights leading to the attic; I breathed in to keep my balance under his massive hands. His mouth, smelling of wine, clamped on mine; his tongue wrapped around my teeth. With my mouth plugged, I stood there estimating how long I could go without breathing while his fingers slipped under my bra. "Remember this," a silly thought raced through my mind as Gennadii was lowering his face to my breasts, "this is what men want."

His head shuttled between my face and my chest, smudging my skin, coating it with a drunken cigarette smell. Not knowing what to do with my hands, I wrapped them around his neck while he was turning my lips inside out in his mouth and squeezing me into the wall with his hips. Then he stopped, as abruptly as he started, and I stood there staring into his open shirt and a black clump of chest hair. I lowered my arms and pressed my wet palms into the wall. My lips felt bloated and chapped, my nipples chilled by air. He peeled my hand off the wall and, with a little guilty smile, led me down the stairs, back into the drunken noise of our apartment.

In my first year at the university, when Nina and I had a discussion about sex, I told her about Gennadii and the stair landing and why it felt like an epiphany. "My head was spinning," I said, failing to mention the Riesling. "He was twenty years older than me and he smelled of tobacco, even his chest hair, even the shirt he was wearing." Nina squinted through our own cigarette smoke and blew out a small menthol cloud. "You're looking for your father," she said and peered at me from above her glasses, a glance that seemed a bit too intimidating to warrant a response.

Was I looking for my father the following year, when my quest took me a step further, for a dose of real sex? *Seks*, blunt and sibilant, so rarely used in public that it sounds like a curse. In our tenth-grade history book—the only place I ever saw the word in print—it was listed among the ugly characteristics of bourgeois society, next to violence and unemployment. I insinuated myself into the bed of a charismatic theater director who ran the university amateur acting studio, by saying that I was lost and needed his direction. Afterward, I peered at myself in a mirror, trying to discern a significant change, a sign of instant maturation and wisdom, manifested by what? There was not a centimeter of difference that I could see, not a wrinkle of a metamorphosis that would brand me an adult, worthy of a place among the ranks of the enlightened and the experienced. It wasn't ugly, as the textbook had warned, but it didn't transport me into a higher realm of being or thinking. The only thing it seemed to have accomplished was to make me more cynical: this sordid, heavily-guarded secret amounted, in effect, to not much more than a few minutes of awkwardness. With lights off, the director's charisma had dimmed, too. Despite all its promised tantalizing danger, sex was nothing out of the ordinary.

Not at all like making love to Boris, which makes me forget his Ukrainian accent and his rantings about the war and Babi Yar. He has a splendid cinnamon tan, and in the dusk I see his body as if through the green prism of water, shimmering along the rocks when he hunts for crabs. It is simple to be with Boris, as uncomplicated as elbowing in line for tomatoes at a local store, as basic as living on the beach. Yet I still feel guilty whenever he rolls up a blanket and we climb into the mountains. This is what sex has become associated with in my mind—a deep sense of shame. Something performed illicitly and in the dark.

Still I could've been partially honest in my postcard sent home and said I had a crush on a guy from Kiev. But I didn't. I'd never admit to such an emotional weakness as falling in love. She's in love, my mother would whisper with an understanding sigh that conveys her pity. She'd feel sorry for me, or worry about me, or give me advice I didn't want. Back in Leningrad, if I feel like seeing Boris, I'll simply buy a ticket for Kiev and tell my mother I'm going to visit some friends. Instead of talking about Boris, or infatuations, or love, we'll talk about the price of a railway fare and the availability of linens on the train.

My sister is not afraid to announce she is in love. When she went on a theater tour last summer, she wrote us a letter every two days pining for the son of the artistic director. All it caused was my mother's injured whispering to a neighbor, her sad tirades that the director's son would never marry Marina because she is too old or because she is an actress, her sighing and lamenting that Marina should have applied to medical school. Yet precisely because she is an actress, my sister doesn't care that she is baring herself to the ears of the entire floor of our apartment building. She is bold; she's above the gossip; she is not afraid. Me? I'd rather die than give my mother the advantage of sighing and pitying me. In my grandmother's words, what's inside you no one can touch.

In her letter, my mother says that her brother, my uncle Vova, who wasn't killed during the war and now lives in the town of Ryazan, is vacationing only five kilometers from where I am, in a House of Rest and Recreation, where he was sent because he is a war veteran. Maybe I can arrange to see him, she says, giving me his Crimean phone number.

I don't mind seeing Uncle Vova. I mostly know him from letters and birthday cards with the poems he likes to compose. They're amateurish poems, but there is a powerful line now and then, a line that sinks deep and rakes up something I've been thinking. So I don't dismiss his poems as I do my aunt Muza's, who rhymes any two words that float into her head and then mails them to us on glossy cards embossed with roses.

Also, I wouldn't mind getting away from our beach for a day. Even the sea, salty and warm and green, can become monotonous if that's all you see for four weeks.

I call my uncle and we meet at a bus stop in the village where he's living, the biggest landmark we can think of. I bring a bottle of champagne made in Novy Svet, at one of the only two champagne-producing vineyards in the country. It's real vintage champagne, made exclusively for export, with a complicated yellow label I've never seen before, not the usual champagne called Sovetskoye, which is cooked under pressure for four months before it is released into the stores. The export-quality champagne was procured from a truck driver Nina and I flagged down because we needed gasoline for our camp stove, a generous driver who siphoned five liters of state gas for us and whom we invited down to the beach for mussels and wine.

Uncle Vova stands on the dusty shoulder of the road, smiling. His smile is a little crooked: the right corner of his mouth seems suspended by an invisible thread, surrounded by scarred, almost white skin, the result of a burn. I've always assumed that the burned skin was a Great Patriotic War trophy and imagined him climbing out of a burning tank or tossing grenades into battalions of advancing Germans. But last year I found out he'd burned his face in a school accident in chemistry class when he was eleven. He was miserable in the hospital, my mother said, wailing in pain whenever they changed the dressing because the bandages kept sticking to the wound, tearing off pieces of burned skin along with the fabric. Then an innovative surgeon came up with the idea to have my grandmother buy bars of chocolate, no matter how expensive or difficult it was to get. After Vova ate the chocolate, the surgeon sterilized the silver foil it was wrapped in and used it instead of bandages for dressing. The skin didn't stick to the foil; the taste of the chocolate was exquisite because it was rare, and Vova recovered in record time.

"Black as a Negro," says my uncle, looking me over with his twisted smile.

"We live on the beach," I say. "We're all black."

"Boys and girls together?" he asks, squinting and pretending to make a serious face.

I like my uncle. Instead of sighing and worrying about my living on the beach with boys, as my mother would do, he winks and asks me about the bottle of champagne I'm carrying. When I tell him the truck driver story, his eyes glimmer with respect and a flicker of admiration at my ingenuity and my guts. Nina and I stood on the road in bathing suits, trying to look helpless, an empty canister for gas hidden in the underbrush.

The truth is that normally I don't have any guts. Back in Leningrad, it makes me cringe to attract the smallest bit of attention to myself, but here, in this new world of Novy Svet, I am fearless, as if it's not even me, as if the sun had branded me with a new identity. Here I can be outrageous and carefree. I sit cross-legged in the warm dust of a road shoulder with a cigarette, attracting punishing glances from passing mothers with teenage daughters in tow. I crawl under rows of vines at a local collective farm, plucking down bunches of grapes. The other day Nina and I climbed onto the biggest rock hanging over our cove and recited Hamlet's soliloquy in English in front of the whole Kiev group, in front of the whole Black Sea, which by that time of night was literally black. Granted, we'd been drinking mugfuls of wine, but I can't imagine reciting anything, in Russian or English, in front of my friends back home, even if it were pitch black outside, even if they'd asked.

"So what do you say if we drink to our meeting?" offers my uncle. To my new, fearless self, drinking on a bench sounds thrilling. As he's already complained to me, the House of Rest and Recreation doesn't allow alcohol on the premises. If I'd wanted a sanatorium, he says, I'd have stayed home with my wife.

We find a bench under a strange gnarled tree that doesn't grow in the north. Uncle Vova pops the champagne open, and we take turns sipping from the bottle. The warm bubbles back up my nose and make me hiccup; to my chagrin, I cannot tell the difference between this export-quality rarity and the Sovetskoye champagne we buy for the New Year's holiday. But my uncle seems pleased, and the other side of his mouth, the unburned side, curls up, too.

We sit in the shade of the strange tree and talk about the Crimea. I tell him about a militia raid, and wine squirting out of vending machines, and seawater fluorescing at night. He tells me that the House of Rest and Recreation has a ten o'clock curfew. Then we walk to where he's staying, a cement building with uniform institutional blinds. In front of it, there are small trees planted in rows, just a hundred meters from the sea. "It's dinnertime soon," he says. "Let's go up to my room and I'll try to sneak in some food from the cafeteria."

The room is small and functional, but what I see through an open door strikes me as almost surreal: in the halo of white tile gleams a bathroom. For four weeks I've washed in the sea, rubbing my hair with a bar of laundry soap, trying to make it lather in the salty water. My uncle's bathroom, with its luxuries of white porcelain and chrome, could have floated directly from the pages of the Western magazines our customs officials routinely confiscate at the border.

"Pretty pathetic, eh?" comments Uncle Vova, watching me freeze on the bathroom threshold. "From a place for war veterans you'd expect something more modern." I truly don't know what he means. The tiles sparkle and blind me; the water gurgles out of the spout, abundant fresh water that makes soap bubble and blaze with every color of the rainbow. I unleash more water—from a bathtub faucet, from a showerhead—and it rushes out in cascades of silver, splendid water without color or taste.

Uncle Vova smiles and closes the door. Water splatters onto my skin, which has become as dark and dense as a hide, so dark that my fingernails glow like pale lights, that I can see a border between the suntanned skin of my instep and my white sole. I soap my hair into a heap of lather; I lie in the tub rubbing my skin free of the four weeks of salt. When I finally stick my head out the door, my uncle says he has to go down to the cafeteria if he doesn't want to miss dinner. "I'll steal something good for you," he promises.

I feel so clean I'm weightless. I glide around the room, around another surreal entity, a bed with sheets. I'll just try what it feels like, I think, the feeling of white cotton against the skin, but the next thing I hear is Uncle Vova's voice telling me I'm missing some great *kotlety* with mushroom sauce he's hidden in a towel. "You've been sleeping for two hours," he laughs. "Don't you have time to sleep on the beach?"

I see a plate covered with newspaper as he unwraps a towel, but my head doesn't want to part with the pillow and my arms seem glued to the sheets.

He takes away the newspaper, revealing two perfect *kotlety* under the blanket of brown sauce, definitely not extracted from a can, that seem as delicious and unreal as a mirage.

He watches me chew with his crooked half-smile, not lamenting that I am not sleeping in a real bed or eating properly, not accusing my friend Nina of dragging me down to the Crimea to live exposed to the elements like a homeless *bomzh*, not asking about Boris or if there is a Boris. And even if he asked, I bet he could keep a secret. After all, he was the one who performed an abortion on my mother when she was between husbands and when abortion was illegal. I know this because in a drawer of my mother's desk I found a blue notebook, its pages covered with her square handwriting, detailing her life before she moved to Leningrad. She must have written it for posterity, and that meant for me. So I read it. And even then, at fifteen, I found it ironic that out of the three siblings in her family who survived the war, my mother, so much in love with order and the proper way of doing things—far more than Uncle Vova or even Aunt Muza—is the only one who has had three marriages, three hasty unions, of which none seemed perfect or even good.

I know this is the last time I will see Uncle Vova like this, just me and him, with no family bustling around to tell us not to swill champagne out of a bottle or not to steal food from the cafeteria or not to do something else disorderly, whatever it is.

We give each other a tight hug and stay in each other's arms for a minute, both cherishing the moment, both knowing it won't happen again. I'm grateful to Uncle Vova for being twisted-lipped and incurious, for not asking and not pitying. I'm grateful for the stolen *kotlety* in mushroom sauce.

I get back to the cove when it's dark and the mattresses are already scattered in their night positions on the beach. It looks tranquil and safe, like a Pioneer summer camp, where days are predictable and easy. Maybe my mother is right, after all, and life under the open sky does have its perils. Sameness, for instance— the sum of perfect weather and the perfect songs Yura keeps strumming on his guitar. Uncensored sex, for instance—with no one to ban or even diminish it with a slant-eyed look, robbing it of tension, smudging it with the dust of the ordinary.

I take off my shoes and wade into the dark water. When I wiggle my toes, grapes of fluorescing bubbles bunch around my feet, making the water glow from within. This happens only in August,

Boris says, the result of sea plankton that floats close to the shore. Around me, the outlines of rocks are slowly dissolving in the dark, and the top of the white moon, like the heel of a loaf of bread, looms above them. Everyone is about to go to sleep in Novy Svet, the new world that suddenly feels so old.

# CHAPTER 17

# Facilitator of Acquisition

Y OU AND YOUR FRIEND Nina can celebrate," whispers
my English professor, Natalia Borisovna, into my ear.
"The head of the department and the leader of our local party
cell have approved your candidacies. You're starting next week."
She wraps her arm around my shoulder to indicate her approval:
I am considered mature enough to teach Russian in the six-week
summer program for American students. I don't know why she
has to whisper; maybe it must be kept secret that there are live
Americans wandering around the university premises in such close
proximity to Soviet citizens.

Nina and I have just graduated from the English department of
Leningrad University. As soon as Natalia Borisovna releases her
hold on my shoulder, I rush across town to tell Nina the good news,
and we celebrate in her kitchen with menthol cigarettes, pondering
through the clouds of smoke how brilliantly we are going to lure
our capitalist students into the world of Russian language and
literature.

At home, I don't feel so cavalier. Aside from a freshman class
I was assigned to teach in my senior, sixth, year, I've never stood
in front of a group of students. Especially foreign students, who

are probably used to teaching methods that are uncommon and advanced, like everything else in America. We get reports from emigrants—stories that reach us through a complicated chain of connections—that in America you can buy mushrooms in March and strawberries in December; that there is never a shortage of books—any books; that a police officer who stopped one such emigrant for speeding asked him to step out of the car because he didn't want to humiliate him in front of his ten-year-old son. The last story seems so unbelievable and maudlin it makes me snicker. What kind of government worries about hurting the feelings of its citizens, especially children? Everyone knows that a government is supposed to govern, not sympathize, as Lenin pointed out in 1918. Ours is busy enforcing residency regulations that ban us from moving, and issuing refusals to emigration petitions, which guarantee that applicants will be kicked out of their jobs and then publicly humiliated. If our feelings aren't bruised, we instantly become suspicious.

I realize I know so little about America it's embarrassing. I've never seen an American newspaper or magazine; decreed subversive and dangerous, they are all confiscated at the border. The only American English I've heard was an interview with Angela Davis, the head of the Communist Party of the United States, whom I could barely understand because she rolled her *r*'s in a way our phonetics professor called "utterly un-British."

I haven't read anything besides what we all read in class— Hemingway's *A Farewell to Arms* (an anti-war declaration) and Steinbeck's *Of Mice and Men* (an exposé of capitalist ulcers). The rest of the books, the ones that don't denounce or expose, trickle in at unpredictable intervals, like deliveries of mayonnaise or imported shoes to local stores. Recently one of our professors snuck in a contemporary novel called *The Other Side of Midnight* from her recent trip to England, and I'm now in line to read it behind all the full-time faculty of the English department. I've estimated that at the present rate it should reach me in about four weeks since the first person in line read the book in two days.

And I've never seen a live American.

CLASSES START IN THE middle of June. I teach three times a week, from 9:00 to 11:50 A.M., grammar and conversation. I've prepared myself for the nauseating feeling of first-day trepidation, a familiar gut jiggle we all know from annual school visits to the dental clinic or from quiet struggles with school authorities who try to arm-twist good students into serving as local Komsomol, or Young Communist, leaders. Yet, surprisingly, I don't tremble inside when I walk through the door of my first class and face fourteen Americans, staring at me with the same intense curiosity with which I stare back at them. My Russian is by far superior to theirs, and since this is an immersion program and we can't use any English during class, I will always have the upper hand, at least linguistically.

As we go through the introductions, I look into their faces, not as foreign as their accents. Lisa from Vermont, blonde and broad-boned, could have come here on a weekend bus tour from Finland; Charles from Virginia, in round spectacles and pimples, looks as if he belongs in the advanced math and physics school, # 239, two blocks from where I live. They look familiar—Steven, Mary, Tony, who immediately become Stepan, Masha, and Anton—yet their otherness is exposed by their open glances, their straight backs, their eagerness to speak our convoluted language, full of conjugations, noun cases, verb aspects, and palatalized consonants that no foreigner can master. They are uninhibited and unafraid. They are earnest and straightforward. They are the opposite of me.

They are from good universities—Dartmouth, Columbia, Duke. I've never heard of any of those schools, but I nod as though I have. This is also a good university, I say, looking around. I don't know if it's true—I have no references, no comparison lists, no guides—but I sound as though I do. They nod vigorously, *da, da*, a very good school. Only the dorm is somewhat *antikvarny*, they say. No, I correct them in a teacher's tone—*staryi*—old, not antique.

They laugh. Of course, not antique, far from antique. What I don't tell them is that it's not even old. It was built five years ago, when I was just starting at the university and passing the building four days a week on the way to school. The rickety scaffolding creaked in the wind, and the workers in quilted *vatnik* jackets and *ushanka* hats staggered around, half-drunk, taking with them at the end of the day everything they could carry—doorknobs, faucets, nails. It was a normal construction site, and the dorm is a normal new building—instantly old and as shoddy as everything else.

The Americans are diligent students. They do their homework and ask questions. During breaks they struggle with case endings to tell me what they saw the previous afternoon after class. The Hermitage and Peterhoff fountains. The cruiser *Aurora*, permanently anchored on the Neva bend not far from their dorm, which signaled the storming of the Winter Palace with one blank cannon shot. Lenin's hiding place in the Leningrad suburb of Razliv, a straw tent with the leader's cap and boots displayed on top of a tree stump. "Only they weren't even his original cap and boots," says Anton in an acerbic voice. Copies, the sign says; originals safe-guarded in the Kremlin. "Safe-guarded?" asks Anton, with amused disdain. "Cap and boots in a Kremlin safe?" "They're afraid someone may steal them," I offer, "some *kapitalisty* like you." They laugh, thinking it's a joke. I meant it as a joke, yet—although I've never been to Razliv, having somehow dodged every school trip that would herd us there—I know this is the reason Lenin's cap and boots in his straw tent are reproductions. Capitalists, as we all know, are enemies not to be trusted, who won't hesitate to stoop to such a lowly thing as pilfering Lenin's real belongings and selling them on the market to the highest bidder.

They tell me about the food at the university cafeteria. *Uzhasnaya*, they complain—awful. As an instructor for the American program, I have a pass to the cafeteria. It's really a faculty cafeteria, but the visiting American students have a meal plan there so they won't be instantly poisoned. When I eat at the cafeteria, I can't help but linger by the desserts enthroned seductively under glass: squares of cake with roses of butter frosting, flaky puffs covered with chocolate, mountains of whipped cream I've never seen anywhere else. I gawk at the stuffed cabbage, whose ingredients include meat, at the carrot salad studded with raisins. For one ruble, I load my tray with delicacies and wolf them down at a corner table, away from other people's eyes. For some reason I feel as if I were here illegally, undeserving of all this hard-to-get food my American students mock.

On Fridays, Nina and I and all the teachers go to the main auditorium to hear lectures on Russian history and literature given to the American students by our best university professors. It isn't that we're so eager to be enlightened about the Decembrists' uprising of 1825 or Lermontov's "useless people." After the lecture, the head of the program, an elegant young woman who is rumored to be married to a KGB colonel, unveils a table with an electric samovar and a pile of big poppy seed bagels called *bubliki*, and, along with our students, we drink tea out of traditional glasses propped in metal holders. The real reason we come here is to hear and speak English.

The English we hear is more robust, more dauntless than the British voices on our language-lab tapes. These vowels split jaws; these consonants clatter. My students don't hesitate now, trying to remember a word or think of a correct noun ending. They are fast and at ease. Navigating their own language puts them in control.

The students from my class have crowded around the samovar and are taking turns swiveling the handle that releases boiling water into a glass.

"You look a little like Natalie Wood," says Charles from Virginia, biting into a *bublik*.

I don't know who Natalie Wood is, but I wrinkle my forehead, not quite sure if I heard the name correctly. "Natalie Wood?" I ask and squint my eyes. She is probably someone everyone knows but me.

"An actress. In movies, you know," says Charles. "Her parents were Russian, you know."

I don't know. But should I know? Should I be happy that he compared me to an actress with immigrant parents?

I smile and nod. "My sister is an actress, you know," I say, trying to carry on this conversation.

Charles utters something in response and I pretend I understand it. I pretend I'm happy.

Then I notice the program director, the one with the KGB husband, giving me sharp looks, and I wonder if I'm pretending too zealously, if she might think that I'm really feeling happy among these students, whom we are glad to introduce to our language and culture but who will always, no matter how innocent they may sound, remain our ideological opponents in the world struggle for mankind's bright future.

I decide to change position and move to where Nina is standing with two of her students, looking just as happy as I must look to the program director. Cynthia and Robert from her class are older, both graduate students in schools whose names come rattling from their mouths, indecipherable, like a good part of what they say.

"Robert is a writer," says Cynthia. "Science fiction. He just had a book published," she boasts, as if it was she who had published a book. "And it's a good one."

Robert rubs his forehead and smiles a crooked smile, half timid, half haughty. His eyes squint through thick glasses, and his hand rakes his hair, so curly his fingers get tangled.

"Robert Ackerman," says Cynthia. "Remember this name," she mocks, wagging her finger.

Robert smiles and rolls his eyes, chagrined but flattered. I also smile, but not too eagerly, because the program director is again looking in my direction.

THE FOLLOWING WEEK, AFTER my class, when I walk out of the building nicknamed "Catacombs" into the drizzly grayness of the university yard, I find Robert leaning against a tree, waiting.

"Nina told me this is where you're teaching," he says, his hands in the pockets of his corduroys, his hair like tiny corkscrews standing on end around his narrow face. Visually he clashes with everything around him—with the birch trunk he is leaning against, with the feeble pansies by his feet, with the cracked and flaking walls behind him—looking utterly un-Russian, looking as if he'd fallen from space. I glance around to make sure the program director isn't anywhere near to witness this unsanctioned, after-class contact with a foreigner.

We walk out of the courtyard through the main building, past the marble staircase and the huge mirror where Nina and I used to meet before classes, into the gray expanse of the Neva Embankment. The clouds are so low that they have swallowed the top of the Admiralty's spire on the other side of the river; the end of the gold needle looks as if it's been broken off.

"It's so damp," Robert says. "Like being under water."

"It's normal," I say. "It's the river, the sea, the swamp, you know." I'm proud of myself for using that American colloquial "you know," which I learned from my student Charles. I feel remarkably nonchalant walking past the university with such a foreign-looking man—both American and Jewish, both unwelcome here—whose otherness announces itself in his long, corkscrew hair and well-fitted corduroys and leather shoes that don't seem to maim his feet. Who, in addition to all these improbabilities, is also the author of a published book.

We slowly walk along the embankment, looking down at the slabs of granite under our feet, not knowing what to say.

"So what do you do when you don't teach Americans how to speak Russian?" Robert asks in his restless American English after a few minutes of silence.

I'm not sure if this is a question about my official life or my private life. Is he asking what I do at the university or what I do at home, what I say to my English professor or what I say to Nina? Which me is he interested in, the proper university teacher and Komsomol member or the real, smirking, cynical person I am with my friends?

"I teach English," I say. "Grammar, reading, conversation. We read Galsworthy's *Forsyte Saga*. Volume One, The Man of Property."

Robert chuckles and scratches the back of his neck. "Isn't it boring as hell?" he asks.

"It reveals the ulcers of capitalism," I say.

He peers at me through his thick glasses to see if I'm serious, to see if it's time for him to remember that he's left a kettle boiling over back in his dorm or some other thing that will require his immediate attention.

"It's boring as hell, you're right," I say and give him a smile. It's not that difficult to choose between the two people inside me. With a Jewish-American writer who has chosen to wait for me, out of all the university women prancing around him with samovars and *bubliki*, I am going to be the real me.

"And what do you do when you don't write science fiction?" I ask.

"I'm a physicist," Robert says.

A physicist, I quickly repeat in my mind, not to be confused with a physician, one of my first lessons from a translation class. Not a physician, as my mother was during the war, a kilometer from the German front.

"Nuclear and astrophysics," explains Robert. "The expansion of the universe, the theory of relativity, black holes. I'm finishing my dissertation at the University of Texas."

I know nothing about physics. In high school, it was the only subject in which I received a final four instead of a perfect five, the four that prevented me from getting a high school diploma bound in red plastic instead of black.

"I also play the oboe," says Robert, trying to soften the hard edges of science with music, probably thinking he's intimidated me with his physics credentials because I don't say anything. Indeed, I am intimidated; I know as little about music as I do about astrophysics.

"And why are you here?" I ask. "Taking Russian classes in Leningrad?"

Robert stops at the granite stairs leading to the water, to the small leaden waves that slurp onto the wet stone, and stares across the river at the gold cupola of St. Isaac's Cathedral. Even in this damp light it radiates a shine that lifts the clouds off its surface, a little halo of insulation against the rain hanging in the air.

"They covered it with gray during the siege of Leningrad," I say. "To make it look like everything else."

Robert focuses on the cathedral as if snapping a mental photograph, then turns to me. "I like the Russian language," he says. "I want to read Russian writers in the original. That's why I'm here."

Now I'm truly awed. I feel undeserving to be standing next to this brilliant American man who solves the problems of the universe during the day and then goes home to play the oboe and sweat over *Crime and Punishment* in Russian.

"Lenin-grad," says Robert. "Doesn't *grad* mean city?"

"Yes, the city of Lenin," I say.

"But the form 'Lenin' is also the possessive of 'Lena,' isn't it? 'Lena's' in Russian is *Lenin*, right? So Leningrad literally means 'Lena's city.' " Robert looks pleased, as if he's just solved a stubborn celestial equation. "This is your city," he says and raises his arm as if bestowing the honor upon my head.

This never occurred to me, but Robert is right. He is even more right than he knows. Lenin's real name is Ulyanov. Lenin is a pseudonym our legendary leader assumed to fool the tsar's police when he was secretly shuttling between Russia and Finland to stir up the working masses in preparation for the revolution, and he chose it from the name of the great Siberian river Lena. So Lenin does literally mean Lena's. Leningrad is literally my city.

ROBERT WAITS FOR ME every day I teach, three times a week, and we walk around the city's center, looking at places he won't find in his tour guide—real places, too ordinary to be included among the glossy snapshots of bronze statues and golden domes. We walk away from the baroque luxury of the Winter Palace to the part of the Neva where necks of construction cranes hang over the water, along the cracked asphalt side streets where crumbling arches lead into mazes of courtyards.

Robert is fascinated with courtyards. He's read Dostoyevsky, and he wants to see those courtyard wells that depress the spirit and twist the soul into a truly Russian miserable knot. As far as I can see, a hundred years have changed nothing in terms of courtyards' contribution to misery, so I delight Robert in stepping with him through the vaulted archways to gawk at aluminum garbage bins that spill rotting potato peels and chicken bones, at broken walls bristling with wires, at piles of rusted sheets of metal brought in at some point for a renovation that never happened.

Robert tells me about Austin, Texas, where he studies, and Trenton, New Jersey, where he lives, the two places fused in my mind, foreign and unintelligible, two black holes in his puzzling universe. He tells me about the films he's seen, the people he's met, the things he's bought, but he might as well be talking about nuclear physics. I don't know what "special effects" or "star wars" mean; I have no idea who "teaching assistants" are; and I have never heard the word "parka." But I nod, pretending I understand, pretending I am sophisticated and worldly. I am a professional at the game of pretense; I've perfected my skills over years of practice. Robert doesn't suspect a thing.

In the beginning of the last week of classes I take him to my courtyard. It is better than many, with a playground in the center—a sandbox and a tall slide made of splintery wood down which I used to glide during nursery school winters. The same ankle-deep puddle in the middle of the yard gleams with a rainbow film of gasoline; "Zoika's a bitch" is scratched into the wall next to the padlocked door where the scary garbageman of my childhood used to shovel the refuse thrown down the chutes.

The chutes are now padlocked, too, and Zoika, who was indeed a bitch ten years earlier, has left her mother to live somewhere on the other side of the Ural Mountains.

"Would you like to see my apartment?" I ask Robert. It's probably against the rules of the department for a teacher to take a capitalist student home, even if a student is from someone else's class. A home visit must normally be set up and approved by the director or, more likely, the director's KGB husband, but we are here already, in my courtyard, and it would be a wrong thing to do, contrary to all rules of hospitality, not to invite him in.

The front door scrapes open, we walk up the eight cement steps to the elevator, and I press the button to summon the rumbling car from above. As we wait next to the bank of wooden mailboxes, a door to one of the first floor apartments opens, the one where the current janitor, a tall woman in a burlap apron, lives. She clangs a key ring to find the one to lock the door, but the search goes on excruciatingly long, and I know, even though I'm standing with my back to her, that she is gawking at Robert, who looks even more alien inside my apartment building than he did out on the street. The janitor doesn't even have to wait for him to open his mouth to tell he doesn't belong here, with his corkscrew hair and his corduroys stamped with metal buttons no Soviet store has ever seen.

The elevator car finally shudders down to the first floor, and I pull the metal door open to let us in. Inside there is a stink of urine, the usual elevator smell, and as the cabin lurches up, we look down at our feet, our backs pressed to a plywood partition that cuts off half the space inside, making the car big enough for only two or three, making it as uncomfortable as everything else here. I curl my toes inside my shoes, embarrassed by this useless partition, by the reek of urine, by the janitor's look of condemnation. It's a stupid feeling, of course; I wasn't the one who built this plywood atrocity, or pissed all over the floor, or branded Robert with a disdainful stare. But I am the one who let Robert see it and smell it. I am, in the words of our American program teacher-trainer, the facilitator of acquisition.

My mother is in the kitchen ironing, bent over an old blanket spread on the table, leaning with all her weight on the heavy iron she's just heated on a stove burner. She's doing the linens: sheets, duvets, and pillowcases that are cotton and wrinkle terribly when she wrings them out in the bathtub.

"This is Robert from my American program," I say, as I wave for him to come to the kitchen. "I was showing him our courtyards, and then he wanted to see a Russian apartment."

My mother straightens up and sets the iron on a metal trivet. Although she smiles back at Robert and stretches out her hand to meet his for a handshake, I can guess what she is thinking: Americans know nothing about manners; according to the proper etiquette, a man must wait for a woman to stretch her hand out first. "It's a pleasure to meet you," she says, taking off her apron. "Please make yourself at home while I organize some tea."

"You can't avoid having tea in a Russian house," I say to Robert, who, I can see, is delighted at the prospect.

My mother is taking this tea very seriously, I can tell: she's rooting in the cupboard for a jar of raspberry jam; she's asking me to bring the good cups from my sister's room. I take the cup assignment as an opportunity to show Robert the apartment, and I now look at Marina's room through a foreigner's eyes: creaky parquet, wavy and unwaxed for years; wallpaper with flowers that were once yellow; peeling windowsills with pots of aloe and feeble scallion shoots my mother pinches off for salad.

I open the balcony door, and the summer street noise tumbles into the room—trams, buses, and a line to the liquor store that snakes around the corner and ends somewhere under the balcony where we stand. "What are they selling there?" asks Robert in Russian—he's switched to Russian completely, proud of his case endings, which make him rub his temples and squint his eyes before they stagger out of his mouth, tortured but nearly perfect.

They aren't selling anything yet. People are lining up because they see a truck parked next to the store, which signals a delivery— of what exactly, no one knows. Yet whatever it is that has just been delivered isn't going to last long, so they stand there waiting, leaning forward in hope of getting a glimpse of what they're queuing up for. "Probably cheap vodka," I say. "Or cheap port. We call it *chernila*, which means ink." Robert smiles, and I know he's just filed the new word away into the coils of his versatile brain.

I'm impressed by Robert's kaleidoscopic talents, so inaccessible to me: physics, music, writing. I'm bewildered by his curiosity, by his willingness to travel to my city—a grandiose ruin hermetically sealed from the rest of the world—and live in it for six weeks. Most of all, I'm awed by his foreignness. I think I am even attracted to him, and if not to him as an individual, then to his otherness, to the classified, unknowable world he represents. The world I've been trying to decipher since I had my first private English lesson with Irina Petrovna when I was ten, the secret and closed place where English is spoken, the place I know so well and yet don't know at all. Everything alien and mesmerizing and seductive has fused together and condensed in one person gawking down from my balcony at the line for cheap ink.

"Tea is ready!" yells my mother from the kitchen, where Robert and I carry the good cups ensconced on good saucers, the gold-rimmed set my mother inherited from her parents. In addition to a bowl with raspberry jam, I see an open box of chocolates on the table my mother has extracted from the reserve cache of jars of mayonnaise and cans of tuna she keeps for holidays and special occasions. I take one and then one more; the chocolates have acquired a white patina of time from sitting in the cupboard for so long.

She asks Robert about the program, but from her absentminded questions I can see this is just polite small talk. What she really wants to know is what Robert does in America. Where he works, where he lives, with whom. Mundane questions, as practical as my mother.

He studies in Texas, finishing his PhD in physics. Robert rubs his forehead, thinking of the correct conjugations and declensions. When he is not in Texas, he is in his mother's house in New Jersey. New Jersey? asks my mother. Close to New York City, he says. On the other side of the Hudson. Hudson? asks my mother. The word in Russian is *Goodzon*, which must sound funny to Robert, as if the Hudson River were a good zone in the middle of the otherwise rotten place.

We spread butter and spoon raspberry jam onto slices of bread, so fresh it gives way under the load. Much better than the cafeteria food, says Robert, chewing and smiling, although I can't see how bread with dacha raspberry jam can be better than the professorial cabbage stuffed with real meat or the bowls brimming with whipped cream.

While Robert is searching for verb endings, my mother gives him pointed looks. She is trying to figure out what to think of this home visit, knowing all too well that I won't be the one to reveal the truth. It's a game we've been playing for as long as I can remember, a game of pretending, not unlike the *vranyo* game we all play with the state. I pretend that my bringing Robert home means nothing, and she pretends to believe me. She knows I won't tell her what I really think about Robert, and I know that she knows that I know.

The truth is I haven't yet decided how I feel about Robert myself.

"Don't be an idiot," says Nina. "This is one chance in a lifetime."

On Saturday, the Russian language program is over, and all the students are flying back to the United States. As I've anticipated, with both hope and trepidation, Robert has said he is sorry to leave. "I don't want to say good-bye to you," he uttered in Russian slowly, in search of the perfect grammatical structure.

"I'm sorry you're leaving, too," I said and sighed.

"Maybe I can come back in six months," he offered. "When the fall semester is over at my university."

"I hope you can. I would like that very much," I said. "Your coming back."

I repeat this to Nina, without mentioning my deliberate sighing. "If I could," she says, "I'd be out of here on the first goddamn plane. This country is doomed, and we're doomed with it. I'd go anywhere. I'd go to Patagonia if I could."

But she knows she can't. She has just married an engineer named Rudik she fell madly in love with, and now they're living in her two-room apartment with her parents and her brother. I visited them recently in lieu of going to the wedding they didn't have. Nina cooked a fabulous dinner, and we drank a bottle of red Bulgarian wine I brought, heating it in a pot with sugar and sliced apples to get rid of the acidic taste. Rudik was tentative, not quite a host in his in-laws' apartment, not quite the passionate romantic Nina had described him to be. He showed me a huge glass vat with coils, which I was certain he'd stolen from a chemistry lab at his job, where from water, sugar, and yeast he produces what he called *idealniy samogon*, perfect moonshine.

"Do whatever you have to do," says Nina, "to get the hell out."

R OBERT WANTS TO SEE a white night, and I take him just before he has to leave. Those of us born here are used to white nights, of course; we close the drapes and sleep right through them without any trouble. But tourists think it's part of the experience to complain that they can't catch a wink of sleep because the sun shines in their eyes. Influenced by the romantic nonsense on postcards, they have to flock to the Neva after midnight to gawk in consternation as the bridges open and slowly rise into the sky to let the ships on their way to the Baltic Sea pass through the city center.

Robert and I are walking on the wrong side of the river, from where the open bridges do not allow us to return until three in the morning. The needle of the Peter and Paul Fortress is glinting in the first rays of the sun, which is rising one hour past midnight, as usual, a copper disk making the brick-colored Rostrum Columns glow in the hues of pale rose. We watch the Palace Bridge split in the middle and creak up into the pale sky. Streams of high school graduates float past us—seventeen-year-olds decked out in dresses sewn by their mothers and suits borrowed from their family armoire, celebrating their new freedom. Their exuberance dances on the steel grid of the bridges, bounces off the stone fence of the embankment.

Robert holds my hand, then puts his arm around my shoulders. I find my ear pressed to the wool of his sweater, which has a foreign, antiseptic smell. I don't know what I want him to do—to hold me closer or to let me go. If he holds me closer, I'll have a chance of getting on an international flight out of here, as Nina thinks I should. If he lets me go, I'll be back to my mother's apartment, to our life of pretense and *vranyo*. I'll be back in my courtyard, which is a much better emblem for our life here than a ubiquitous hammer and sickle: the crumbling façade with locked doors and stinking garbage bins behind it.

Robert tightens his embrace, touching his lips to my temple, and we stand there, like so many other couples around us, gawking at the open bridge with its arms stretched to the sky.

I TIPTOE INTO THE hallway of my apartment around four in the morning, when the sun has crept past the cupboard and is glinting on the kitchen stove. In her ghostly nightgown, my mother is shuffling toward the bathroom, her hair, mussed by sleep, slithering down her back in a skinny braid. Robert and I said good-bye in Decembrists' Square, halfway between his dorm and my house. He was going to see me home, but I wanted to be sure he could find his way back.

"What are you doing up so late?" My mother squints in my direction. It takes her a minute to see that I am dressed in street clothes. "Where have you been?" The light beams in her eyes as she lumbers closer. "It's the middle of the night," she says, shielding her face from the sun.

I haven't told my mother anything about Robert, just as I haven't told her anything else about my life that is of any importance. I don't want to face her lecturing, or her guilt-provoking tirades, or her advice. What could she possibly advise me regarding a fledgling love affair with an American, my mother who was born along with the Soviet state? What advice could she give me about anything?

In our brief interactions I inform her about my university classes and private lessons—always the summary of the outcomes, never the curves of the process. I recite the courses I've taken, the new students acquired. She seems to think she is in control of my life.

"It's white nights," I say and look out the window at the tide of the gleaming roofs that roll toward the horizon. "The whole city is awake. Everyone's out on the streets, everyone's in love."

"I don't care about everyone," says my mother. "I worry about you. You're my daughter, and at four in the morning you should be safe at home. Where were you?"

A wave of fatigue rolls over me, a lull of exhaustion. I have been so diligent in slicing my soul in two and keeping the real half to myself, away from the outside, away from my mother, who wants me to be safe.

"Out on a date," I say, scraping with my fingernail at something stuck to the oilcloth. "With a foreigner, an American. The one who came to see our apartment."

I see my mother gasp as her face begins to twitch with restrained tears.

"An American?" she squeezes out as if the words themselves would blemish her. "American" and "date" in the same phrase, as I should've known, have fused into a powerful compound fraught with explosive consequences. She glowers at me, swallowing the oncoming tears. "Aren't there any Russian fellows around? Nice university graduates?"

She waits for my response, for some indication that I am open to normalcy. Out of the corner of my eye I see her swallow hard as I deliberately continue to trace the oilcloth flowers with my fingernail.

"What's wrong with you?" she yells. "You're exactly like your father—stubborn as a goat."

Strangely, I feel removed from this whole scene, watching the action from the wings, like a director during a performance.

My mother, the tragic heroine of the second act, admonishing a prodigal daughter. Robert's taste is still lingering in my mouth; American kissing and groping are no different from what they are here. Although my mother's voice is trembling, suspended on the brink of crying, I can't help thinking of a joke Nina has told me: *A mother barges in on a daughter in bed with a man and laments, Next she'll start smoking.*

On my way to the kitchen door, sharpening my voice like a knife, I turn to my mother, hunched over the table.

"And, by the way, I also smoke," I say and shut the door behind me.

What comes out of my mouth is driven by anger: at my righteous mother, who refuses to look out the window and see there is no bright dawn on the horizon; at my black-hearted country that inspired her, forged her into steel, and deceived her.

# CHAPTER 18

# *Waiting*

*DEAR LENA,* WRITES ROBERT from Copenhagen, where he had to change planes on the way back to the United States. *I'm in the airport, waiting for my flight, thinking about you. There are no border patrolmen with gold epaulets and no guns, but every store sells salted herring, just like in Leningrad. Will write again from the States.*

I receive this postcard a month later, when Robert is back in New Jersey, or Texas, having long forgotten about Danish herring, but not about Leningrad. Soon after the postcard, a long envelope arrives with my name written in a careful foreign handwriting, and then a letter appears in my mailbox every week. *I miss you,* he writes, in English and Russian. He wants me to respond in Russian, so he can practice his grammar. *I've already begun inquiries into coming back in December,* he writes. *Getting a visa is a tortuous process and needs to be started early. It's difficult to get to talk to someone in the Soviet Embassy in Washington—they don't answer the phones.*

Nina just laughs when I tell her about the Embassy phones. In August, we were given temporary full-time teaching jobs in the Philology department we'd just graduated from. Natalia

Borisovna pats us on the shoulders and says that our summer work at the American program has strengthened our prospects. After a few years of temporary teaching, if we take an active role in Komsomol and union activities and if some faculty member drops dead or decides to retire, we may be considered for a permanent university teaching job. It's a remote possibility, whispers Natalia Borisovna, I won't deny it, but if such an opening happens to come up, I won't recommend anyone but you. We are very grateful, says Nina, who knows what to say in every social situation. It will be a great privilege and honor to work in this department by your side, she adds.

I am not sure Natalia Borisovna would be so helpful if she knew that a student I met at the American program, where I worked on her recommendation, has been calling the Soviet Embassy in Washington to get a visa to see me again in December. I'm not sure she would be helpful at all if she knew that he sends me a letter every week with reports about his life and graduate studies at the University of Texas. The stories about his teaching assistantship and his Indian roommate are as incomprehensible to me as if they were written in Farsi, the language he tried to learn when he went to Afghanistan as part of the Peace Corps five years earlier. I don't know what the Peace Corps is, but I suspect it may actually have something to do with world peace, unlike our own House of Friendship and Peace, where I worked as a secretary to the departed director.

*If you want to see the U.S.*, Robert writes in one of his weekly letters, *maybe I can help you. Maybe you can come as my friend, on a visitor's visa.*

I read this sitting at the desk in my mother's room and snicker. I know I'm supposed to feel appreciative, and I do, but I also feel frustrated. Who in his right mind would allow me or anyone else within the borders of the Soviet Union to go visit a friend in a capitalist country? Who would allow me to see that there are lifestyles more illuminated than our own bright future? The few exchange delegations that are permitted abroad, as I learned working in the House of Friendship and Peace, are carefully selected from the internal ranks and assiduously screened to make sure they are free of such compromising traits as foreign friends or Jewish relatives. A foreign friend is a liability we try to conceal, a handicap that instantly makes us untrustworthy and suspicious.

I think of how liberating it must feel to be able to visit friends who have never heard of Komsomol meetings that vote on the fate of a prospective tourist, or character reports required for foreign trips, or our infamous OVIR, the visa department. The visas that OVIR allegedly issues from time to time—not to most applicants and not cheerfully—are visas to leave the country, a notion that made Robert squint in confusion when I tried to explain to him what our country thinks about foreign travel. "You need a visa to leave?" he asked and scratched his forehead, although I expected him to know more about our bureaucracy. "In the rest of the world you need a visa to enter a foreign country."

"We're different from the rest of the world," I said, thinking that Natalia Borisovna would be proud of this statement, thinking that in some perverted way, I was proud of it, too. "There's something else we need to do when we leave the country," I said, adding more weight to my twisted pride. "We have to go through customs. It's not only what you bring in that must be ransacked by law, but also what you take out."

"What is there to take out?" asked Robert, looking around.

Unable to control the impulse to laugh off such an outrageously misguided statement, I fumbled for an example of an exported commodity. "Rubles, for instance," I said, but Robert scrunched his nose as if inhaling a smell from the garbage bins in my courtyard, letting me know that rubles are worthless beyond our borders. "Lacquered Palekh boxes," I said, thinking of the exclusive shelves of the *Beriozka* shop I was allowed to glimpse in the ninth grade, with all its glamour of salami and Pasternak poetry—as Robert pleated his lips into a smirk. "Icons, for instance," I said, reaching for the indisputable, thinking of Marina's first film role in Rimsky-Korsakov's *Tsarist Bride*, shot in a tiny village in Central Russia, whose church had been promptly relieved of its religious artifacts by the insightful movie crew.

"Icons?" said Robert and rolled his eyes. "Where could a tourist get an icon anyway?"

He was right. Not in a tiny village tucked under birches and fir trees in the European part of the country where there might still be a babushka or two who, in their pre-revolutionary ignorance, keep clutching at the idea of the divine. No foreigner would be allowed to go to such a village, of course, even if he was willing to pay for the ticket in the hard, dependable currency of a capitalist country.

So it was at this point that I realized the futility of my argument, the futility of every argument, present or future, Robert and I might have. The problem we face is that under his un-Russian curly hair presides an American brain, which is fundamentally different from my Russian brain. If I had to place us on the Darwinian origin of species tree, Robert would sit on the end of the top branch, while I would dangle off a side, dead-end stump. The fact that we can speak each other's language is as irrelevant to our mutual understanding as my mother's loaded silences and pointed looks.

On the desk where I'm sitting there is a picture of my mother in my grandparents' garden in Stankovo, standing by an apple tree holding up a branch that sinks under the weight of apples. Next to her stands my smiling grandma, her face creased with wrinkles. The photograph was taken six years ago, just before she died "from her heart." That's what my anatomy professor mother said with uncharacteristic imprecision: she died from her heart, like most Russians. It was an expected death, at an age when most of our compatriots already lie in cemeteries, just a year before Dedushka, my grandfather, died from his heart, too.

I don't know why I keep looking at my grandma's photograph, at her smiling eyes behind round glasses, at the black and white apples on sagging tree branches, the garden I've always resented as much as my own dacha. I can almost feel the worn-out-cotton softness of the dress she's wearing in the picture, the dress I suddenly remember so well that its dry, woody smell of her oak armoire rises to my nostrils. *Mamochka*, as my mother used to call her, the diminutive of *mama*—a plain, non-endearing form I use to address my own mother. What would Grandma, with her arms as soft as her dress, think of moving to America? What would she think of me? "Whatever happens, happens for the best," she always said in her calm, liquid voice when things happened that no one liked.

THEN MAYBE I CAN *invite you as my fiancée,* writes Robert. *I've inquired at the State Department, where they told me there is such a program. You can come here and stay for up to a year to see if you like it.*

I reread the word fiancée, which sounds frightening and thrilling. It sounds as if it has floated from a more old-fashioned life, from the world of Pushkin and Tolstoy, when women, before they married, became engaged after they danced with some officer at their first ball and then faithfully waited for him to return from a battle with the French army or an exile to the Caucasus.

I reread the words "if you like it." I know I'll only be a make-believe fiancée, but as such, could I really see with my own eyes what we've only been allowed to glimpse in books? Could I really step through the looking glass and wonder if I like it there? I know that in our locked-up universe an exit visa for a fiancée is as far-fetched as that for a friend, yet I sit at my mother's desk and think of America. It is clearly a waste of time: the images are foggy and monochromatic; they shift with every breath I take because, like our bright future, they are based on nothing. I try to imagine where Robert lives, but all that drifts into my head are Leningrad courtyards and flaking façades with yellow windows peeking through the dusk. I try to imagine an American airport, but all I can see is the one-story shack of Pulkovo, with two rusty toilets and a dozen planes scattered on cracked asphalt taken over by weeds.

When I stop trying to conjure up the unimaginable, I go to work. In the corridors of my university's catacombs, where I teach grammar and reading to my eight classes of first- and second-year students, I run into an ex-classmate, whose name I can barely dredge out of my memory. She beams a toothy smile, towering above me on her slender heels, and I remember she almost flunked out in her senior year because she had just begun modeling for the state House of Fashion. "I'm getting married," she announces as soon as she corners me in the nook behind my classroom. "My fiancé has just flown in from Düsseldorf." "Germany?" I ask, stupidly. "Of course Germany," she giggles, flashing glamorous teeth that have not yet been ruined by Soviet dentistry. "I couldn't think of what to ask him to bring, so he brought me a tennis outfit and a racquet. I keep asking, where are we going to play tennis?" she says, laughing.

Where, indeed? I am thinking that she should have asked for something more practical, like a pair of boots, or a winter coat. Or at least a pair of jeans. Last year, when an American movie called *The Domino Principle* was released into our theaters, everyone marveled at the fact that even prisoners in American jails were wearing blue denim. "If they dress their convicts in jeans, life can't be too bad there," my mother announced when we were walking out of the theater, a straw of hope to keep her afloat. As I watch the movement of my classmate's crimson lips, I can only think that she is foolish not to have asked her fiancé for a pair of blue jeans.

I am also thinking it is strange that he had to ask what to bring at all. Surely he has been here before to see what we have in our stores—nothing. A pair of pantyhose would make a girl insanely happy. A pair of winter boots that don't look like felt peasant *valenki* would generate a cry of ecstasy. A denim jacket would bring on tears. But foreigners don't understand this. They stubbornly refuse to give practical gifts, bringing instead packages of flavored tea, or tablecloths that don't fit Russian tables, or tennis outfits complete with white hair bands.

"Could you visit your fiancé in Germany?" I ask, being as practical in my question as my mother. "I heard it may be possible to visit before they actually have your passports stamped." Of course, I heard nothing of that sort, but I feel that I need at least one outside opinion before I write back to Robert.

My ex-classmate frowns for a second, as if utterly confused. "Why would they allow that?" she says, wagging her head so that strands of her thick, model hair fall across her face. "If they allowed such visits, can you imagine what would happen to this department?"

I can imagine, so I nod.

I write to Robert about what I've learned. Then I think of our different brains and add a couple of sentences of my own, direct and to the point: *Engagement, like friendship, is an unbinding relationship, not written into the Soviet law. Only in the West, where the individual seems to trump the collective, can it be considered a legal foundation for such a serious procedure as a visa.* I write this in English to make sure he understands every word. Then in Russian I write about mundane things: the classes I teach and the early November snow that fell on the columns of the demonstrators marching under my windows to celebrate yet another anniversary of the Great October Socialist Revolution.

In the university corridors I run into two other ex-classmates, Natasha and Luba. They, too, are getting married to foreigners: Natasha to a Finn, Luba to a Swede. Natasha tells me that on his way out of Leningrad her fiancé was escorted into a little room off the customs area and locked up for two hours so he missed his flight to Helsinki. Luba tells me that she was not allowed into a hotel for foreigners where her Swede was staying, accused by the doorman of being a prostitute—although everyone knows there are no prostitutes in our country, just as there are no homeless or unemployed. "These social ills afflict only the West," I said to Luba, "where they fester like maggots upon the flesh of unjust societies, contributing to their gradual rot and imminent demise." I wanted to force a little smile out of her lips because she had begun to sniffle when she told me that the doorman reached out and squeezed her butt as she was leaving.

I listen carefully to this exclusive, firsthand information, wishing I could share in the wisdom of the shadowy sisterhood that has sprouted, unsurprisingly, at the university's foreign language department. After all, the professors of scientific communism were right when they used to terrorize us at their seminars: nothing good can possibly come out of someone who speaks a foreign language. We are hopeless and warped; we are unreliable and confused. We don't know what's good for us. "When things are good you don't search for better," a Russian saying goes, one of my mother's favorites.

But all my former classmates are marrying Europeans. Finland is only a bus ride away; Sweden is just across the Gulf, its proximity the reason for the city's first fortress; Germany, as everyone knows, was reached on foot in 1945. America, on the other hand, is all the way on the other side of the Earth, in the same hemisphere as parrots, feathered Indians, and Brazil. I might as well tell my mother that I'm thinking of traveling through a black hole.

As usual, I tell my mother nothing. I know what she thinks, and she knows that I know. She hands me long American envelopes when she takes them out of the mailbox. She bangs silverware in the kitchen drawer and blames my friend Nina for luring me into the American program summer job. When she asks about Robert, I say he is probably going to travel here for New Year's. I know that she knows why he's coming, but she wants me to say it. I tell her he's studying Russian customs and needs to see a real New Year's tree.

What would my father say about Robert? Was he disillusioned enough with our life to consider this possible marriage a positive move? Or would he, like my mother, lament it and worry? I think of him sitting in a boat, rowing into the Gulf of Finland, into the murky waters that separate us from the West. I wonder if he ever thought of crossing that invisible line, of rowing toward the big black ships that crawl along the horizon; I wonder if it ever occurred to him to leave behind his ordinary life: the director's desk, and the dacha he didn't want to paint, and the "cow chow" salads my mother chopped for him. He was a loner, my father, a man with no past; he could have kept gliding in his boat, working the oars. Was this the reason he loved fishing—that possibility of rowing away from the shore, toward the horizon?

ROBERT ARRIVES ON DECEMBER 20, 1979. He has somehow arranged with the university to stay in the same dorm where he lived in the summer. I go to the airport to meet him, and when I glimpse him through the glass, opening his suitcase for a customs official, he looks completely unfamiliar in a winter parka, a strange foreigner with corkscrew hair and silly thick glasses. A strange foreigner to whom a strange word has now been attached—*fiancé*. When he emerges from the customs area, his suitcase ransacked, he smiles and pecks me on the cheek. I brought you a present, he says, and pulls out a silk scarf.

In my last letter, when I wrote that our government would not permit a fiancée visa, Robert, with the directness of a scientist, asked this question: let me know what will work to bring you here. And although I didn't have time to write back before he arrived, I had a suspicion that he knew the answer, just as I did. He knew the answer then and he knows it now, shouldering his way out of the customs trap full of flustered tourists and smug men in ill-fitting gray uniforms. It's quite obvious, even to a visitor, that there are only two ways to leave this country: Jewish blood in your veins or a foreigner to marry.

Robert's arrival signals to everyone that we may be getting married. What other reason can there be for him to willingly jump the hurdles constructed by the Soviet Embassy in Washington and trudge across the globe to minus-25-degree, snow-blanketed Leningrad?

It is an awkward subject I try to avoid with Robert. But I also, rather clumsily, try to steer toward it since he is here for only two weeks and we don't have much time. If he goes back to Texas with nothing said, I might as well go back to my apartment and ask my mother for the recipe for borsch.

Robert seems to feel as awkward as I do, so our first two days together are filled with silent sightseeing and complaints about the cold.

On the third day Robert says what I've been waiting to hear. We are walking toward my apartment building, the air so cold that it feels like shards of glass scraping down my throat. Marina has made a pot of sour cabbage *schi* according to her own recipe, so we are expected in my kitchen at three.

"If you want to leave this country," he says as we clutch on to each other because the sidewalk is solid ice, "I'll marry you. I'll do it if that's what it takes to get you out of here." He is composed; he rubs his temple under his hat; he sounds as noble as a character from Tolstoy. "But please understand, I'm not ready to be married. I don't know if I ever will be." I glance at his profile, so serious and foreign, so close to my face that I can see tiny drops frozen inside his mustache. "I want to see other women," he says. "I want to continue seeing Karen."

I must have a puzzled look on my face because Robert stops, takes off his glasses, and starts wiping them with his scarf. "I've known Karen for a long time," he says. "As long as I've been in Austin, four years. She's a professor at the University of Texas Slavic department. We're good friends, and I want to keep seeing her."

I stop too and blow into my mittens to warm my fingers, but I'm really giving myself time to think. I'm standing under a huge icicle that hangs off a windowsill straight above my head, thinking about Robert's proposal, but instead of an appropriate response, a string of bitter questions unwinds in my head. So why do you need me at all, I want to ask. You already have someone who can correct your Russian. Can't we pretend that we are really going to get married, at least for a little while?

I know how to pretend well, I want to say, and I'm willing to pretend that we are a couple. I'm willing to pretend that I love Robert as much as I loved the Crimean Boris, as much as I loved Slava from my sister's theater. I'm willing to pretend that I love Robert as much as I need to.

But I don't say anything. I don't want to show what I am thinking. It's a lifelong practice, a tribute to Grandma's words, What's inside you no one can touch.

"I understand," I say—although I really don't—and hook my arm around Robert's elbow. Then I add a mousy "thank you" that puffs out of my mouth and hangs in the air in a small cloud of frozen breath.

IN MY APARTMENT, OVER Marina's *schi* and the meatballs with buckwheat, Robert announces that we've decided to get married. The air in our kitchen seems to have hardened into lead as I stare into my plate, afraid to face my mother. I feel as if we are in the silent scene at the end of Gogol's *Inspector General*, so finally I look up and utter the words "Gogol's silent scene," an idiotic phrase that gets stuck in the leaden air, having explained nothing.

Marina gets up and rinses her plate under the faucet. I know that theoretically she, like Nina, thinks one should hop on the first available plane pointed out of this country, but in life things aren't that simple. In real life, my mother sits frozen over a plate of buckwheat, her eyebrows creased together in a frown, her eyes like shattered glass. Maybe she was hoping that when it came to a crisis, such as a marriage proposal from an American, I would be able to shake off all that acquired philological decadence and return to my innate Russianness. Maybe she was still hoping I was normal.

Robert looks at me quizzically and I look at Marina, who is conveniently staring down, scrubbing her plate.

"Wait," says my mother as her face becomes older. "What does this mean, you're getting married?"

I don't know how to answer her question. "It means we have to go to the Acts of Marriage Palace, the central one on the Neva, and find out about the procedures," I say, grasping at an opportunity to switch to the clear-cut matters of bureaucratic routine. "Tomorrow is Wednesday, so we'll go tomorrow. It's all right," I add, a signal to Marina to save her stage voice, a signal to my mother that I've made up my mind.

"So when are you planning to . . . get married?" asks my mother, pausing before the last two words, as though her mouth cannot contort to their shape.

I feel strange hearing these words directly aimed at me. I'm twenty-four, and no one but Robert has ever contemplated marrying me. Yet it is not my advancing age and a fear of remaining single, like my sister, that have made me accept Robert's offer.

It feels like a revelation, although somewhere inside me, where familiar things are stripped naked, I have known this all along. I want to leave this country, which, it dawns on me, is so much like my mother. They are almost the same age, my mother and my motherland. They are both in love with order, both overbearing and protective. They're prosaic; neither my mother nor my motherland knows anything about the important things in life:

the magic of Theater, the power of the English language, love. They're like the inside of a bus at a rush hour in July: you can't breathe, you can't move, and you can't squeeze your way to the door to get out.

From his guest chair at the head of the kitchen table, Robert gives my mother an uneasy, regretful smile, as if to apologize for planning to take me to the other side of the Earth, to a place so faraway that the thought of it alone has filled her eyes with tears, making her blink.

THE NEXT DAY, DESPITE my plan, we don't go to the Acts of Marriage Palace. Our Supreme Soviet announces that it has sent troops to Afghanistan in order to help it rid itself of the atavisms of capitalism. The news is all over the front pages of *Pravda* and *Izvestiya*, in long articles with fat headlines explaining that if we didn't invade Afghanistan, it would be gobbled up by the war-mongering United States. "*Chorny pauk*—like a bloodthirsty black spider," reads Robert from a *Pravda* on the kitchen table, "the U.S. is always on the lookout for new opportunities to strangle socialism and catapult the world back to the dark, retrograde, pre-revolutionary past."

"Gobbled up by the United States?" asks Robert, raising his eyebrows. "I've been to Afghanistan; there's nothing there worth gobbling up."

We trek all over the city center in search of an English-language newspaper that will explain what's really happening. In the lobby of Hotel Europe on Nevsky Prospekt, where I sneak in on Robert's heels while a doorman is gawking at a parked BMW, we find the *Morning Star*, published by the Communist Party of Great Britain, and the *Daily World*, published by the Communist Party of the United States. "I've never seen these papers," says Robert. "In America or England." But he doesn't buy them, even out of curiosity. He wants to read the real news, he says. He wants to know *pravda*, the truth, with *Pravda*, stacked up in piles everywhere we look, being the last place to find it.

We fumble through a stack of papers in Polish, Bulgarian, Serbo-Croatian, Italian, and French, until Robert pulls out something with wobbly lines printed on pinkish paper, the *Financial Times* of India. We hurriedly leaf through the pages of unsteady print that gives me an instant headache, looking for some mention of the Soviet invasion of Afghanistan, until I glance at the date and see that the paper is a week old.

I wish I could shield Robert from the onslaught of all this media nonsense on both TV channels, from announcers with serious voices and pensive eyes. I am immune to the lead articles in *Pravda*, vaccinated against the official line by Aunt Polya back in nursery school. I don't pay any attention to the somber drone of the television program *Vremya*, which my mother switches on at nine before she goes to bed. I walk right past the grainy clips from military parades, past marching soldiers and banners unfurling in the wind that are supposed to stir up our patriotic fervor. The only thing that currently concerns me is how this new international development is going to affect the regulations for marrying a foreigner, my future visa prospects, and the Aeroflot plane schedule between Leningrad and New York.

I LEAVE ROBERT IN the Russian Museum and go to the Bureau of Foreign Marriages to find out what papers they require. My mother goes with me, to provide support against pigheaded red-tapists, she says, and I don't mind. She has her own scores to settle with bureaucracy. Ten years ago, her medical institute put her in charge of advising a group of students from Hungary, who spent most weekends of their academic year in our kitchen, cooking goulash with stringy beef and red paprika they'd brought from home in little canvas bags. The students—grateful to my mother, who tutored them in anatomy and Soviet survival skills—

invited her to visit them in Budapest, where she could meet their parents and taste the proper goulash made from real meat. But the miscreants from the visa department, after she'd bought a caseful of souvenirs for gifts and collected a dossier of required character reports, refused her a visa. It was un-Soviet, they said, for a professor to visit a foreign student's home.

The Foreign Marriage Bureau is on the Neva, one of those former mansions that remain from our despotic past. The application office is on the first floor, under the marble stairway barred with the kind of thick red velvet rope used to cordon off museum exhibits. The building is solemn and empty; there don't seem to be many foreign marriages. Behind the office door is a woman in her forties with graying hair cinched in a bun, her face as round and rosy-cheeked as my provincial aunt Muza's.

"What documents are needed to marry a foreign citizen?" I ask nervously, my voice echoing off the five-meter ceiling of a home that used to belong to a count or a prince.

"What country?" asks the woman, and she peers at me as if trying to guess the answer.

"Se-Sh-Aa," I say—the sounds hiss out of my mouth, more sibilant in Russian than the English "USA."

The woman blinks and turns to my mother as if seeking confirmation of this statement, even more outrageous since December 25, when our government successfully preempted the American efforts to usurp Afghanistan. My mother holds her gaze and sighs.

The woman sighs, too, signaling her understanding of my mother's silent suffering, then comes from behind her desk and stops in front of me. "My dear," she says and cranes her neck trying to peer into my face. "You've fallen in love, is that it? With someone from a faraway land?" She smiles a motherly smile—too motherly—but I cannot show her what I think. I know I have to play the game and respond to her cue. I know that the fate of my leaving this place has now been placed in her hands.

I smile sheepishly and nod.

The woman steps back and lifts her chin, assuming a pose for delivering an important message. "Well, the rules for capitalist countries are actually the same as for socialist ones," she says. "This is one area where we don't discriminate. Marriage is marriage, and the wife should follow her husband no matter where he lives." I'm relieved to hear this piece of medieval wisdom, but it sounds a bit too accommodating for an official line, too suspiciously easy.

"Both you and your fiancé must fill out an application here in person." She recites the rules with inspiration, as if they were lines from Pushkin's poetry. "You need your passport, your proof of residency in Leningrad, your birth certificate. He needs his passport and his visa. Then you wait three months."

"Wait?" I ask. "Wait for what?"

"We give you this period in case you change your mind," she says, smiling.

"But we're sure we aren't going to change our mind," I say.

"Then in three months you come again and we register your marriage," says the woman and cocks her head to underscore the benevolence of the state rules. "Both of you. In person."

"But that means he has to travel here again," I say, raising my voice involuntarily. "All the way from America. All the way from Texas!"

The woman shrugs her shoulders, undoubtedly having heard this before. "What can you do?" she says, pretending to sympathize with me, exchanging glances with my mother. "Rules are rules."

"So then he will have to come again in March," says my mother, her voice laced with the hope that he won't.

"Can't we come back in two weeks?" I ask pointlessly, knowing the answer. "He is only here for two weeks."

The woman walks back to her desk and peers into a calendar. "March twenty-seventh," she says. "That's if you show up here tomorrow with all the papers in order, both of you."

\*

"MARCH TWENTY-SEVENTH?" SAYS ROBERT. "Can't we come back in two weeks? Or in a month; I can stay here until the end of January."

"This is the Soviet Union," I say in a solemn voice, hoping that this will somehow explain everything. "We should be grateful that they're allowing this at all."

I don't know if Robert thinks he should be grateful for having to be here during the coldest winter since the Leningrad siege of 1942 and having to pay in hard currency for the decrepit university dorm without heat. I don't know if he thinks he should be grateful for having to arrange yet another trip here, visas and all, when the Soviet Consulate in New York has just been closed down in protest at the Soviet invasion of Afghanistan.

He gives his cheek a rub and sits there, thinking.

# CHAPTER 19

# Wedding

FOR THE THREE MONTHS before our scheduled wedding, I'm not planning anything because I don't believe it is really going to happen. In my mind, I've played out everything that could go wrong: Robert will come to his senses; the Soviet Embassy will refuse to issue a visa on learning that he's going to marry a Soviet citizen; the border patrol will seize and detain him the moment he steps onto Soviet soil.

I go to work as usual, teaching my classes and chatting with Natalia Borisovna as if nothing were about to happen. I ask her advice on facilitating conversational fluency, and she whispers the latest gossip about the department secretary, who is marrying a Georgian and moving to Tbilisi. I'm afraid to think what she would say if I told her that I am marrying an American and moving to Texas. She might say nothing; such an announcement would most likely choke her.

Am I really going to marry an American and move to Texas? I feel as I did when I was eleven, standing on a diving board just before they kicked me out of the district pool for my lack of swimming ability, with ten meters of void between my toes and the green water below, clear and hard as glass. I never had the guts to jump, but I've always wondered what it would have been like, taking that step forward, plummeting through the chlorine-smelling air, splattering into the water that would reluctantly part and swallow me and seal over my head in caps of white foam.

Some days I'm free from doubt, confident that I am indeed going to marry and move, that I am only a few months away from a new life. And some days I'm not so certain. Some days I have to look at myself in the mirror to make sure that this person who uses the words "America" and "marriage" in the same sentence is really me. Aside from convicts dressed in blue jeans, I know nothing about America. I know what is not likely to happen to me: I won't be sleeping under a bridge, as my mother whispers to Marina in the kitchen; I won't be begging on the street, as the news report announces Americans are forced to do—by whom? I won't be doing any of the things we are warned against by our press and by posters with fat men in top hats trampling over the huddling workers in chains. I know all this is a lie. But what is the truth? The only thing I can tell so far is that those convicts in blue jeans don't seem to have that bad a life.

But sometimes, at night, when I stand at a bus stop where the only light is an amber square from a first-floor window, and the wind rattles in the round metal drainpipes chained to the façades, I am frightened. I shiver at the silence, at the cold, wet, empty air, at the nothingness of the night. If nothingness exists here, where I know everything, what will I have there, where I really know nothing? Where the bus stops and the air and the drains and the night are all so different that I may not even recognize them at all.

I want to tell my mother or, even better, simply bury my face in her breasts as I did a long time ago when I got lost in the woods. But I am no longer ten and cannot seem weak and show how scared I am, especially to her. It would frighten her, too. It would confirm that she was right all along when she gave Robert a first hard look, when she wanted me to apply to medical school instead of the philology department, when she raised her eyebrow in disdain fifteen years ago hearing that I wanted to learn English.

TWO WEEKS BEFORE ROBERT'S arrival, the phone rings in my apartment, and I hear the voice of Boris, whom I met in the Crimea. In the last year we've talked on the phone only twice: I called him on his birthday, and he called me on mine. He was planning to go to Novy Svet again that August, and we reminisced about boiling mussels on the beach and stealing grapes from the collective farm that made exported champagne. I no longer feel a melting in my belly when I hear his voice; I no longer feel like dropping everything and rushing to join him wherever he is.

He is in Leningrad, he says.

In Leningrad? He has never come to Leningrad before, not when I sent him a telegram as my mother was walking out the door to spend a week with her sister in the provinces, not when I bribed a conductor in Simferopol to put an extra person on a train headed north. And now, when I didn't beg or bribe, he is here.

Can I meet him somewhere in the center so we can go to a restaurant?

I am not sure which makes me more nervous—seeing Boris or going to a restaurant. In my entire life, I've eaten at a restaurant only once. A surly waitress, who looked as if Nina and I had personally insulted her by sitting down at her table, tossed down a ten-page menu, only to announce that they had nothing but beef stroganoff. It was stringy, lukewarm, and expensive, and we swore never to go to a restaurant again. It was not a sincere promise; we both knew there were other, more exclusive places that actually had food, places guarded by unflappable doormen towering pompously in front of "no seats available" signs.

"So, can we meet?" asks Boris, notes of impatience around the edges of his voice. Or maybe he isn't impatient; maybe he is nervous, too. After all, I am the one who is sitting in my apartment, a marriage stamp soon to decorate my passport, while he is propping up the wall of some telephone booth with buckled rubber tile on the floor and a smell of urine in the air.

I put on the two best pieces of clothing I own: a pair of corduroy Levis a girl from my American class gave me last summer and a jacket of rough suede Marina brought me from her theater tour in Riga five years ago. The day is too cold for such a flimsy jacket, but it looks so much better than my wool-padded winter coat. I spit into a container with dry, caked mascara, which we sometimes also use as shoe polish, and drag a little plastic comb over my eyelashes. The mascara congeals in clumps, and I carefully break them with a sewing needle, separating the eyelashes so that they look as thick and long as those of any American woman.

I see Boris first when I elbow my way out of the Nevsky Prospekt metro station. He stands with his hands in the pockets of his jacket, his eyes blue as the Crimean sky. When he makes me out in the crowd, his lips stretch into a smile that three years ago would have stopped my heart.

"I got on the train as soon as I heard," he says, taking me by the shoulders and kissing my cheek. "Natasha called me yesterday and told me."

He sounds as if he were speaking of a disaster, a terrible accident that forced him to hop on the train and rush here. "Told you what?" I ask.

He peers at me to make sure I'm not joking. "That you're marrying a foreigner and leaving." His voice rises at the end, almost like a question. We're walking along Nevsky Prospekt, two specks in its afternoon crowds, and for a few seconds I don't say anything as I shoulder my way through a cluster of people getting ready to storm a bus, the air filled with the clang of faulty transmissions and the shriek of brakes. "That you're marrying an American," he says, the word *amerikanets* hissing out of his mouth the same way it hisses out of my mother's.

I don't know how Natasha from Kiev, who sighed and gave Boris sad, longing glances back in our Crimean cove, could've learned that I'm going to marry Robert and leave. I look at Boris and shrug, letting him know that Natasha was right, that I am indeed responsible for this catastrophe that required him to abandon his engineering duties in Kiev and race to Leningrad.

We walk a little longer without saying anything, absorbed in the street noise, in the clatter of buses, trolleys, and trucks, in the ferocious whistling from a militiaman trying to prevent a few girls from jaywalking. Then Boris stops in front of a door with the words "Kavkazsky Restaurant" written in big neon letters on the façade above it, one of those places where no one can get in.

Boris tells me to wait and walks over to the doorman. His hand fumbles in his pocket and then produces a red and white pack of Marlboros, something I've seen only once because it's a black-market item, just like blue jeans and Grundig radios with frequencies reaching beyond our jamming range that can tune into the Voice of America and the BBC. Is there also a red ten-ruble note stuffed under the Marlboro pack? I can't see from where I stand, but the doorman, whose silly uniform looks like it was dusted off from Gogol's "Overcoat," steps away and does what he has theoretically been put there to do, open the door. Boris extends his arm, inviting me to enter, a little smile glowing in his eyes, the usual Boris who is older and wiser and knows everything.

When we get to the dining room, it is nearly empty. Unoccupied tables with white tablecloths stand on gleaming parquet, a potted ficus tree behind a grand piano, an air of withered luxury more suited to a town in a Chekhov story than the first proletarian city on earth. A disinterested waiter in a white shirt and a black jacket with an oily stain on the sleeve unhurriedly crosses the room to bring the menus. I pretend to study rows of unfamiliar appetizers, but pretending is all I can do. Boris orders a bottle of champagne and, as the waiter drags his feet to set the table with glasses and napkins, sits back and stares at me, as if he'd been sitting in such restaurants his whole life, as if he hadn't just spent his week's salary on the pack of Marlboros and the bribe to get in.

I gaze back at him, and that's what we do for a while, stare at each other. I don't know why Boris is here. Beyond the August in the Crimea, I was always the one to initiate phone calls and trips to see him; I was the one who forced him to admit finally that I was too different from him, with all my Leningrad arrogance and cynicism and glorification of Western lifestyles gleaned from foreign books.

The waiter shuffles in with the champagne and Georgian appetizers and interrupts our staring. Boris nudges the plates toward me and instructs me to try the red beans with spices and chicken in walnut sauce, although I don't know how, living in Kiev, he can be so familiar with Georgian cooking. We carry on a safe conversation about our Black Sea cove and the two border patrol boys who descended from their observation point on a hill, lured by our potatoes and our wine. When the champagne is finished, he orders a bottle of cognac. The waiter, his face scrunched in reproach that we are making him carry all those heavy trays, warily sets down plates with skewers of lamb and chicken *tabaka*, flavorful and spicy and so much unlike our own food. After a toast of cognac, Boris stops reminiscing about the Crimea and turns to my impending marriage.

"Why are you doing it?" he demands.

I am almost ready for this, so I pick up my cognac glass and drink what's left in it, a honey-colored liquid that definitely—my mother was right—smells of bedbugs.

"You're marrying an American and going to live in America," he says, an accusation I cannot deny. "Don't you realize they'll never let you back?"

"They'll let me back," I say quickly, as if saying it would make it happen. "I still have my Russian passport. I'm not Jewish; I'm not emigrating to Israel." If I were, it occurs to me, Boris wouldn't be sitting at this table, plying me with Georgian food in a place I never dreamed I would see. I still remember his harangue about the Ukrainian Jews during the war, his bewilderment at how they marched to their own graves in Babi Yar. The present-day Jews who want to leave the country are ordered to surrender their passports and their nationality, so they can never return. "I'm still a Soviet citizen. They have to let me back." I say this in a knowing, deliberate voice, but inside I'm not so cavalier. Will I really be able to come back to visit? Maybe Boris is right, after all. Why would they allow me to return, a traitor who took advantage of the university's language labs and seminars in Chomskyan grammar, who learned everything there was to learn from books about a London she could never see, then turned around and married a foreigner and left?

But Boris doesn't stop here. "And if you did return, do you know what would happen?" he says. It feels eerie, as though he could see through my skull and read my thoughts. "You'd be marked. No one would want to be around you. Even your closest friends."

I gulp more cognac, but it only makes me dizzier. I'll be *vrag naroda*, enemy of the people, just like Uncle Volya, my mother's uncle who was arrested in 1937 and then shot—the time we don't talk about, the time that makes sense only in the West, where they publish Solzhenitsyn.

"I still don't understand why," he says. "You graduated from a great university. You have a good teaching job. Your future is set. The department trusts you. Everybody trusts you. Why are you throwing it all away?" I don't know if I want to continue this conversation about good jobs and trust. "Do you really want to live in a country where all they think about is money?" he goes on. I'm not sure where Boris learned this tidbit about America and money. Maybe he read Maxim Gorky's *The City of the Yellow Devil*, about his visit to New York in the 1920s, when our writers were still allowed to travel abroad. "Here," he says and stretches out his arm, presenting to me our dirty plates with bones and empty skewers, "we don't count every kopek. Here if we party, we party." He reaches for his glass and drinks all of its contents, as if teaching me an example of the proper partying etiquette. "Here our life is more than work and the stock market."

"Actually," I say, "it's less. We don't have a stock market."

He leans back in his chair, failing to hear my remark or maybe simply ignoring it. "Our life here is about friendship and love," he adds.

"Friendship, yes," I say, "but not so much about love. You certainly didn't seem to be in love with me."

What I really want to tell him, what I've never been able to tell him, is how it felt when he didn't move a finger to come to Leningrad to rescue me, even for a weekend. When I concocted plans and counted days and he didn't. It felt humiliating. It felt like I'd turned loathsome and worthless, a worm inching across our dacha compost pile.

A woman in an apron lumbers out of the kitchen and begins to pile the dirty plates onto her forearm. Boris looks down, busy examining the stains on the tablecloth, and I now have a chance to hold in my gaze his face, already touched by the first Ukrainian sun and his hair falling over his forehead in soft, yellow strands. This is the face that compelled me to borrow fifty rubles from Nina and hop on a plane two months after we'd met in the Crimea, having lied to my mother that a linguistics professor had sent me to a conference in Kiev.

The waiter, a forced creepy smile on his face, sidles up with a bottle of Georgian wine we didn't order, but Boris is too cocky to send it back, especially since he has just demonstrated the advantages of Russian partying. The bottle is opened and poured into chipped glasses, a syrupy red called Khvanchkara that the oily waiter proudly announces was the favorite wine of Stalin. For a minute, he stands over our table, as if waiting to be invited to salute our former leader, as if he doesn't see that Boris frowns and stares at something stuck to the bottom of a glass, collecting thoughts for an important statement. When the waiter finally departs, Boris plants his elbows on the table and leans toward me. "Whatever you may think of me," he says, "you're making a mistake you'll never undo. The biggest mistake of your life."

"And why do you care?" I say. Stalin's wine tastes like compote made from sweetened ink. "You never came to Leningrad before. I was the one who went to Kiev and then to Moscow when you were staying at your friends' place, that communal mousetrap with no hot water." A narrow, mothball-smelling corridor pops up in my mind, and a bony babushka with accusing eyes. "So what are you doing here, haranguing me about my mistakes? Maybe that was a mistake, coming to see you. Maybe the summer in Novy Svet was all there was supposed to be."

I'm not sure why this tirade has tumbled out of my mouth because all this, as my mother says, is last year's snow. In two weeks I'll be married to Robert Ackerman, who resides in Austin, Texas, which makes Boris Kravchenko from Kiev, despite his blond hair and impossibly blue eyes, quite irrelevant. But is he? In all his sermonizing about collective trust, there are grains of something I've been thinking, little crumbs of truth that wake me up at night and make me lie in bed, listening to the breathing of my mother in the bed next to mine.

"*Nu, nu,*" says Boris, reaching across the table and covering my hand with his, benevolently granting me the right to be angry. "All I wanted to say is congratulations." He grasps my ring finger, leans across the table, and touches it with his lips. "Congratulations and best wishes for a happy life and healthy children," he says, the drunken words, like wet laundry, tangled in his mouth. He lets my finger go, reaches for the cognac bottle, still half full, then puts it back. "But they will never see

Leningrad, your children," he says. "No Hermitage or white nights. No bridges, no Kirov Theatre."

Strangely, I'm sober enough not to get involved in a conversation about children. "Borya," I say and lean across the table to get closer, "why are you here?"

He looks down and stares into his empty glass. For a few moments, it seems that he may answer my question, that he may stop lecturing about collectives, about the Hermitage and the Kirov. It seems he may finally admit that the August in Novy Svet, with its unfailing sun and turquoise light, has burned a mark into his soul, just as it has into mine.

Then his old, all-knowing face is back. "How about some chocolate?" he offers. "You must have chocolate before your wedding."

He waves at the waiter, who unhurriedly reappears with a bar of chocolate peeking out of its foil wrapping, displayed on a serving dish as if it were an exotic cake. I get up as the waiter scurries over with a bill, which, I'm certain, contains things we didn't order. But Boris, of course, is above doing the itemizing and the addition, something they would stoop to only in the money-obsessed West, which doesn't know how to party or how to love. I rewrap the chocolate bar and take it with me because I don't want the greedy waiter to have that, too.

We go out onto Nevsky. I am not sure what time it is, but it seems late, and we walk pointlessly along the canal, where the black water licks at the walls of the embankment. Icy wind whips in from the Neva and blows the fog out of my head. We walk past the Kirov, past the Theatre Square lampposts, their glow nestled in the lace of wrought iron. The last Intourist buses are pulling out of the square. Their passengers are on the way back to their hotels after a day in our museums and former churches, where guides instruct them to stay together, as if these uninhibited people in leather shoes could somehow be mistaken for one of us.

It is ironic, I think, that I'm walking with Boris around Leningrad now, two weeks before my marriage to someone else. This is what I've wanted to do since that August in the Crimea—dazzle him with Leningrad's baroque balconies and marble statues and benches in the shade of linden trees; unfold before him the magic rug of avenues beaming out from the Neva toward the center of Nevsky and sparkling with the gold thread of spire needles. Parade in front of his eyes our fountains and our Bronze Horseman, our pearly domes of light-blue cathedrals and our wrought-iron fences sheltering the silent gardens where Pushkin composed poetry.

And although it isn't beautiful now, on a freezing March night, when most windows are extinguished and the sidewalk is a porridge of dirty snow, I wonder if Boris is right and I am making a mistake. What city on earth can possibly trump Leningrad? I'm leaving a place people from all over the world come to see from the high-perched seats of their Intourist buses. I'm leaving the only place I know.

We stop on the corner to let a streetcar clang by, and Boris puts his arms around me. He holds me close, my face in his wool scarf, and we stand like this for a minute. It is dangerous to be so close to him, especially when we've just mixed champagne and cognac with Stalin's wine, especially when this nostalgic walk has stirred up some sentimental questions in my head. Just as he starts to breathe into my ear, I wiggle out of his arms. "I have to go home," I say, shaking my head as if to shake him off for good. "I'm glad you came to say good-bye."

He looks at me, his eyes still a little glassy, trying to understand what has just happened. "Who is this *amerikanets*, anyway?" he asks.

"It doesn't matter," I say. "Just a nice guy. I have to go."

His eyes are now focused and dark. He runs his fingers through my hair and steps back. "Good luck, silly girl," he says, "in your America."

Then he walks to the middle of the intersection to get me a cab. When a car appears, he flags it down with a V sign—the sign for double fare—and the taxi obediently stops where he's standing. Boris's figure is etched against the light green car—shoulders leaning forward, hair tossed by a wet, briny breeze.

I say good-bye and kiss him on the cheek. His cheek is stubbly and prickles mine, but for a few moments I stay pressed to his face. Then I give him a last kiss on the lips, salty and raw—the taste of the Black Sea, the taste of this windy night.

ROBERT ARRIVES ON MARCH 24. They detain him at the airport, but only to turn the pockets of his parka inside out and to spend a half-hour leafing through his address book. My phone number, I'm certain, is now registered at the Interior Ministry, but then, considering my English-speaking past, it has probably been in their files all along.

To meet Robert we arrive at the airport in a Volga that belongs to Marina's friend Grigorii Isaakovich, Gris for short, who is almost bald and much older than Marina. After we wait for an hour, we see Robert's head bobbing above the barrier that separates the Soviet Union from the West. He gives the glass door a push and crosses over to our side of the world. "*Svolochi,*" he mutters in Russian, zipping up his jacket—bastards. He doesn't need to say anything else; we all know who the *svolochi* are.

I'm glad Robert's mind is still on our zealous border guards, so I don't have to think how to greet my husband-to-be, who has just flown from the other side of the world for our wedding. He shakes his head as if he were ridding himself of a bad dream as I smile an apologetic smile, although I wasn't the one who demanded, or frisked, or intimidated; I wasn't the one who made him reach for the Russian words we don't use in the presence of my mother.

"Here, this will get you into a better mood," says Gris, back in the car, as he pours champagne into four mismatched teacups he brought from home. "Here is a toast: to the two of you and to your life together. A better life." We raise the teacups and drink the syrupy champagne, so cold the bubbles feel like needles of ice and make me numb.

SINCE ROBERT AND I are getting married in two days, we are allowed to stay in the apartment that belongs to my older half-sister Galya, my father's daughter. It is in a new district an hour away from the center, a cluster of tall, dirty-white buildings with low ceilings, called *Khrushchevki*, built during Khrushchev's reign, around 1960. The apartment is a co-op, and my father was able to buy it because he had connections. Galya is the only person I know who owns the place where she lives.

For the two weeks of Robert's stay, Galya has agreed to move in with a friend, but not without the silent comment of compressed lips and a raised eyebrow. Her sentiments are shared by my mother and my aunt Muza, who arrived from Stankovo a week earlier. They all sit in our kitchen, pointing out how inappropriate it is for two people to live in one apartment prior to the moment the state pronounces them officially married. "You should've stayed here until the day after tomorrow," says Aunt Muza in the soft, patient voice of a pedagogue, trying to teach me a belated lesson. In response, my mother throws up her arms, demonstrating that it is futile to fight against the decadent morals of the rotting West.

I think of Uncle Vova, who couldn't come to the wedding, but who wouldn't frown at my staying in an apartment with Robert the same way he didn't care about Crimean Boris or my sleeping on the beach.

But there is a more important message Aunt Muza wants to drive through my head, her final attempt to shake me into sanity. "Maybe you could still find someone else to marry," she continues wistfully, looking into my face with searching eyes. "A good Russian fellow." She stresses the word "Russian," which makes me think of my cousin Fedya, her middle son, who has just emerged from a three-day drinking binge. "We were born here," coos Aunt Muza, "so what do we know about their Western life?" She exchanges glances with my mother, who shrugs to underscore the fact that we certainly know nothing. All my family, with the exception of my sister, wish the West had already collapsed, as our newspapers promise, so they wouldn't have to deal with this scandalous wedding.

On the other hand, Marina, who now openly supports my foreign marriage, thinks the West is perfectly healthy and it is our country that needs surgical intervention. She spits emphatically when my mother unfolds *Pravda* on the kitchen table and makes my provincial aunt wince by telling the story of the last general election, when Marina and I crossed out Brezhnev, the only name on the ballot, and wrote in Sakharov with a blue ballpoint pen. She rolls her eyes and laughs a devilish laugh every time Muza asks Robert about the West or utters the words "inflation" and "apartheid."

"Apartheid?" Robert squints in confusion. It doesn't matter to my aunt that apartheid is happening on the other side of the world from America. The West is the West, no matter what continent. All capitalist vices here get entangled and rolled together, like mismatched threads of wool, into one hairy ball of international evil.

IN OUR TEMPORARY APARTMENT, Robert and I pretend we are getting married. We both know it's a game, but it's not quite a game because we have invited six real guests to the ceremony scheduled at the Acts of Marriage Palace in three hours. We both know it's not quite a marriage, but a marriage nevertheless, for which he has brought a suit borrowed from a friend. He doesn't own suits, he says proudly, putting on dark brown pants that are an inch too short.

I stand over Galya's table ironing my wedding dress, made from sparkly polyester the color of lilac that wrinkles at the slightest touch. I bought the fabric at Gostinyi Dvor on Nevsky, and Marina stitched it into something she saw in a coverless fashion magazine left lying around her theater. We didn't know if the magazine was published this month or even this year, but the girl in the picture looked experienced and worldly, just as I wished to look.

I glide the iron over the staticky fabric, feeling guilty that I'm not as deeply in love with Robert as the woman at the Acts of Marriage Palace assumed I was. I wish my knees had gone weak when I saw him walking toward our side of the world at the airport; I wish my gut melted when he kissed me hello. I wonder if in the deep corner of his soul he really is in love with me—that kind of love, exhausting and irrational, the kind that infected me for a year or two after I met Boris in the Crimea. Is that why Robert has taken so much trouble to arrange all this, to come here for the third time this year? Yet nothing is irrational about Robert; nothing is overwhelming or even spontaneous. I've never heard him spit out a real curse; I've never seen him blush. Having been through a number of our parties where a bottle of vodka for two is just a start, he's not once stumbled in drunken stupor or even looked glassy-eyed. Maybe, in some strange way, he is like me, hoarding his feelings inside and locking them up against strangers' eyes, as if they were precious logs of Hungarian salami or hard-to-get Finnish boots. Maybe we are so similar that he'll promptly forget Karen the Slavic professor and we'll spend our days reading Gogol's *Dead Souls* together and practicing the palatalized consonants that elude every non-Russian speaker.

"He is simply a horse. He's taking you out of here," Nina said the other day. "So what do you care if it isn't a real marriage? Count your blessings and enjoy the ride."

I don't really care that Robert still thinks of Karen. I'm glad I'm marrying him because I like his foreignness. I like that he represents the forbidden and the unknown, that his nationality makes people gasp. I like that Robert has lifted me above the collective and now I can be the opposite of what we are all here, cynical and meek. The opposite of what our souls have become, cleaved and schizophrenic. I can heal and fuse the two parts of me together—the real, hidden self and what I let others see. And Natalia Borisovna will never dare volunteer her slippery advice again, powerless to condemn me for rolling my *r*'s in a most un-British way. I like that I am no longer, as I was in Vera Pavlovna's third grade, a yearning Pioneer vying for attention, a gold nugget to Zoya Churkina's diamond.

I may even love Robert. When we first found ourselves in bed, we were both tentative, as if afraid to discover in each other something alien and ghastly. But the only foreign part of American sex turned out to be a supply of prophylactics.

"Do you know the story of a Soviet couple traveling to Cuba through Ireland?" Robert asks, as I stuff the condom wrapper into my purse so Galya won't find it. "They had four hours in the Dublin airport. They'd learned the English word 'protection' for a condom and they asked the owner of a drugstore for protection. The owner called the police because he thought they were asking for political asylum, and they ended up in the police station." Robert shakes his head, amused at the bad luck of the two heedless Soviets. "But do you see the irony?" he asks, chuckling. "Ireland is a Catholic country, so they don't sell condoms. They will give you political asylum, but not a prophylactic." I see the irony, but also wonder what happened to the Soviet couple after asking for prophylactics, let alone for political asylum. I wonder what's going to happen to Robert and me.

Out of Galya's first-floor window I stare at naked birch trees the color of the dirty snow on the ground, at a boy in *valenki* boots and an unbuttoned coat pulling an empty sled along a footpath. Robert, struggling to knot a tie that he also borrowed from a friend, looks toward where I'm looking, but the boy has already disappeared behind a corner. What is a boy, who should be in school, doing pulling a sled over the last patches of frail snow? What lie did he tell his mother when he left home?

I think of my imminent marriage as a play with a punch-line ending that is going to stun the English department of Leningrad University into near unconsciousness. A recent graduate is moving to America, students will whisper in the hallways, voices tinged with respect and envy. A young adjunct from the philology department has wiped out her future by marrying a capitalist, the dean will announce.

Then we will all play our usual game. Nina will pretend that she is shocked. Natalia Borisovna will pretend that she doesn't know me. I will pretend that I'm sorry to leave.

WE STAND IN THE center of the wedding room of the Acts of Marriage Palace. In front of us is a woman in a red dress with a wide red ribbon across her chest, reciting a speech about the creation of a new society cell. The speech is modified for international marriages: there is no reference to our expected future contributions to Soviet society or to the cause of Communism. I was written off the list of trustworthy citizens three months ago, when we filled out the marriage application. "I wish you to live your life in the spirit of internationalism and friendship among all the peoples," she says, a scolding note in her solemn voice, a dash of condemnation of a Soviet citizen who has chosen to marry a foreigner.

Behind us is a small flock of my relatives and close friends. This is probably the smallest wedding this vast room with its soaring pre-revolutionary ceiling has ever seen: besides my mother, my sisters Marina and Galya, and my provincial aunt, there is Nina, who is six months pregnant under her tent-like dress, her husband Rudik, my aunt Mila, who arrived from Minsk a day earlier, and behind her, as if hiding from the gaze of my family, Marina's Gris in a navy suit.

Each sentence of the speech, which is delivered with grave pathos worthy of a Party Congress plenary, echoes in the crystal drops of a bronze chandelier, the only piece in this room untouched by the sure hand of Soviet design. The crystal drops click faintly, then fade to silence as the woman ends her speech and invites us to join her on the podium for the ring exchange and paper signing.

As I walk across the room, the polyester dress clings to my legs, making the sound New Year's Bengal fireworks make, the spitting sound I'm sure everyone in this room can hear. The woman motions in the direction of a red velvet banner, hammer and sickle embroidered in gold thread. On the wall above the banner a sign reads, "Forward, toward the victory of communism!" The exclamation mark has partially come off and is hanging at an angle, like a collapsing drunk. She shows us to the place on the podium where she's installed a box with the rings—the harvest of my trip to a special store where every citizen-to-be-married can buy two rings made of real gold with written proof from the Acts of Marriage Palace.

"You can exchange the rings," the woman commands, and Robert picks up the smaller gold band. As I extend my right hand, he suddenly freezes and just stands there, making me freeze, too, making me instantly think that he has changed his mind and come to his senses.

"Which hand?" he whispers.

"The right one," I whisper back, bewildered. What kind of question is this? Everyone wears a wedding ring on the right hand—everyone who could get a written proof from the Acts of Marriage Palace to buy one.

He pushes the ring up my finger and extends his right hand for me. Then we all file out of the grand wedding room into a less grand corridor where Nina's husband, Rudik, is already pouring into glasses the two bottles of champagne included in the ceremony. I down my glass and someone else's. Nina comes over and embraces me. Instead of the usual perfume, there is a new smell around her, a scent of ironed laundry and freshly made soup. "Good for you," she says as her big stomach presses into my dress. "Congratulations."

Then a photographer appears, herding us all onto the front stairway so he can arrange us on different levels according to the guests' importance, as if we were coming down the marble steps. Robert and I are ordered to stand next to the carved banister, my family behind us, my friends above on the upstairs landing. The photographer, a short man in a wrinkled suit, runs between our group and the camera, perspiring, yelling instructions, pressing the air between his palms to tell us to stand closer.

I am grateful for all this commotion. I'm glad my aunt is lamenting the empty champagne bottles and not my failure to marry one of "our Russian fellows." I'm glad my mother is worrying about the photo album and not about my leaving. I squeeze Robert's hand as my aunt stretches her arms out to grab him by the shoulders and kiss him on the cheeks three times, a good Russian custom she is now bestowing on an undeserving foreigner. No matter what she thinks of American apartheid or of Robert, he is now family, and she has no choice but to apply to him the same generosity she applies to any in-law, in spite of his curly Jewish hair and his watch that sports the incomprehensible word "Seiko."

At home, the refrigerator is packed with meat stew and a dozen salads. "We're going in a taxi," says my mother, pointing to two cabs idling by the entrance. She would prefer a white Volga provided by the Acts of Marriage Palace—two intertwined golden rings on the roof and a doll in a white dress on the hood—but that was where I drew the line.

"Where is your coat?" asks my mother with a frown. "You'll get cold and get sick." I don't know where my coat is, just as I don't know what they've done with my marriage certificate and my stamped passport, which are now much more crucial to my life than coats or any other warm things. Across the street, below the granite embankment, the zinc waters of the Neva churn around the stone pillars buttressing the Liteiny Bridge, the last chunks of ice dipping and rising in their flow like huge bobbins on invisible fishing lines. A gust of wind knifes in from the river; my mother, I reluctantly admit, was right about the coat.

In the backseat of the cab, Robert and I stare at our ringed hands. "In America it's the left one," he says, making me feel silly about the moment on the podium. "I wonder what that woman would've done if we'd put the rings on our left hands."

Only someone who wasn't born here could think of such a bizarre thing, such a deliberate flouting of rules. But since I know we have different brains and Robert cannot understand how impossible this thought would be to any of us here, I pretend I am considering the option. "She'd probably say that as long as you are on Soviet soil, you must do things the Soviet way. The right way, you know," I add and skew my eyes to see Robert's reaction. "The right-handed way," I say and we both giggle.

I look out the window at the façades fringed in slushy snow, at the yellow building with white columns, the railroad ticket office, and think of what happened here just a few days before. I know Robert would appreciate this story, a uniquely Russian scene that I describe to him in Russian. At around one in the afternoon, after I'd been standing in line for an hour to buy Aunt Mila a train ticket back to Minsk, two ticket sellers simultaneously barricaded their windows with handwritten signs, the word "lunch" scribbled on cardboard in purple indelible pencil. In front of me, an African man in a sheepskin coat—a foreign student from one of Leningrad's schools—politely suggested that shutting two out of the three open windows for lunch when the queue curled out the front door might not be the most efficient way to serve the people. "They're wasting their time in line instead of contributing to the society and the Five-Year Plan," he said quietly, with a serious face, using correct, docile grammar. The crowd grew silent, a sea of white around a single dark face. Then one of the ticket-sellers shoved the "lunch" sign aside and leaned out of the window, her polyester bosom hanging over the counter. "We taught you Russian," she barked, glaring at the African, stressing every word as if she were reading Lenin's decree—a glare of condemnation for his well-fitting coat, for his quiet voice, for his otherness. "We taught you Russian, so now you shut up!"

I wiggle closer to Robert on the scratchy taxi seat. "So now you shut up," I whisper into his ear, and he puts his arm around my shoulders. I taught him about Russia, and he gave me the power to leave it. He smells of the blue shampoo he brought with him, a cold, antiseptic smell. He smells of America and a different life.

# CHAPTER 20

# *Farewell*

I AM ON A SECOND-FLOOR landing of the philology department, in the "philodrome"—a place to meet, smoke, and gossip. The gossip nowadays is about me: a temporary instructor and a possible graduate school candidate who has married a capitalist and is leaving for America.

After the wedding, three weeks of paper collection have finally produced a complete package accepted by the visa department, and now I'll have to wait for my exit visa. My work record has been copied from a shelf in the university archive and notarized, my Leningrad residency rescinded, permission to leave signed by my mother, and my Komsomol membership card safely stowed away in a safe in case I decide to come back and reenter the ranks. At home, the talk about these red-tape hurdles and surly clerks allows me to avoid the talk about leaving.

I must be in the dean's office in ten minutes, an appointment I was ordered to keep by the department's party secretary, who was so livid that he hardly said anything because he couldn't unclench his teeth. This meeting is going to be another expression of official outrage, a pro forma scolding.

I've never seen the dean before, the only proof of his existence an impatient signature on the department's rules posted on billboards, Dean Maslov. I timidly knock on the door, as if I don't want him to hear it, as if his not hearing it would excuse me from this visit. But the voice inside commands me to come in, and I creak the door open. His office is cluttered with chairs, filing cabinets, and papers spilling out of folders; it smells of tobacco and dust. A wrinkle-free Brezhnev in oil frowns from the wall above the desk. Dean Maslov is short and dense, his weight solidly packed inside a suit. He looks like a pirate, one eye covered with a black patch, a pipe jammed between his fingers. A communist pirate, a pirate dean. He blows out smoke and motions to the chair on the other side of the desk.

"So what have they been telling me," he says, peering at me through the smoke, "you're leaving us?"

"I'm married to an American citizen, so I guess I'm leaving." Before coming here, I assembled a few stock phrases from the dustbin of jargon used in speeches and administrative orders tacked to door frames.

He draws on his pipe, squinting—whether from the pleasure of the tobacco or disgust at seeing me, I don't know.

"Isn't it a shame—as soon as we raise a decent student, a candidate for graduate school, she's snatched away by the West. Well, too bad. We will have to be more careful hiring young single women to teach American students."

I know this is a threat—not to me, but to future foreign-language majors applying for summer teaching jobs. It means that from now on these jobs will go only to women who are married, preferably to KGB officials, like the director of the American program.

"Everyone wants to go to America." His pipe leaves a trace of smoke in the air as he throws up his arm. "America, America— that's all we hear. America the paradise. America the land of abundance. Strawberries in the winter and a car for every citizen."

He pauses and peers at me with his one eye.

"I'm not leaving because of strawberries in the winter," I say since he expects me to say something. "Or even a car."

"Not even a car, eh?" He cranes his neck as if to take a better look at me. "Well, why then?"

Although he is sharp enough to know that I am not going to tell him the truth, Dean Maslov leans back and waits for me to respond. He looks the same way Nadia from my high school looked at me yesterday when I ran into her in the street. Nadia is now a *refusenik*: she is Jewish, and nine months ago her application to leave the country was refused by the local visa department. Her parents, her grandmother, and her husband are now blacklisted and shunned. I felt guilty that I can leave and she cannot, too embarrassed to admit to her that my real reason for leaving has nothing to do with the cause of political freedom. It has to do with my mother. Two years ago, if Boris had asked me to marry him, I would have hopped on the first train headed for Kiev, a thousand kilometers away.

"I got married," I say. "People get married and leave."

The dean sets his pipe down in a heavy crystal ashtray on his desk and gets up. He was not really expecting to get an answer. According to procedure, he has to check off in a book that the talk has taken place.

"Where are you going in America?" he asks, leafing through papers on his desk.

"Texas."

"Ah, the land where they kill presidents." He walks over to the bookshelf, stops, and runs his fingers over the book spines. "Well, good luck." I don't really know what killing of what presidents he is talking about. "I've been to America, you know," he says. "I lived there for a year—a cultural exchange in the early sixties. A fascinating place." Dean Maslov stuffs his hands into his pockets and rocks on his feet, his eye on the window, where little sticky leaves curl out of buds on poplar branches. "But you don't want to get fired there, or get sick, or get old. There is no safety net, no collective to help. You are on your own." He half-smiles for the first time. "It made me feel grateful for my guaranteed ninety-ruble pension."

This is about what I expected to hear, the talk about collectives and ninety-ruble pensions, although I thought that university deans, considering their ideologically sensitive positions, made more than ninety rubles. I thought that Maslov would limit this talk to a pointy reprimand or, possibly, an angry accusation of squandering the state's resources, wasted on my education.

"What do you mean, the land where they kill presidents?" I ask.

"You don't know?" He wags his head to show me how hopeless he thinks I am. "In 1963 an American president was killed in Dallas, Texas. Didn't you know that?" He looks familiar now, an authority lecturing an underling. "*Your* president. You should brush up on your history."

I am not sure how I'm supposed to know what happened in America when I was eight as I cannot even find out what is happening there now. Yet he is right: I am as ignorant of my new country's history as I am of everything else.

Dean Maslov moves back to his desk, to his spilling papers and his pipe. He must be in his mid-sixties, my mother's age, which means he also went through the post-revolutionary chaos and the two wars. Maybe that's why he's tried to warn me about America. Like my mother, he comes from the first Soviet generation, from the time when *vranyo* was still fresh, still a little curly sprout. He comes from the time when it hadn't yet morphed and metastasized and tunneled its way through our tissue the way my father's cancer wormed into his bladder and his lungs. When it hadn't yet crept through every millimeter of our flesh—this lie, which my father helped cultivate after he'd lost his teeth to scurvy, which my mother, busy organizing union meetings and funerals, barely noticed. Maybe Dean Maslov played the same crumb game my grandmother—everyone's grandmother—invented during the famine; maybe he, too, saw a piece of bread swell into a whole mountain of crumbs.

He feels the pockets of his jacket for a box of matches, squints his one eye, and lights his extinguished pipe—not quite a pirate, not quite a pundit or a leader—an old man ready to retire on ninety rubles a month.

A silly thought floats into my head: this is what it has all come to—a mountain of crumbs.

I get up and carefully close the door behind me. The pro forma talk has taken place.

I AM ON A bus, clutching a handbag with my exit visa and an Aeroflot ticket to America. The Aeroflot office on Nevsky was empty, as always, since it deals exclusively with international travel. I went in and asked for a ticket to the United States. The girl perched on a high seat behind the counter winced, sized me up with stiff eyes outlined in imported mascara that doesn't have to be mixed with spit, and scrutinized my visa while I stood on the other side, staring at her chin. Then, with angry reluctance, after taking my passport to the back room to consult her KGB supervisor, she wrote out a ticket in her diligent official handwriting, reserved for foreign destinations.

I get off three bus stops before my house and walk home in the August evening light. I walk across Theatre Square, past a monument to our composer Glinka, past a Kirov poster announcing the opera *October*, scheduled for tomorrow. My mother and I saw it when I was nine, so it has been playing there for at least fifteen years. In the second act of that old *October*, after the people had grown disillusioned with the tsar, after a chorus of soldiers had brandished guns toward the Winter Palace and a quartet of children had begged for food, an actor with a goatee and a bald wig thrust his arm out, Lenin-like, and announced that the October Revolution had prevailed. The crowd onstage burst into cheers, and then Lenin's chest heaved as he took a deep breath to launch a high note that should have trumped everything that came earlier. Everything, from the first disgruntled peasant to the pack of sailors hoisting a red flag on top of the Winter Palace, even the lemonade and éclairs in the buffet during the intermission. For a second the note teetered on the brink of the required triumph, but then it collapsed into such a grinding bray that the whole audience, including people like me, with no musical ear whatsoever, simultaneously gasped.

I stop in front of the *October* billboard, which pictures the same singer whom I heard here fifteen years earlier. I imagined then how terrible it must have felt for him to stand there, in front of everyone in the twenty-four orchestra rows, four tiers, and the former tsarist box in the center, having in one second ruined the defining moment of Lenin's life and the cause of the Revolution itself.

I gaze at the poster: the same disgraced singer, the same dishonored country.

MY SUITCASE GAPES OPEN on the couch, with a new pair of sandals between two shirts Marina crocheted for me. The shirts, green and purple, the only colors of thread she could find in the stores, are designed in elaborate patterns of leaves and flowers. Marina spent days bent over at a window, a tiny metal hook dipping between her fingers. I've seen her resew clothes—convert a pair of old pants into a patch-pattern skirt or rip out the lining of a jacket from the mothball darkness of the storage space above the refrigerator and turn it into a silk blouse—but I never suspected that such intricate elegance could emerge from under her hands.

"They're beautiful," I say. "It's unfair that one person can have so many talents."

I open the armoire and stare at the clothes dangling from hangers, none worth lugging across the Atlantic. A flowery polyester dress my mother bought for me that I have never worn; a shapeless cardigan with elbows stretched out; a sweater punctured with sparkling thread, lint clinging to its sleeves.

"Don't forget the warm things," says my mother, lumbering in with a load of wet laundry she begins to pin on two clotheslines crisscrossing the room.

Warm things, according to her, are as essential as soup for proper nutrition or fresh air for healthy lungs. One should always have a good amount of warm things—hats, gloves, scarves, and coats—to ensure survival.

"I won't need any warm things," I say. "I'm going to Texas. It's warm there all year long."

"It's warm now," she says, pinning up a sheet, "but come winter and you'll be sorry you don't have them." She bends over the pile of laundry and quotes one of her proverbs, "We don't cherish what we have, then cry when we lose it."

I'm about to say that Texas has no winter, but I don't. In the past few weeks my mother's sayings have strangely begun to make sense; it has occurred to me that maybe all those little lines we've heard since nursery school sound like such clichés precisely because they are true. "Without work, you won't even pull a minnow out of a lake," or "Don't get into someone else's sled," or "If you knew where you'd fall, you'd put down some straw"—they all, I'm reluctant to admit, are beginning to feel like unlearned lessons of wisdom, too late to start acquiring now.

When my mother is finished pinning up our duvets and pillow-cases, she goes into the kitchen to make dinner. Marina is home tonight, too, and as I stand in the hallway under the coatrack among the crinkly raincoat sleeves, I hear the muted sizzling of their voices. My mother's voice trembles with fear; my sister's sputters with contempt for anyone who feels alarmed about leaving for the West.

"What do we know about America, really?" says my mother. "People beg on the streets and sleep under bridges and everyone walks around with a gun."

"Good," says Marina. "If I had a gun here I'd know what to do with it."

There is a pause, a clinking of pots. I want to go in and tell my mother that I won't beg or sleep under a bridge.

"And how is this nearsighted writer going to support her?" asks my mother. "He is a student, isn't he? Do they have stipends for students over there?"

"How do I know?" barks Marina in a stage whisper. "She doesn't need any stipends from him. She speaks English. She'll do just fine."

I hear my mother sigh, then sniffle.

I pop my head into the kitchen door. "Did you hear that?" I say. "I'll do just fine. I promise." I straighten up and bend my elbow in a Pioneer salute. My mother shakes her head and blows her nose, but I can see a little smile struggling to rise to her lips.

I go back to the room divided by the wet laundry, to my half-empty suitcase. I pack the *American Heritage Dictionary* in its red jacket, a present from Robert, the second most valuable thing I own after a pair of corduroy Levis. From the dresser I scoop several bottles of perfume I bought with my private-student income. I carefully wrap each one in newspaper and place them between the shirts.

The rest of the twenty kilograms Aeroflot allows is presents. Russian souvenirs for Robert and his family that my mother and sister have been piling on the couch. Wooden spoons painted in the red and gold colors of *Khokhloma*, black metal trays with roses, linen tablecloths with matching napkins. On the television set beams a chrome samovar my mother obtained through her medical connections, a present I've refused to take. I could see myself in an American airport, swaddled in kerchiefs and scarves, cardboard samovar boxes tied with string weighing down my hands.

When I'm finished packing, Marina comes into the room. She straightens the sheets on the clothesline, closes my suitcase, and pulls it down onto the floor. We sit wedged into the corner of the couch, without talking, in a space darkened by the hanging laundry.

"What do you think America's really like?" I ask.

She stares at my suitcase, thinking. "It's like a corridor of light," she says. "You know, what people are supposed to see before they die—this shining light, a passage to somewhere else."

I don't know why I'm asking Marina, who clings to superstitions and believes in everything our dacha Gypsy neighbor tells her when she fans a deck of cards. I don't know why I'm listening to my sister, who went to St. Nicholas Cathedral two blocks from our house in Leningrad and paid five rubles to get baptized by a drunk charlatan with dirty hair. I'm also not grateful to her for this dubious analogy. I'm not planning to die tomorrow. On the contrary, my life is just about to begin, as far as I can see.

She looks into my face and moves closer. "It's our bright future, this light," she says. "The future we've been promised since nursery school, since 1917 and the storming of the Winter Palace. Only no one has told us it's on the other side of the Atlantic Ocean."

We sit quietly for a minute, without moving.

"You have to tell Mama," I say. "About the bright future."

She nods and puts her arm around my shoulder.

"It's scary, like the first day of school," I say. "First grade, when I was seven. Everyone came wearing white aprons over their uniforms, but I didn't know—and Mama didn't tell me; maybe she didn't know either—so I wore the regular black. I stood there, the only one in black among the crowd of white, not even knowing what my teacher looked like, not even knowing where I was supposed to go. With a stupid bunch of gladioli Mama stuffed into my hand."

"From our dacha, no doubt," says Marina and wiggles even closer.

"Yeah," I say. "Where else?"

*

GRIS, WHO HAS VOLUNTEERED to drive me to the airport, arrives at two-thirty, ten minutes early. When Marina opens the door, all we can see is a huge bunch of flowers Gris is holding in front of his face.

"Here, here." My mother hurries out of the kitchen with a vase. "Peonies are very fragile; they can't survive long without water." She sets the flowers on the table in the room with my desk and Marina's couch. It is Marina's room now.

I check my handbag: my passport, which still smells of the printing press; an Aeroflot ticket, a glossy rectangular booklet with red carbon-paper pages; one hundred and thirty dollars, the allowed amount of currency for departees, exchanged yesterday in the vaulting emptiness of the central bank.

My suitcase is by the door; everything is ready. We awkwardly stand in the hallway, not knowing what to do.

"Well, let's go," says my mother.

"Where are you going without sitting down first?" snaps Marina. A superstition for a safe trip and the hope that a person who is leaving will return: everyone sits down for a minute, silently; the youngest gets up first.

My mother, Marina, and I sit on the couch in Marina's room, Gris on the corner of the chair in front of the desk. My mother looks at me; Marina, with stage concentration, gazes at the flowers on the table; Gris stares at the floor. An ambulance—or a militia car—wails in the distance, the siren growing louder as it screeches around the turn and races past our windows.

Marina motions for me to get up. We crowd in the hallway, our shoulders bumping, keys clanging, doors swaying open. A meaningless commotion, a spurt of last-minute chaos.

Gris lifts my suitcase and carries it out to the elevator.

In the courtyard, where children from my old nursery school are playing in the sandbox, I look up at the square of the sky, at the fleet of burly white clouds casting a temporary shadow. A girl with two skinny braids stops her sandbox digging and gazes at the circle of the sun glowing through the cotton cloud.

Gris loads my suitcase into the trunk and opens the car doors for us. My mother, as the oldest, sits in the front. Gris slowly drives past the playground and pulls through the courtyard archway into the street.

With one hand on the wheel, he weaves around trolleys and trucks in the unmarked width of Moskovsky Prospekt. People line up at the bus stops, emerge from grocery stores, their arms weighed down by string bags. Children hold their parents' hands on their way to libraries and piano lessons. A usual Tuesday afternoon.

The massive buildings lining the avenue change to matchbox apartment complexes and then to barren fields dotted with commercial hothouses. "Summer," a big sign reads, the name of a vegetable factory that occasionally produces lines of people waiting for watery cucumbers and stalks of yellow dill. When the sign fades in the distance, the road swerves to the right, where the international wing of Pulkovo Airport looms on the horizon.

Nina is already there to see me off, a fan of customs declarations in her hands. I fill in the required items to declare: a gold wedding band, the silver bracelet I received from the British boy Kevin when I worked as a tour guide in the ninth grade, a bank exchange receipt for one hundred and thirty dollars. The international terminal is dark and cramped, a small wing walled off for a few foreign flights. I squint at the customs declaration, trying to make out the tiny letters that warn me against exporting rubles, precious metals, and works of art.

"Check-in begins for a flight to Moscow to connect with flight number 37 to Washington," a voice drones from a loudspeaker, muffled as if underwater. Since the invasion of Afghanistan, Aeroflot hasn't been allowed to land in New York, so Robert said he would borrow a car from his friend, the same friend who lent him the wedding suit, and drive to Washington to meet me. "The passengers are asked to clear customs at this time."

"Already?" asks Mama and looks around, her usual pre-departure surveying glance, as if we were surrounded by scores of string bags. "It's still so early . . ."

"Well, you better go," says Marina. "Who knows how long it'll take those bastards to nose through your suitcase."

Gris lifts my bag and wraps his arm around me, pressing his cheek to my ear. "*Schastlivo*," he says, releasing his embrace and winking. "Good luck to you. Find out how everything is there, really."

A Spanish student who is part of a visiting tour, his size doubled by his backpack, sideswipes Marina as she hugs me, and this jolt pulses through to me in a tighter embrace, in a firmer kiss. I press my face into her hair, which glows under the light, the color of the apricot jam she once brought from a theater tour of Armenia. "Write to us," she says.

I look at Mama's crumpled face and catch her gaze, open, like a fresh wound. She steps forward and I snuggle into her wet cheek. She smells of kitchen and mushrooms, the same familiar smell as years ago, when I got lost in the woods on a mushroom hunt, when the crunch of her footsteps led me to the safety of her embrace.

"*Pishi*," she whispers, "promise to write often." New tears swell in her eyes and spill over. "Are you sure you have everything?" she asks, swallowing and blinking. "Did you take the scarf I left out for you?" She swipes a finger under her eyes, folds her hot hands around mine, and I feel something small and heavy drop into my palm. "Take this with you. It's your grandma's watch, solid gold, French. They don't make them anymore."

I know that the law prohibits taking out of the country anything made before 1957, anything made in a foreign country, anything made of gold. But at this moment the law is as irrelevant as the visiting students with their machine-gun Spanish. I hold the watch in my palm, then drop it in the pocket of my jeans.

"We'll come to visit you," says Gris. "First we'll send Mama, as soon as she's done with the dacha and her apple jams. Then Marina will be next, and then we'll all be there and you won't know how to get rid of us."

"Yeah," I say and give Mama a smile. "I'll start the paperwork as soon as I land."

The current of the student group picks me up and carries me to the glass door, the border demarcation between us and the rest of the world. Behind it, in an automatic movement, a customs official in a gray uniform begins to riffle through my bag. I recognize him from my senior-year university lectures. He unwraps my bottles of perfume, one by one, lifts them up to the light, and stares at their contents. He opens my wallet and counts my money. He thumbs through the pages of my address book. A university graduate rummaging through luggage. He doesn't recognize me, or pretends not to. Feeling the metal of the watch on my thigh, I look into his eyes, the deadened KGB eyes that can still, as long as I am in the international airport zone, drill right through my untrustworthy head, accuse me of being unpatriotic and delinquent, and order me to stay here. We stare at each other until he looks away—a philologist of Germanic languages busy analyzing underwear and socks—and pushes my violated suitcase off the belt.

When I finish repacking, I look back, at all of them clustered together before the glass door. Nina waves vigorously over my mother's head. Gris stands next to her, his cap pushed over his forehead, his hands in his pockets. Marina is trying to shove in front of the guard, squeezing him out with her shoulder. I can only see a part of Mama, a small fragment of her face, her hand with a handkerchief blotting her eye.

If my father were alive, would he be standing next to her, waving me good-bye, reassuring me I won't end up under a bridge? Or would he be fuming at a friend's dacha, angry at my leaving, doing what he did when I was born? He was as stubborn as a goat, according to my mother, just like I am. I think of the dream I had about him when I was eight, in which he sat in his rowboat and spoke about theater, about the audience holding their breath and growing silent the moment before the curtain is about to go up. The anticipation of magic, he called it, the expectation of illusion. The moment when the noise stops. The moment you're no longer ordinary.

I wonder whether in real life he knew anything about magic. Could he have recognized that moment, my unknown father?

Can I?

"Walk forward, let's go," commands a border patrolwoman, pushing me toward a metal detector that doesn't work. But we have to pretend it does, and I obediently step through the metal arch, benevolently silent. When I am done, the border woman turns to the two British-looking ladies in pantsuits, explaining to them with her hands that they must pretend, too.

I stand on the other side of the world, looking back, saying good-bye. I think of the bulky clouds chugging over the city toward the Baltic Sea, pausing over my courtyard. I think of pocked walls, windowsills covered with soot, crumbling stairs leading to doors permanently barred. I think of the dilapidated sandbox in the middle of the playground. On its ledge crouches a small girl with braids. I know that face: green eyes slightly slanted, betraying the drop of Tatar ancestry in every Russian; faint freckles, as if someone had splashed muddy water onto her skin.

She looks up at me, and the bows in her skinny braids flutter like butterflies. I squat next to her, but the freckles grow darker, a wave of pink floods her cheeks, and her slanted eyes evade mine. She is tense and distant, like the still lindens behind her, like this mute courtyard, like prematurely aged Leningrad. A flock of pigeons pecking at the dirt lift their wings and with a startling clatter rustle up to where the wind rattles over the rooftops. We sit there in the sandbox, on different sides of the world, caught in a time warp—

both waiting, both staring at the square of the courtyard sky and wondering what lies beyond it.

When I look back again, my family and friends are no longer visible. All I see through the horseshoe of the broken metal detector, all that is left of my country is a glare of glass.

# Epilogue

M Y MOTHER WALKS AROUND my house switching off lights. She unloads my dishwasher, sweeps the leaves off the patio, and feeds the dog. She arrived here twenty-one years ago, when I waddled through my last weeks of pregnancy, her hair as white as our winter courtyard. According to my sister, it was my divorce from Robert—our different brains, the hot strangeness of Texas—that precipitated that dramatic change in hair color. My remarriage to someone she hadn't met, my husband of now twenty-eight years, did not make things better. No one could believe that my mother's hair was brown and then a month later, white, and then brown again once she settled with us in Nutley, New Jersey.

On the way home from Kennedy Airport, where she landed in June 1988, after we rolled across Manhattan toward the Lincoln Tunnel, a young woman in tight shorts approached our car at a red light on Forty-second Street. My husband turned his head toward her, and as she lifted her tank top above her chest, my mother winced and stiffened. I knew what she was thinking. She had been right all along, lying awake at night, combing through newspaper headlines for crumbs of transatlantic news. America is the mouth of a shark, just as *Pravda* had promised.

Much has happened since then. In 1991, we watched the Red Square barricades on CNN and gaped at Yeltsin perched on an armored vehicle with his arm thrust into the future in front of the Moscow Parliament called the White House. After that, the map of the Soviet Union shrank at the edges, Leningrad became St. Petersburg again, and *Pravda* ceased to exist. The English department of my university opened a private division where learning English is no longer free; the dean turned from guarding the party standards to investing in privatized oil companies. Marina answered a personal ad from a Louisiana newspaper and married a good man who loves her cooking and her sewing. She gave up acting and now devotes her talent to cultivating persimmons and tomatoes in a suburb of New Orleans. The rate for international phone calls dropped from three dollars a minute to two cents.

My mother still reuses paper napkins and plastic bags from the supermarket produce section, neatly folding and piling them under her bed. In her basement apartment, she reads memoirs about the Great Patriotic War and watches Russian National Television, which is again owned and controlled by the government, just as it was when I lived there. Between Moscow news and militia dramas, she fills a notebook with stories from her past. Every week, she dials her sister Muza and her stepdaughter Galya back in Russia and tells them all about our life here. She tells them about her ninety-fifth birthday party, when Marina flew here and cooked for two days; she mails them packages with gloves and sweaters, the necessary warm things.

She no longer needs to control and protect. There are no commissars and no lines bristling with elbows; there is no KGB, or shortage of mayonnaise. But old habits linger, and I have to catch myself not to react as I used to when out of the deep new pleats of skin gleam the eyes of my Leningrad mother. Every time I load her shopping cart with buckwheat and cottage cheese, she questions the prices and scrutinizes her receipts in search of errors, ready to find she's been deceived by greedy cashiers. She gives us a slant-eyed look when we go to a restaurant, in brazen disregard of the refrigerator full of perfectly good food. But she is also practical, my mother. She knows her life is good, and as her saying goes, "When things are good you don't search for better." On holidays, she buys us cards with puppies and roses. To help me, she cuts out quick dinner recipes and piles them on the kitchen counter, along with advice on college majors for my daughter from the Russian-language newspaper published in Brooklyn.

I am the one now who worries about scarves and schools, soup and order. I am the one expected to protect and control. In my head, pictures of the perfect life grow like our dacha strawberries, in model rows. I want my daughter to speak Russian, to read Turgenev, to memorize Pushkin's verse the same way we memorized it in school. I want her to love theater and spend nights in the kitchen pontificating about personal happiness and the meaning of life. I want to infect her with the germ of Russia so she stops being American and becomes like me.

But I don't. My daughter's native language is English, and KGB and *Pravda* are just the names of expensive bars in New York.

In my New Jersey house, with my mother's apartment the size of our place in Leningrad, we all enjoy privacy, something I tried to find in the Russian language and my Russian life, something that didn't exist there. I'm glad I left that life twenty-nine years ago; I'm happy my family is here with me. I am closer to my mother and sister now than I ever was in Leningrad. But then, we are probably not the same people we were back in Russia. In our private American space, we can splice the cleaved halves of our souls and heal; we can change if we want to—transform ourselves, as my actress sister knows how to do—and no one will say we've betrayed the collective. We can simply live, and keep the door open, and wait. We can be in flux, just like the new Russia.

"Whatever happens, happens for the best, as Mamochka used to say," murmurs my creased, once again white-haired mother. Her *mamochka*, my grandma, as soft and wrinkled, smiles at us from a photograph on the wall, which hangs next to my young mother's portrait, painted by her brother Sima. We don't talk about such things as forgiveness, understanding, acceptance. We simply sip black currant tea, my mother's favorite, and I don't say anything to question Grandma's wisdom.

# *Acknowledgments*

I AM DEEPLY GRATEFUL TO my agent, Molly Friedrich, extraordinary in every way, for taking a chance on this first memoir and for guiding me ever since; to my editor, Priscilla Painton, for her insight, grace, and sharp eye; and to Jacobia Dahm, my reader who first called it "a book." My gratitude also goes to Victoria Meyer, executive director of publicity at Simon & Schuster, for her enthusiasm about the book, and to Loretta Denner, for her exactitude and style. Lucy Carson, Michael Szczerban, and Dan Cabrera, thank you for your support.

The inspiration for this memoir came from Frank McCourt's seminar at the Southampton Writers Conference, where the intelligence and energy of my exceptional classmates challenged expectations and created magic. I have learned from the conference's many mentors and friends, and I am grateful for their wisdom and gracious advice. My special thanks to Robert Reeves, the conference director, and Jody Donohue, a poet and a friend.

I am thankful to my fellow writers Pearl Solomon, Patricia Hackbarth, and Ruth Hamel, whose suggestions have improved many chapters; to Nadia Carey, an old friend from Leningrad, for setting some facts straight; and to Eleanor Oakley for her enormous heart.

My appreciation goes to Donna Perreault of *The Southern Review*, Stephanie G'Schwind of *Colorado Review*, Robert Stewart of *New Letters*, and Lou Ann Walker of the *Southampton Review* for publishing chapters from the memoir; and to Juris Jurjevics of Soho Press for his generous support. My gratitude to the late Staige D. Blackford of *The Virginia Quarterly Review* for his kind words dating back to the twentieth century, the first encouragement I received from an editor.

*Spasibo* to Irina Veletskaya, Anna Graham, Luba Borisova, and Olga Kapitskaya for their friendship, the Russian kind.

I thank my sister Marina for her soul filled with talent and my mother for her head filled with memories. Also, I am indebted to my remaining family in Russia, although they would have probably told a different story of our past.

And finally, this book would not be possible without the two closest people: Laurenka, who may have been touched by Russia more than she knows, and Andy, my most ardent advocate, exacting reader, and unwavering supporter since my first years in this country, when the English language was still a mystery. To you, my love.

# MARINA ENDICOTT

# Good to a Fault

'There's heartbreak, there's joy, there are parts where you cry - and it's very high quality writing. Well done!'
MARGARET ATWOOD, GILLER PRIZE JURY REMARKS

Absorbed in her own failings, 43-year-old Clara Purdy crashes her life into a sharp left turn, taking the young family in the other car along with her. When bruises on the mother, Lorraine, prove to be late-stage cancer, Clara moves the three children and their terrible grandmother into her own house while Lorraine undergoes treatment at the local hospital.

We know what is good, but we don't do it. In *Good to a Fault*, Clara decides to give it a try, and then has to cope with the consequences: exhaustion, fury, hilarity, and unexpected love. But she questions her own motives. Is she acting out of true goodness, or out of guilt? And most shamefully, has she taken the family over simply because she wants one of her own?

In *Good to a Fault*, award-winning writer Marina Endicott examines what we owe in this life and what we deserve. And the result is a profound and unforgettable novel.

'Witty and wise, light and dark, with many unexpected moments.'
COLM TÓIBÍN

'Good to a Fault is one of those novels you want to tell people about. It's unpretentious and affecting, with characters to remember and themes that linger and resound'
MEG WOLITZER, AUTHOR OF THE TEN-YEAR NAP

# Helen Rappaport

# Ekaterinburg

A vivid and compelling account of the final thirteen days of the Romanovs, counting down to the last, tense hours of their lives.

On 4 July 1918, a new commandant took control of a closely guarded house in the Russian town of Ekaterinburg. His name was Yakov Yurovsky, and his prisoners were the Imperial family: the former Tsar Nicholas, his wife Alexandra, and their children, Olga, Tatiana, Maria, Anastasia and Alexey. Thirteen days later, at Yurovsky's command, and on direct orders from Moscow, the family was gunned down in a blaze of bullets in a basement room.

Ekaterinburg is the story of those murders, which ended 300 years of Romanov rule and began an era of state-orchestrated terror and brutal repression.